Rapid

Appraisal

Methods

WORLD BANK

REGIONAL AND

SECTORAL STUDIES

Rapid

Appraisal

Methods

EDITED BY

KRISHNA KUMAR

The World Bank
Washington, D.C.

338.90068
R218

The World Bank Regional and Sectoral Studies series provides an outlet for work that is relatively limited in its subject matter or geographical coverage but that contributes to the intellectual foundations of development operations and policy formulation. These studies have not necessarily been edited with the same rigor as Bank publications that carry the imprint of a university press.

Cover design by Sam Ferro

Library of Congress Cataloging-in-Publication Data

Rapid appraisal methods / edited by Krishna Kumar.
    p. cm. — (World Bank regional and sectoral studies)
   Includes bibliographical references.
   ISBN 0-8213-2523-X
   1. Economic development projects—Evaluation. I. Kumar, Krishna.
II. Series.
HD75.9.R36   1993
338.9'0068'4—dc20   93-21584
                                                         CIP

Contents

v

Boxes

Figures

Tables

Foreword

SOCIAL RESEARCH METHODS, though powerful, are not often used to meet the pressing information needs of decision-makers in development. This has sparked a growing interest in an array of less structured data collection methods called "rapid appraisal," which aim to supply needed information in a timely and cost-effective manner.

This volume outlines five rapid data collection methods—key informant interviews, focus group discussions, group interviews, structured observation, and informal surveys—that have been used by the exponents of rapid appraisal. Eight case studies illuminate the use of these methods in development settings, particularly for the appraisal and evaluation of development projects and programs.

The authors take a reflective, if not critical, look at the data collection enterprise and draw practical lessons for the development community. They describe the nature and types of data generated and the problems encountered with each method. They also discuss the strengths, limitations, and applicability of the methods in different settings.

The implicit message of the case studies is that formal social science research and rapid appraisal are complementary. For example, rapid appraisal methods have often been used to design complex socioeconomic surveys as well as to interpret their findings and conclusions. In many instances, both methods are used sequentially. In situations where a choice is made, it is dictated by such factors as the nature, purpose, and ultimate use of the information; available technical and monetary resources; and time constraints.

For the development community, this may turn out to be an indispensable guide to monitoring and evaluating development projects.

Robert Picciotto
Director General
Operations Evaluation
  Department
The World Bank
June 1993

Acknowledgments

SEVERAL COLLEAGUES AND FRIENDS have helped me in the preparation of this volume. Annette Binnendijk, director of the Office of Evaluation, at USAID's Center of Development Information and Evaluation (CDIE), enabled me to organize a three-day workshop during which some of the papers included in this volume were presented. Janet Ballantyne, the former director of CDIE, encouraged me to edit the workshop papers for a wider audience. John E. Eriksson, the associate assistant administrator of USAID and Jock Conly, chief of CDIE's Program Operations Assessment Division, took a personal interest in this endeavor. Dennis Casley, former chief of the World Bank's Operations Monitoring Unit, not only reviewed all the chapters, but also wrote a thoughtful introduction. Graham Donaldson, chief of the Agriculture and Human Development Division in the World Bank's Operations Evaluation Department, took upon himself the responsibiiity of getting this volume published. I wish to record my deep gratitude to these colleagues and friends.

I dare not thank individual contributors who authored different chapters and were most gracious in making suitable revisions. After all, this volume is as much theirs as mine. I would also like to acknowledge my debt to the six anonymous readers who reviewed the first draft of the manuscript and made valuable comments. This book is undoubtedly improved because of their suggestions. Last but not least, I am grateful to publisher James Feather and managing editor Kenneth Hale at the World Bank for the publication of this volume.

Krishna Kumar
U.S. Agency for International
Development
June 21, 1993

B K Title

Introduction

Dennis J. Casley

THE GROWTH IN THE ACADEMIC RESPECTABILITY of so-called rapid appraisal (RA) methods in the 1980s has demonstrated the frustration of many working in the development field (particularly rural development) with the contribution made by surveys designed by statisticians using sampling theory. In the early days, there was a tendency by some proponents of such methods to make a virtue of damning statistics and sampling theory, so that there was a danger of claiming that in almost any development context, purposive sampling of an arbitrary, limited number of sample units was a defensible alternative, to the application of formal sample size determination and selection. Fortunately, this danger is diminishing. More and more, it is being realized that rapid surveys involving open-ended interviews of purposively selected or self-selecting cases provide a complement to the use of random sampling and structured questionnaires.

Krishna Kumar and I emphasize this complementarity in our two books (Casley and Kumar 1987, 1988) on monitoring and evaluation of agriculture development projects—particularly in the second volume, in which we describe in some depth the use of such techniques as key informants, focus groups, and the like. It is giving away no professional secrets to say that it was Kumar who provided the expertise in this area, for my own experience was based largely on formal surveys and an adherence to probability sampling methods. I have always argued that such surveys need not be large, cumbersome, slow, or excessively expensive, so there is no need to introduce other methods to overcome these disadvantages. This is not to say that, misguidedly, many survey practitioners (often ill-trained in sampling theory) have not produced such monstrously useless and expensive surveys. However, this is an indictment of those individuals, not of the discipline of statistics.

No, the advantage of the methods that Kumar describes in his overview is that they fill a gap in the data collection spectrum. There is a place for enumerators following a detailed structure in interviewing randomly selected respondents, and there is a place for a skilled team undertaking open-ended probing conversations with purposively selected groups. If I were a project manager of a major development project today, I would demand that information flow using both methodologies. If I needed a regular update on the number of farmers responding to project initiatives, I would call for the statistician to design the adoption rate survey and require that precision levels set by me are met. If I needed to know why farmers in Zone C are relatively slow in embracing my services, I would call for one of the authors in this volume to put together a skilled team to visit the area and exercise their craft. And if all I had at hand was a young, inexperienced monitoring officer, I would recommend that he or she consult closely his or her well-thumbed set of Casley and Kumar, and also pay attention to the experiences of the authors represented in this present volume.

This brings me to the reason I am happy to be associated in a minor capacity with this book. One of the problems with rapid appraisal is that it has been difficult to lay one's hands easily on a set of experiences in which the practitioners set out what they did in some detail, warts and all, with a frank assessment of what they achieved, including the limitations. There have been growing exchanges among those using rapid appraisal methods, but for the uninitiated or the survey designer trained in formal statistical methods, access to such examples has been limited.

Nearly all the contributions in this book provide examples of information gathering in which—given the aims of the study in each instance—the non-random selection of respondents is clearly appropriate. Some indeed illustrate cases in which no sample as such is involved. In these instances, the appraisal process was applied to the actual micro-area in which a community-assisted development activity was occurring or was being planned. One of the contributions does provide an example of purposive sample selection in a situation in which most survey practitioners would consider orthodox sampling procedures appropriate. I return to their individual cases a little later.

One of the underlying themes in nearly all the case studies is the value of seeking out and soliciting in an unprejudiced manner the views, ideas, and aspirations of those who are the participants in and, to some extent, the subjects of the development process. There is perhaps a tendency by some current practitioners of rapid appraisal studies to assume that this was not a common practice hitherto. In my experience, this is not so. Development banks, development agencies, individual government departments, and smaller, private funders of development projects have engaged in a vast amount of project preparation and appraisal work which, at least in a substantial number of cases, involved travelling within the areas concerned and talking to local people. It is a myth that international staff stay in the main cities and do not muddy their expensive footwear in the "bush." In my 30 years' involvement with government, Food and Agriculture Organization of the United Nations (FAO), and World Bank undertakings, I have witnessed a vast amount of diligent effort to get to and talk to small farmers, rural traders, women attending clinics, and so on. As long ago as the 1950s, I was encouraged by my then-colonial superiors to spend three months with a tent, living in various parts of rural Uganda in order to get a feel for the pattern of small farming systems and economics.

No, what the contributors to this volume and others are doing is to codify these information-seeking processes and to improve the manner in which they are conducted. For myself, I would have benefited a great deal in my earlier years in Africa if I had known how to organize, for example, a focus group meeting.

Kumar and I have described the monitoring function as having three components: physical and financial monitoring, beneficiary contact monitoring, and diagnostic studies. Our second component we set in the context of monitoring penetration and adoption rates, which requires probability samples, although there is room within this category for selective application of the techniques described in this volume. It is for the third component of monitoring—namely the diagnostic study—that rapid appraisal techniques come into their own. When the reactions of the participants, or a subset of them, are unexpected or exhibit changes from an earlier trend, the project manager needs a diagnosis of the likely cause or causes, and such diagnosis is needed fast. A skilled team spending weeks rather than months in seeking out the opinions of the participants through open-ended discussions is likely to be the best way of providing such a diagnosis.

In the opening chapter, Kumar provides an overview of the methods most commonly used by rapid appraisal practitioners. He includes very important sections on both the limitations and advantages of these methods, as viewed from the perspective of a rapid appraisal practitioner. It is indicative of the improved understanding between such practitioners and statisticians that the limitations receive such equal coverage. The claim that RA techniques can provide more accurate information when used in appropriate circumstances hinges on the broad definition of accuracy. Statisticians tend to equate accuracy with quantifiable measures of sampling and non-sampling errors. Kumar, for his part, is concerned with accuracy, in terms of achieving a true insight into a respondent's feelings through a communication process which is more revealing than that achieved in a structured interview. One may put it thus: the non-sampling error measured in a structured survey may reveal the incidence of incorrect replies, but not the incidence of *correct but superficial* replies. It is the latter that Kumar believes can be minimized using the techniques he describes.

Following the overview, this volume contains eight examples of recent experiences in applying these methods in practice. Of them all, I consider the first by Scudder to be both one of the most important and one of the most controversial. It is important in that such an effort to monitor and evaluate the Mahaweli Program is a rare example of a sustained, consistent input over a number of years despite many problems, including the common one of needing to survive the danger of being the messenger who bears bad tidings. Many such efforts have been cut off from funding and access when early results embarrassed the executing and funding agencies.

It is controversial, in that the small sample was selected in about as non-random a way as would be possible to devise and was then maintained almost without rotation over a number of years. The author presents very clearly the dangers of such biased samples, but on balance believes other advantages accrued. Nor does the breaking of sample survey orthodoxy end here.   Some of the sample households were actively assisted with capital or lobbying of government agencies to overcome bureaucratic delays or advice, but were still retained in the sample.   The most worrying confession by Scudder, however, is that despite this emphasis on convenience and continuity, the data base has not been maintained in an easily retrievable format. This seems to obviate the advantages sought of such a methodology for which such a price in unknown biases was paid. Nevertheless, for those who employ a similar method, there is much to be learned from this example, including Scudder's own warnings.

Kumar gives a good example of an assessment based on group interviews in a classic context in which the groups—farmer's clubs—are well defined. Once again, as the author notes, there is the danger that the selection of the clubs was biased toward those performing well and those more readily accessible geographically. This must surely be the most common problem with rapid appraisal methods and should not become one that practitioners too readily accept, for the limitations then imposed on data interpretation are extreme. The Kumar example does provide a very clear and useful guide as to how to conduct group interviews, particularly in the care needed to obtain balanced participation and control pressures that build up within groups. His conclusions, too, largely avoid unjustified generalization of the findings—a good example of interpreting the information within the limitations imposed by the method.

Haggerty and Armstrong describe an example that combines the methods of interviews and focus groups. There is an intriguing use of a coordinating committee in the role of moderator, and a very detailed splitting of the main issue into over 30 component parts, with a questionnaire to be completed by the group for each part. Reading this, I wondered at times whether this was a description of a rapid appraisal method or of how to run a workshop. But this, perhaps, is merely a semantic issue, although the selection process for participants in the workshop is clearly of major significance when interpreting the findings.

The use of focus groups to assess a weaning food in Nigeria is very well described by Cabañero-Verzosa, Johnston, and Kayode. In this case study, one gets closest to classic market research techniques. Again, some rapid appraisal practitioners (and I do not refer to the authors of this study) are not aware of how much they owe to such earlier developments. Certainly, focus group interviews have been used by market researchers for many years. The novelty in this instance is not the technique, but its use in an underdeveloped, rural setting. The conclusions of this study provide a particularly good example of the non-random nature of the participant selection being of little concern, in terms of the accuracy of the results.

A blend of methods different from that used by Haggerty and Armstrong is described by Holtzman in the description of his study of vegetable seed marketing in Nepal. In this case, a combination of key informant interviews and direct observation were the methods of choice. In this contribution can be found a well-argued case for seeking out progressive farmers and marketers when agricultural market research is being undertaken. It is almost refreshing, given the current emphasis of development literature, to find a researcher who is prepared to defend not seeking out the vulnerable groups in certain circumstances when the potential for change is being assessed. Once again, ease of access played a role in site selection and, not for the first time in the case studies in this volume, one is concerned at the slowness of analysis compared to the speed of data collection.

Blumenfeld, Roxas, and de los Santos illustrate the direct observation technique in a very appropriate context; namely, the diagnosis of problems in health care delivery in the Philippines. The author's justification for the method adopted is very well argued and the description of the survey details should be of considerable value to other practitioners. Here again we have sampling controversy. The selection of the only province included in the study was influenced by "practical consider-ations of geographic accessibility, interest and cooperativeness of re-gional and provincial staffs." Health units were selected systematically from a ranking of all 54 according to the quality of care deemed to be provided—an interesting example of selecting from a list ranked by a qualitative attribute. But here, too, geographic accessibility and security influenced the final selections. Also important here is the point made by the authors; that the health units studied were likely to be better than average in the quality of their facilities and services, so that problems detected in these cases were likely to be at least as prevalent in others. Important, too (in a methodological sense), is how easily the direct ob-servers were accepted and soon merged into the general background without apparently altering the behavior of those being observed.

In the next-to-last case study, Appleby avoids the purposive sam-pling problem by adopting a complete coverage approach and going to some trouble to reach even remote centers, which in Zaire can mean some trouble indeed. Simple direct observation, counts, and listings of commercial activities in urban centers and marketplaces were the main data collection tools. This study also provides an example of a suitable use of key informants to provide background information on the local-ity. Another interesting aspect of this case is the application of such data when monitored over time to assess the impact of rural development within the context of central-place theory. The author recognizes the theoretical basis and designed his study accordingly.

In the final case study, Kabutha, Thomas-Slayter, and Ford present a very detailed Kenyan example of the preparation of a development project, which closely involves the intended participants in the appraisal process. No sampling controversy is involved here, because the data collection and analysis are conducted in the community in which activi-ties are to be identified and pursued. The use of simple tools such as sketch maps, village transects, and local preparation of historical time series are well described. The most interesting aspect of this example is how the data are used to prepare options for discussion and decision-making by the local community.

There are, I believe, many lessons to be obtained from a close reading of the examples of rapid appraisal methods, as applied in practice by seasoned practitioners. From my own experience, I noted two of the most common occurrences that arise singly or together in many of the contributions—excessive emphasis on convenience in selecting respon-dents and sites, and insufficient planning of the analysis relative to the planning of the data collection.

I stated earlier in this introduction that most of these studies were inappropriate for probability sampling methods. But there is room for concern in some cases at the neglect of even minimum safeguards required to reduce the dangers of misleading conclusions being drawn. Speed and cost constraints are insufficient justification for the acceptance of "geographical convenience" or "proximity to roads" that affected the selection of respondents in these cases. And there is little to be said for speeding up the data collection process if the analysis is to take as long as some of the examples of formal surveys often quoted by rapid appraisal practitioners in justification of the need for new approaches.

The value of these contributions is not least in the frankness with which the authors reveal these points of potential criticism. This, with the value-added effect of bringing together in one volume such varied experiences, all with something to commend them is, I believe, sufficient justification for the effort that Krishna Kumar and all the contributors have made.

References

Casley, Dennis J., and Krishna Kumar. 1987. *Project Monitoring and Evaluation in Agriculture.* Baltimore, Maryland: John Hopkins University Press.

_____. 1988. *The Collection, Analysis, and Use of Monitoring and Evaluation Data.* Baltimore, Maryland: John Hopkins University Press.

1

An Overview of Rapid Appraisal Methods in Development Settings

Krishna Kumar

In this chapter, Krishna Kumar provides an overview of rapid appraisal methods, focusing on their nature, types, limitations, the rationale for their use, and appropriate roles.

According to Kumar, rapid appraisal methods fall within a continuum of informal and formal modes of data collection used to provide decision-related information in development settings. At one extreme are the highly informal methods that rely on intuition, experience, and common sense, and which do not generate information that can be verified. At the other extreme are highly formal methods developed and refined by social and economic researchers. Such methods generate quantitative data that can be statistically analyzed to draw conclusions.

The author suggests that the rapid appraisal methods lie between these two ends of the continuum. They are neither highly informal nor fully formalized, and require more than common sense on the part of the investigator. He identifies five methods—key informant interviews, focus group discussions, community/group interviews, structured direct observation, and informal surveys—that constitute the core of rapid appraisal methodology.

Several limitations of rapid appraisal methods are mentioned by the author. First, the reliability and validity of the information generated can be questionable in many instances, due to factors such as the use of informal sampling, individual biases of the investigator/interviewer, and the difficulty in recording, coding, and analyzing the qualitative data. Second, rapid appraisal methods do not generate quantitative data from which generalizations can be made for a whole population. And finally, the general credibility of these methods is low compared to formal survey methods. These limitations should be weighed against the obvious strengths of rapid ap-

praisal methods. Such methods can rapidly generate relevant infor-
mation with relatively low investment of resources. Moreover, expe-
rience shows that they can provide in-depth understanding and
information in the project or program setting.

The author suggests that rapid appraisal methods should be used
rather selectively, depending on the purpose of the study, availabil-
ity of resources and, above all, the nature of the information re-
quired. He concludes this chapter by identifying situations in which
their application is particularly appropriate.

DURING THE PAST DECADE, development practitioners have developed, tested, refined, and applied many rapid appraisal methods to gather information and ideas for the design, implementation, monitoring, and evaluation of projects and programs. They have published papers, articles, and monographs articulating the nature, underlying premises, strengths, and limitations of rapid appraisal methodology. They have also held many regional and international conferences on the subject, bringing together experts from different disciplines and backgrounds. As a result, the phrase "rapid appraisal" and its various synonyms (rural reconnaissance; rapid, low-cost methods; intermediate methods) have entered the vocabulary of the development community. The methodology has acquired an intellectual legitimacy never dreamed of by its early proponents, who invented it while grappling with the problem of gathering relevant information for agricultural and rural development initiatives with limited time and resources. We can indeed paraphrase Victor Hugo by saying, "Rapid appraisal is an idea whose time has come."

This chapter explains the nature of the rapid appraisal methodology and the various methods that are generally subsumed under it. It also describes the methodology's strengths, limitations, and general applicability. The purpose here is not to resolve considerable confusion and controversies still surrounding this methodology, but to state our position in order to provide a framework for the case studies included in this volume.

Rapid appraisal methodology is discussed here in the context of the goal of applied research; that is, to provide timely, relevant information to decision-makers on pressing issues they face in the project and program setting. The aim of applied research is not to solve theoretical puzzles contributing to the generation and verification of social or economic theory, but to facilitate a more rational decision-making process in real-life circumstances. This distinction is important because the success of applied research is to be judged, not only by the scientific criteria of validity and reliability, but also with reference to the relevance of the research to the problem and its timely delivery in a cost-effective fashion.

Methodological Paradigm

The exponents of rapid appraisal methodology have come from two entirely different intellectual traditions with differing perspectives on the nature and style of social and economic research.

The first paradigm, which has been developed by social phenomenologists or symbolic interactionists (although significant differences exist between them, we have coupled them for the sake of simplicity), questions the premise that objective reality can be captured by social science methodology. Its proponents view social or economic phenomena as constituting not one, but a set of over-arching multiple realities. The usual simile given is that of peeling an onion: as one layer is peeled, another comes to surface. In the same fashion, various investigators researching a phenomenon encounter multiple layers of realities, which are largely, though not totally, exclusive.

According to this paradigm, the premises, preferences, and interests of various investigators largely condition their construction of the reality. For example, a development intervention is likely to be construed differently by its various stakeholders—the donor agency, the host government, the bureaucracy that manages it, the clients for whom it is designed and implemented, and finally, the other actors who constitute its wider environment. Each of these stakeholders, the exponents of this paradigm argue, is likely to perceive the role of the intervention differently, to emphasize different sets of issues, to highlight different achievements and failures, and invariably, to make different recommendations. Thus, there is no single reality that can be obtained by an investigator.

Within the context of this paradigm, many experts view rapid appraisal as a tool to articulate the opinions, concerns, judgments, and perspectives of those who are often ignored by the social scientists researching development interventions. Thus, they stress the use of rapid appraisal methods for discovering such "indigenous knowledge" as the views of small farmers—particularly women and the landless—and the perspectives of deprived groups, and not as a pursuit of objective reality by an objective investigator.

In sharp contrast, the logical positivist paradigm is based on the premise that a social or economic phenomenon exists not only in the minds of individuals, but also as an objective social reality. The fact that it may be viewed differently by individuals does not negate its existence, nor does it imply that it cannot be objectively described by investigators. Consider, for example, the case of an initiative designed to reform the macroeconomic policies of a developing country. The various actors involved may have varying conceptions of it and may stress different effects. In fact, often the people who may be most affected may not understand the initiative or its impacts on their lives. However, this does not mean that economists cannot examine the initiative and its intended and unintended effects on the concerned people.

Logical positivists believe that the primary task of social and economic research is to go beyond the superficial, partial reconstructions and arrive at the objective reality as physical scientists do by using established procedures for gathering and analyzing information. Its purpose is to discover and describe social phenomena and processes, systematically explain their causes, and identify contingencies under which they occur. Rapid appraisal is construed here as one of many sets of data gathering methods to achieve this objective.

Formal and Informal Modes of Data Collection

For us, rather than debating the above alternative views, rapid appraisal methodology can be better explained as falling within a continuum of various informal and formal modes of data collection that are used to provide decision-related information in development settings.

On one extreme are highly informal modes of data collection for which precise procedures are not established. These informal approaches rely on intuition, experience, and common sense, and do not generate systematic information that can be verified. Examples of such modes are conversations with concerned individuals, general perusals of official records, and short visits to existing or planned project sites or institutions. For example, a project manager who wants to know whether small entrepreneurs are satisfied with the technical assistance provided by the project might talk with some of them or have a simple discussion with a few field staff. If enough time is available, the project manager may even visit a few firms that have received technical assistance. On the basis of such meetings and visits, the manager may be able to reach a conclusion. The majority of decisions made in development bureaucracies are usually based on the data gained through such informal methods.

The strengths of informal approaches to data collection are that they are quick and inexpensive, and usually do not require outside assistance. Often the decision-maker alone is able to gather relevant data in a readily usable form. However, the problem with informal approaches is the uncertainty concerning the quality of the information gathered. Personal biases and prejudices can affect the reliability and validity of the information collected. Often the investigator finds what he or she wants to find and overlooks what does not support his or her thinking or intuition. As a result, the credibility of such information, and consequently, of the decisions based on it, tend to be low in the eyes of others.

On the other end of the continuum are the highly formal data collection methods that researchers have developed and refined over the years. These methods, which include cross-sectional and longitudinal sample surveys, censuses, experiments, and non-reactive data collection, have contributed to significant advances in social, economic, and behavioral sciences. Their procedures are largely specified, and the investigator is expected to scrupulously follow them in theory if not in practice. Such methods generate quantitative data that can be statistically analyzed to draw conclusions within specified confidence margins.

The most important strength of formal methods is the relative accuracy of the data generated by them. Although the problems of individual bias and erroneous inferences are not completely solved, they are greatly reduced. At least, other investigators can easily examine the studies based on formal methods for such limitations. Consequently, the study findings have credibility in the eyes of decision-makers.

Despite their accuracy and wide popularity, formal methods have their own limitations in many development settings. Often, they require greater time and resources than are available to the managers of the development interventions. For example, a medium-sized sample survey may take four to six months to complete, and a larger survey may take even longer. Moreover, large sample surveys cost thousands of dollars, especially when an expatriate specialist is involved. Above all, there is the question of whether managers really need the type of precise and often extensive information these studies produce.

Between these two extremes lie rapid appraisal methods, which are neither highly informal nor fully formalized, and which require more than robust common sense and understanding on the part of the investigator. The investigator using rapid appraisal methods must have sufficient grounding in formal data collection methods to use them effectively. Although the investigators generally have considerable flexibility, they should make every attempt to systematically report procedures so that others can scrutinize them for accuracy and relevance. In most cases, rapid appraisal methods do not generate quantitative information from which generalizations can be made in a statistical sense to populations larger than those in the immediate cases examined.

Core Rapid Appraisal Methods

The following five methods constitute the core of rapid appraisal and have been used in various permutations by experts in the project or program setting.

Key Informant Interviews

Perhaps one of the most important methods is the key informant interview, which is widely used by development practitioners. In fact, a majority of evaluations and policy-oriented studies conducted by international development organizations rely largely on key informant interviews. As the name indicates, such interviews involve interviewing a select group of individuals who are in a position to provide the needed information, ideas, and insights. Two special features of key informant interviews can be mentioned here.

First, key informant interviews are essentially qualitative interviews, and are carried out with interview guides that list topics and issues to be covered in a session. The interviewer frames the questions in the course of interviews and subtly probes the informants to elicit more information. The atmosphere is informal, resembling a conversation among acquaintances. The interviewer takes extensive notes that are developed later. It is the unstructured nature of the interviews that invests them with special meaning and relevance in the context of rapid appraisal.

Second, only a small number of informants are interviewed who are selected on the basis of their specialized knowledge and experience on the subject under investigation. Depending on the nature and scope of an inquiry, the investigator identifies appropriate groups from which the key informants may be drawn, and then selects a few from each group. Thus, for example, if the researcher is interested in learning about the functioning of agricultural credit institutions, he/she would first identify groups most likely to include people who can shed light on the subject, such as traders, moneylenders, village chiefs, farmers, local government officials, and other experts. The investigator would then select a few informants from each category so that diverse viewpoints and concerns are fully represented. The number of informants usually ranges from 10 to 25.

The accuracy and depth of information obtained from key informant interviews depends primarily on the care that is exercised in selecting the informants, developing suitable interview guides, training interviewers, conducting interviews, probing informants, and recording responses.

Focus Group Interviews

Another method, recently added to the repository of rapid appraisal, is the focus group interview. Focus groups have long been used by marketing researchers to gauge the reactions of potential consumers to new products and services. In recent years, development experts have started using focus groups to design, implement, and evaluate health and family planning projects. There is no reason, however, why they cannot be used in other sectors as well.

Focus group interviews are conducted to discuss a specific topic in group sessions. Participants discuss ideas, issues, insights, and experiences among themselves, and each member is free to comment, criticize, or elaborate on the views expressed by others. The premise underlying the focus group method is that free discussions generate fresh ideas and insights because the participants stimulate each other.

Focus groups are limited in size to 8 to 12 carefully-selected participants. Such small groups tend to facilitate the free flow of discussions. As much as possible, groups are homogenous in composition, with members sharing similar background and experience. A session generally lasts one to two hours, although in some cases it can be longer. The moderator introduces the subject, keeps the discussion going using subtle probing techniques, and tries to prevent a few participants from dominating the discussions. Generally, several sessions with different participants are held on a specific topic. The composition may vary among the groups.

Community Interviews

Unlike in focus group discussions, in which participants discuss a subject among themselves, in community interviews, the investigator(s) asks questions, raises issues, and seeks responses from the participants. The primary interactions are between the interviewer(s) and the participants rather than among participants.

Community interviews take the form of public meetings open to all community members. The date and location of the meeting are announced in advance. The number of participants tends to be large (more than 15 persons), although past experience shows that, unless concerted steps are taken, certain groups—especially women and people of lower socioeconomic strata—are often underrepresented because of social and cultural barriers. Community interviews are ideally conducted on the basis of a carefully prepared questionnaire that lists all important questions to be asked. The advantage of having a well-designed questionnaire is that questions can be phrased in language that the participants can understand.

Every effort is made in community interviews to make the discussion interesting and to ensure the participation of all those present. Although community interviews can be conducted by one interviewer, a team of two or more is preferable, because it is difficult for a single individual to preside over the meeting, ask relevant questions, and record the answers.

Structured Direct Observation

Structured direct observation is yet another rapid appraisal method that has been used with considerable success in developing countries. It involves careful gathering of data based on well-designed observation forms, which are designed to take into consideration the nature of the object to be observed. In most instances, direct observation also involves individual or group interviews, or both.

Structured direct observation should not be confused with the ethnographic method of participant observation. Three major differences between the two may be noted here. First, the participant observation method is a long-term process; a researcher observes a phenomenon or process for months, even years. In contrast, studies based on structured direct observation can be completed within days or weeks. Second, while participant observation focuses primarily on social and cultural phenomena, direct observation can deal as well with physical objects, such as roads, dams, or agricultural production. Finally, in participant observation, the observer tries to empathize with the people being studied to gain an insider's perspective. This is not always the case in direct observation.

Direct observation is better conducted by a team of experts than by a single individual. A team approach contributes to more comprehensive data collection and helps to prevent individual biases.

Informal Surveys

Finally, informal surveys have emerged as an important tool in rapid appraisal studies of agricultural and rural development interventions. Such surveys are usually conducted on the basis of an open-ended questionnaire that permits respondents to answer questions in their own words. The sample size for informal surveys usually ranges from 25 to 50 people, who are selected on the basis of non-probability sampling techniques. One popular technique is convenience sampling, in which respondents are interviewed in markets, shops, public meetings, organizations, and other places selected on the basis of easy accessibility. Finally, the interviewers enjoy considerable flexibility in asking questions and are not constrained by the given questionnaire.

Although informal surveys are in many ways similar to key informant interviews, important differences exist between them. First, while the key informants provide information about others, respondents in informal surveys answer questions about themselves. Thus, to understand the problems faced by the owners of micro-enterprises, in a study based on key informant interviews, the investigator will not only interview the enterprise owners, but also others who might be knowledgeable about them, such as project staff, concerned government officials, traders, executives of owners' organizations, and other experts. An informal survey, on the other hand, will primarily target the owners. Second, while similar if not the same sets of questions are asked of each respondent in informal surveys, this is not the case in key informant interviews. In fact, different sets of questions are often put to key informants of different backgrounds and experience to obtain a more balanced and comprehensive understanding of the subject. Third, the number of respondents in key informant interviews is typically smaller than in informal surveys.

Limitations of Rapid Appraisal

Before examining the strengths and potential of rapid appraisal methods, it is important to recognize their limitations. Because of the initial success of many rapid appraisal studies in generating relevant information and enlarging understanding, there exists considerable euphoria about them. As a result, practitioners tend to minimize or ignore the following shortcomings.

First, the reliability and validity of the information generated by rapid appraisal methods may be questionable in many cases. In the language of social research, validity refers to the soundness of the research findings. If the answer to the question is sound, the research is supposed to be valid, and vice versa. Reliability is one of the constituent elements of validity and refers to the extent of random variation in the results of the study. Three factors may contribute to the low reliability and validity of the findings of rapid appraisal studies.

Probability sampling is not used in the selection of individuals or groups for such studies. Investigators rely largely on their convenience or on expert judgment to select the people to be interviewed, the sites to be visited, or the activities to be observed. As a result, it is quite possible that the sample is not representative of the whole population. For example, when communities are selected using non-probability sampling, outside investigators are more likely to select communities that are easily accessible by transportation. Moreover, poor and deprived groups are likely to be underrepresented in community interviews, unless efforts have been made to ensure their participation.

During the data collection stage, individual preferences, judgments, and views of the interviewer/observer may significantly affect the conduct of inquiry. This happens, not because of any deliberate attempt on the part of the researchers, but primarily because the research instruments used in rapid appraisal investigations are usually open-ended. The interviewer/observer enjoys considerable flexibility in framing and asking questions, observing phenomena, and recording answers and observations. While such flexibility contributes to more in-depth discussion, it also leads to increased probability of introduction of biases and distortions.

For example, one persistent problem with key informant interviews, focus groups, and group interviews has been that unless investigators are extremely careful, they hear what they want to hear and ignore what they do not want to hear. Still worse, they may not even be aware of this problem. For instance, in many focus groups, we find that moderators unknowingly introduce biases by reacting with enthusiasm to comments that confirm their preconceived views, while showing indifference to opposing views; by being patient with those who seem to be supporting their positions, while demonstrating impatience with others; or by not probing those who articulate a different viewpoint or volunteer information that contradicts their preconceptions. In any case, the result is that data, opinions, and arguments that do not support the pre-existing framework of the investigator are not always fully presented in the groups.

Qualitative data, by their nature, are difficult to record, code, and analyze objectively. This problem is not unique to rapid appraisal methods, but is found in ethnographic investigations as well. Only recently have anthropologists and sociologists started focusing on developing and refining techniques for recording and analyzing qualitative data and for improving the data's reliability and validity.

A caveat is necessary here. While there is little doubt that validity and reliability can be a major problem in many rapid appraisal studies, this is certainly not a universal limitation. In fact, most investigators using rapid appraisal methodology usually take several steps to improve the accuracy of their findings. First, they use a well-articulated conceptual framework, which is often—though not always—empirically grounded. Thus, they try to solve the problem of validity by focusing on what researchers call "external validity." Second, they employ many strategies used in ethnographic investigations to minimize the element of bias during the collection and analysis of data. Third, they try to use more than one rapid appraisal method so that data generated by one source can be cross-checked with those produced from the other sources. Fourth, many practitioners are becoming increasingly aware of the problem of subjective bias, and therefore critically scrutinize their own procedures.

Second, rapid appraisal methods do not generate quantitative data from which generalizations can be made for a whole population. They can give a relatively accurate picture of the prevalence of a phenomenon, attitude, perception, or behavior pattern, but not of its extent or pervasiveness. For example, an investigator may learn that farmers are not availing themselves of the short-term agricultural credit offered by public sector banks because of the cumbersome delay in processing loan applications. However, the investigator could never know what percentage of farmers in the project area are being deterred by this factor. Even when some quantitative data are generated by some of the rapid appraisal methods, they cannot be the basis for making generalizations for the entire universe.

Finally, there is some problem with the credibility of the findings reached by using rapid appraisal methodology. Most decision-makers are more impressed with precise figures than descriptive statements. For example, the finding of a sample survey that 83 percent of the local entrepreneurs were satisfied with the technical assistance provided by a project is likely to carry more weight than the conclusion based on key informant interviews, that most of the entrepreneurs interviewed seemed satisfied with the technical assistance.

Rationale for Using Rapid Appraisal

Why should investigators use the rapid appraisal methodology if it has these shortcomings? The simple answer is that it has several advantages in the context of development projects and programs that must be weighed against its limitations.

First, the most compelling reason for using rapid appraisal methods is that the cost of such studies is usually much less than others that use more rigorous methods. For example, one sample survey conducted by a U.S. firm is likely to cost US$100,000 to US$200,000, an amount that can support three to four rapid appraisal studies. The costs of these studies is low partly because of the smaller sample size and more focused nature of the investigation.

It should be recognized that under the conditions of scarce resources prevailing in developing countries, the opportunity cost of resources spent on information-gathering is high because these resources can be easily expended on activities that would more directly contribute to increased production and incomes. Thus, the US$200,000 needed for conducting a socioeconomic survey of farmers could instead be used to provide farmers with agricultural inputs that would have a tangible, positive impact on agricultural production and incomes of the concerned households. By reducing the overall cost of studies, rapid appraisal can therefore help project and program managers optimize the use of available resources.

Second, rapid appraisal studies can be completed quickly, thus ensuring that the findings and recommendations are available to decision-makers when needed. For example, through community interviews, an investigator(s) can reach eight to ten communities or villages within a week, thereby soliciting the views of hundreds of people. Such a course is not possible in the case of a carefully conducted sample survey. Likewise, focus group interviews enable the investigator to benefit from the judgment of concerned people within a matter of days, rather than months. This is indeed a very important advantage, because in project and program settings, administrative deadlines and not the requirements of field research determine the time span available for conducting studies. Seldom do managers have the option of postponing crucial decisions in anticipation of information. In most cases, managers must make important decisions at a given time—with or without information. The timely availability of data and findings is important to them, even if these are not as precise or elaborate as might be wished.

The widespread interest in rapid appraisal methodology was initially heightened by the realization among development practitioners that studies based on formal methods are often too time-consuming. Therefore, even when such studies generated valid and reliable findings, they were of little use if these results were not available at the time a decision had to be made. (It should be recognized, however, that with careful planning and the use of micro-computers, the time required for sample surveys, and even censuses, can be reduced.)

Third, in many instances, especially when an interpretive understanding of a phenomenon or process is required, rapid appraisal methods are successful in obtaining relevant data, ideas, or recommendations.

A major limitation of many formal methods is that they tend to focus primarily on quantifiable information, and much information is lost in the process of "operationalizing" social and economic phenomena. Thus, they are often of limited value in studying complex socioeconomic changes, highly interactive social situations, or people's underlying motivations, beliefs, and value systems in project and program settings.

Much of this kind of information can be captured by rapid appraisal methods.

Finally, rapid appraisal methods provide flexibility to the investigator to explore new ideas and issues that may not have been anticipated in planning the study, but that are relevant to its purpose. For example, suppose in the course of a study, a key informant indicates that one of the main reasons entrepreneurs are not taking out loans in the micro-enterprise development project is the complex and cumbersome loan application procedure. The investigator can pursue this issue with the other informants, even though it was not included in the interview guide. Such a change is not possible in sample surveys or censuses once the questionnaire is designed and the investigation is underway.

Appropriate Role for Rapid Appraisal

Perhaps the most important question that can be asked about rapid appraisal methods is, "When should they be used in development settings?" In answering this question, it should be recognized that the choice of appropriate methodology—formal or rapid appraisal—should be dictated primarily by the information requirements of the decision-maker and the resources and time available for conducting an inquiry. It should not be determined by some abstract notion of validity and reliability, which, though essential for basic research and theory formulation, is only one of the many considerations in designing, implementing, and evaluating development interventions.

Three factors should be examined in choosing appropriate methods in a given situation. The first, obviously, is the purpose of the study. If the primary purpose of an investigation is to make major policy choices or programmatic decisions, the need for employing formal methods, which are more likely to generate precise and valid information, is apparent. For example, if the objective of an evaluation is to assess the effects of structural adjustment programs on lower socioeconomic strata or to test the effectiveness of a highly innovative agricultural development program introduced in a country, comprehensive longitudinal and cross-sectional surveys will undoubtedly be necessary. In such cases, the stakes are too high to rely on less reliable measures. On the other hand, if the objective of a study is to make a simple assessment of how a project has been doing, what services it has been successfully providing, and what implementation problems it has been encountering, rapid appraisal methods may better serve the purpose. This is, in part, because very precise information is not really needed and the risks involved in arriving at less accurate results are likely to be limited—if present at all—and may be small compared with the resources and time saved.

The second factor, which logically follows from the first, is the nature of the information required. One should not assume that formal methods are always efficacious in answering all kinds of questions. In fact, many questions that require in-depth, inside information can be better answered through rapid appraisal methods. Such methods are particularly appropriate for the following situations:

- *When descriptive information is sufficient for decision-making.* Such information may pertain to assessing organizations and institutions, socioeconomic conditions of an area (village and communities, for example), or characteristics of the relevant populations, including cultural patterns, behavior patterns, and values and beliefs. In fact, rapid appraisal studies have been most promising in stimulating insightful, extensive discussions of smallholders, the economic and social environment in which they live, the institutional constraints they face in adopting recommended innovations, their views and perceptions about development interventions, and their suggestions and recommendations. It is hardly surprising, then, that farming systems specialists have been the most outstanding exponents of these methods.

- *When an understanding is required of the motivations and attitudes that may affect people's behavior, in particular the behavior of target populations or stakeholders in an intervention.* Rapid appraisal methods are quite successful in answering the "why" and "how" questions. For example, key informant interviews or focus group discussions are more likely than sample surveys to provide insightful answers to such questions as, "Why are farmers not adopting the recommended variety of seeds?" or "How is the internal politics in an agricultural university affecting its capability to do strategic planning?" or "What institutional barriers are coming in the way of promised policy changes in the health sector?" or "How are macroeconomic policies being implemented in the country?"

- *When available quantitative data must be interpreted.* Usually, donor agencies, hosts governments, and project and program managers have access to routinely-generated quantitative data (for example, data about financial outlays, targets reached, volume of inputs and services provided to the participating populations, or beneficiaries contacted) or data gathered for other purposes (for example, data collected by donor agencies, projects, or host governments). Many of the rapid appraisal methods are extremely useful in interpreting such data, resolving inconsistencies, and deriving meaningful conclusions. Suppose, for instance, project records show that female farmers are not using the technical package recommended by the agricultural development project. Interviews with selected key informants and one or two focus groups can shed light on the factors that explain this behavior.

- *When the primary purpose of the study is to generate suggestions and recommendations.* In many cases, the prime reason for an investigation is to solve a problem facing a project or program. What is needed is a set of practical recommendations. For example, the manager of a contraceptive social marketing project may be more concerned with finding out what can be done to augment contraceptive sales than with conducting an in-depth, quantitative study of the subject. The manager's needs can be better served through interviews with the concerned doctors, pharmacists, medical workers, traders, and current or potential users to elicit their suggestions. An alternative may be conducting a few focus groups on the subject.
- *When the need is to develop questions, hypotheses, and propositions for more elaborate, comprehensive formal studies.* Key informant and group interviews, along with the literature review, are widely used for this purpose.

The third and final factor that should be considered in choosing between formal and rapid appraisal methods is the available resources. These include money, technical expertise, time, and the institutional support for research. All must be considered in any given situation.

23 - 55

2

Monitoring a Large-Scale Resettlement Program with Repeated Household Interviews

Thayer Scudder

In this chapter, Thayer Scudder describes the methodology of the repeated informal surveys he and Kapila Vimaladharama conducted to assess the impact of the Accelerated Mahaweli Programme in Sri Lanka. This major irrigation and resettlement project was designed to bring under irrigation 50,000 hectares of new land and to improve irrigation facilities of another 10,000 hectares of already irrigated land.

To understand the project's effects on the lives of the settlers and the problems they faced, Scudder and Vimaladharama repeatedly interviewed the same households over a ten-year period. The number of households interviewed ranged from 19 to 45. Over time, they established rapport with these households, and the interviews were conducted in an informal atmosphere. In addition to giving information about themselves, the respondents were asked to give information about other households who were in the same irrigation turnout or came from the same community of origin. They supplemented interview data with those obtained from community interviews.

The author mentions that their methodology generated useful information, insights, and understandings that could have helped the project management. For example, as early as in 1983, their data indicated that the full potential of the project was not likely to be realized, as the net income of the settlers was not sufficient to generate major multiplier effects in terms of enterprise development and employment generation. The findings of the 1984 survey further confirmed this conclusion by showing that the living standards of the sampled households deteriorated or remained stagnant. The report of the 1985 survey also noted that Tamil-speaking settlers

were not being fully incorporated into the program. All these find-
ings and conclusions proved to be correct with hindsight.

   Three limitations of this methodology should not be overlooked,
however. First, since the sample is both small and opportunistic,
there exists a high probability of bias in the findings. In our judg-
ment, the sample seems more appropriate for highlighting problem
areas to be further explored than for making generalizations about
an entire population. Second, the researchers' familiarity with the
respondents—and the latter's expectations of help from them—
might have influenced their responses. For example, it is not un-
likely that the respondents over-stressed their problems and under-
stated the benefits they obtained in anticipation that the author
would exercise his influence to obtain greater assistance for them.
Third, a time interval of one or two years is too long for accurate
recall. Despite these limitations (which can be easily overcome with
more careful planning, and by using a larger sample), this method-
ology has great potential for monitoring and evaluation.

NOW IN ITS 12TH YEAR, an ongoing review (Scudder 1979, 1980, and
1981a, and Scudder and Vimaladharma 1984, 1985, 1986, and 1989) of
the settlement component of Sri Lanka's Accelerated Mahaweli
Programme (AMP) has three major purposes. The first is to evaluate, in
very general terms, the impact of the AMP on over 50,000 households
settled on irrigable lands in the Kala Oya, Mahaweli, and Madura Oya
basins since the mid-1970s. The second is to assess the implications of
those impacts for realization of the AMP's major goals as they relate to
employment generation, increases in production and productivity, rising living standards, and regional development. The third purpose is to
report findings to the relevant Sri Lankan government agencies, to the
United States Agency for International Development (USAID), and to
other interested donors within a fortnight after completion of each field
survey. Throughout, USAID has funded the study—through its Office
of Evaluation up to January 1979, and thereafter, through the Institute
for Development Anthropology, or through the Clark University/Insti-
tute for Development Anthropology Cooperative Agreement on Human
Settlements and Natural Resource Systems Analysis (SARSA) with
USAID's Bureau for Science and Technology.

   To date, eight project-related surveys have been made, including two
in 1979, and one each in 1980, 1981, 1983, 1984, 1985, and 1989. Brief
visits were also made in 1988. Further assessment is to be undertaken
during 1990 and 1991. In-country evaluations last four to seven weeks,
with a report submitted during the final week. Costs, involving two
senior investigators, international travel for one, and in-country travel

and per diem for both, range between $20,000 and $40,000 per evaluation.

Even though most USAID funds went to one irrigation command area (System B), it was agreed from the start that the study should include the three major settlement areas of the AMP (Systems H, C, and B). It was also agreed that the investigators would have the flexibility to follow up on unexpected findings.

The settlement of large numbers of people in problem-prone environments can be expected to have a wide range of impacts, most of which have policy implications. Included are impacts on the natural resource base, human health, community organization, political relationships between different categories of settlers, and living standards at the household, community, and regional levels. This case study's scope covers all of these, along with the effectiveness of the planning and implementing institutions. Throughout, however, the main emphasis has been on household living standards. The key aspect of the methodology for surveying these living standards has been repeated interviews with a small, stratified opportunity sample of households.

A fundamental assumption of the investigators is that it is the rising disposable income of hundreds of thousands of small-scale producers that drives development forward during the early stages of industrialization (Mellor 1986). As disposable incomes rise, low-income producers not only diversify their household economies in predictable ways, but also buy a remarkably similar range of locally- and nationally-made goods and services—the demand for which increases the generation of a widening range of non-farm enterprises and employment (Johnston and Kirby 1975).

Such behavior is especially characteristic of households colonizing new lands (Scudder 1985). Conversely, if settler households are unable to move beyond subsistence, or if incomes fall, goals relating to increased production for the market, to employment, and to regional development suffer. Either way, concentrating on changes and continuities in settler living standards enables evaluators to assess the extent to which project goals are being met.

Country and Program Setting

The Accelerated Mahaweli Programme

Sri Lanka's first major attempt at regional development, the Accelerated Mahaweli Programme, is one of the largest development projects currently under way in the tropics and sub-tropics. In 1977, the Sri Lankan Government decided to accelerate the development of the country's dry zone that had been outlined in a number of UNDP/FAO-assisted feasibility studies. Four mainstream dams on the Mahaweli, Sri Lanka's largest river, were the key intervention. Increasing the national supply of electricity by about 50 percent during the AMP years, these dams—in conjunction with hundreds of kilometers of main canals, and other dams in the Kala Oya and Madura Oya Basins—would also store sufficient water to intensify production on approximately 10,000 hectares of previously irrigated land, and also to bring under irrigation approximately 50,000 hectares of new land in north central and northeastern Sri Lanka. System H was settled first, with ongoing settlement still underway in Systems C and B during 1990 (Figure 2.1). With donor assistance totaling over US$1.0 billion dollars, project costs to date approximate US$2.0 billion dollars.

The Settlement Component of the AMP

As planned by a small interdisciplinary task force in the early 1970s, the implementation of the settlement component of the AMP involved a comprehensive program of land reform whereby each head of household, including married sons over 18 years of age, was to receive one hectare of irrigable land and a 0.2 hectare homelot. This size was based, not on income calculations, but rather on the amount of irrigated land that experimentation had shown could be double-cropped by family labor alone.   After the 1977 election, a parastatal organization, the Mahaweli Authority of Sri Lanka (MASL), was created to accelerate implementation.

Though intended to catalyze a process of integrated area development, the AMP was planned and implemented primarily as a paddy production scheme. Four kinds of settlers were involved. Priority was given to the host population already resident in Systems H, C, and B, and to at least 30,000 evacuees who had to give up their lands and/or homes to make way for dams, reservoirs, canals, and other infrastructure. The numbers in both categories were seriously underestimated. This reduced the number of outsiders from different electorates throughout the country that could volunteer for settlement and who made up the third category of settlers. Most of these government-sponsored settlers were selected on the basis of landlessness and family type (young couples with small children were preferred). As for the fourth and smallest category of settlers, this consisted of spontaneous settlers who had moved into a given Mahaweli command area prior to a cutoff date, after which more recent spontaneous settlers were ineligible for selection.

Figure 2.1 Accelerated Mahaweli Program

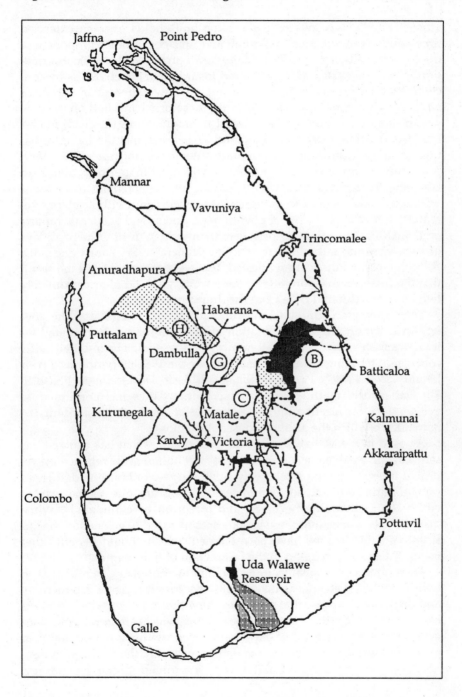

Methodology

The repeated interviews with the same households over an extended time period were the most important and time-consuming component of the survey methodology. These interviews provided the basic information for assessing project impacts and institutional effectiveness by concentrating on project-related problems, on how different members of each household attempted to cope with those problems, and on the new circumstances in which settlers found themselves. In the field, household information was checked against, and complemented by, information obtained from larger community interviews and interviews with government officials and other knowledgeable people. Back in Colombo, household data were further complemented by discussions with headquarters staff in government agencies and with academic researchers, and by a review of government, donor, and academic reports on the AMP. Draft final reports were then written during the final days of each visit and submitted to the Government of Sri Lanka and AID. Although comments were requested, few were received, with the result that the final report—submitted after a waiting period of approximately two months—differed little from the draft final report.

The two-person survey team proposed in 1980 to AID and the government that an ongoing evaluation of the AMP based on repeated interviews with a relatively small number of households be initiated. AID concurred, building annual evaluations for the 1981-86 period into their January 1981 Project Paper on Mahaweli Basin Development Phase II. Since then, the methodology for such interviews has continued to evolve, the most recent addition being greater emphasis on studying the networks to which the 45 1989 households belong.

As used in the Mahaweli case, the methodology that has evolved has some major weaknesses. Some of these are inherent in reliance on repeated interviews with a relatively small number of households. These can be mitigated, but not eliminated. Others are due to the way in which the methodology evolved and these *can* be eliminated. While there is no evidence that these weaknesses have led to erroneous conclusions, valuable lessons have been learned, which should benefit other users. These are discussed in the last section of this chapter.

There are several justifications for this methodology. Emphasis on household living standards makes sense because it is rising productivity and disposable income that will determine the extent to which projects like the AMP meet their goals. Repeated interviews are important, since goal achievement can not be expected to occur within a five- to ten-year period in a project in which the main producers are thousands of households pioneering a new habitat with a problem-prone technology.

Keeping the sample size small is essential, since large-scale surveys based on random sampling are seldom repeated because of their high costs, in terms of money, personnel, and data management. Even where benchmark surveys are completed, their costs often delay the publication of results by years, as opposed to the months involved in producing reports based on repeated interviews—as in this case—with a small number of households.

Repeated Interviews

Repeated interviews also provide more reliable information, since researchers are better able to evaluate the accuracy of the information given, and household members are more likely to provide thoughtful answers to interviewers who are knowledgeable about their affairs. The methodological weaknesses during the early years of the study notwithstanding, another justification of the Mahaweli study is that none of the major conclusions has subsequently been shown to be erroneous. A major purpose of repeated interviews with 30 to 50 households is to identify problems affecting the realization of project goals as they arise. If one-third of a small sample are having problems with the preparation of, or water delivery to, their one- hectare holdings, and if over half are having problems with malaria and the repayment of their seasonal agricultural loans, it is reasonable to assume that malaria is a problem and that land preparation, water delivery, and provision of credit are defective. Similarly, if only a small minority of households have moved beyond subsistence over a five- to ten-year period, one can assume fewer multiplier effects, in terms of employment generation and non-farm enterprise development.

The purpose of such evaluations is not to produce statistically significant correlations for academic publications, but rather, timely information for policy-makers, planners, and implementing officials. Repeated interviews with a relatively small number of households produce just that type of information. While complementing them with large-scale surveys will provide more "reliable" information, there is apt to be a major cost, in terms of the prompt initiation of corrective action associated with its delayed receipt. Such delays suggest that a more cost-effective approach would be to improve methodologies based on repeated interviews with small samples.

The same two-person research team has been involved in the study since its commencement. One member (K. P. Vimaladharma) is a senior Sri Lankan civil servant with a special interest in irrigated land settlement schemes as a development intervention. The other member (T. Scudder) complements his colleague's Sri Lankan expertise with knowledge of land settlement elsewhere in Asia, Africa, and the Middle East. This combination has proved exceptionally fruitful in developing the survey methodology.

Sample Selection and Size

The basic unit for sampling is the household. In large-scale agricultural development projects, households selected should be stratified according to location, background, and wealth criteria. Table 2.1 shows the number and characteristics of the selected survey households in 1981, 1985, and 1989, with all of the 1981 households incorporated within the 1985 sample, and all the 1985 ones incorporated within the 1989 sample.

In the Mahaweli case, location criteria meant selecting households within the three Mahaweli systems and, to an extent, from different areas within each system.

Table 2.1. Accelerated Mahaweli Programme Household Sample

Category	1981	1985	1989
Sample size	19	33	45
Type of settler household			
Host [a]	5	9	13
Evacuee	8	12	14
Selectee	3	7	12
Spontaneous	3	5	6
Location			
System H	13	15	15
System C	5	8	10
System B	1	10	20
Language and religion			
Singala (Buddhist)	19	33	40
Singala (Muslim)	0	0	1
Tamil (Hindu)	0	0	3
Tamil (Muslim)	0	0	1

a. Although hosts are mainly residents of long-established *purana* (villages), in four cases, they are settlers who were recruited in the 1970s in connection with older settlement schemes or land development programs.

Background criteria should vary according to type of project and participant households. In the AMP-type of household (hosts, evacuees, government-selected, and spontaneous settlers), language (Singala and Tamil) and religion (Buddhist, Hindu, and Muslim) were emphasized, although Tamil-speaking Hindu and Muslim households were not selected until 1989, because over 95 percent of project households through 1985 were Singala-speaking Buddhists.

Two simple wealth categories were used: those within the project with sufficient capital to invest in off-farm enterprises and improved housing from the start, and those (the large majority) who were initially dependent on government and kin-based assistance, on their Mahaweli 0.2-hectare homelot and one-hectare field allotments, and on income from wage labor and artisanal and other skills. A disproportionate number of households were selected in the first category to increase the proportion of "key informants" in the sample. Tending to be entrepreneurs and local leaders, anthropologists have found such informants to be an excellent source of information on development constraints and strategies and on community affairs. They were also disproportionately represented in the AMP on the assumption that development constraints adversely affecting such informants would have worse effects for households with fewer resources.

Analysis of interviews suggests that 30 carefully selected households are sufficient for identifying major problems if a disproportionate number of "key informants" is included; if supplemental information is gathered on a reference group about which each household is knowledgeable; and if household interviews are combined with interviews within the community with relatives and neighbors. In the Mahaweli case, the number of households has been increased to 45 (see Table 2.1) as the AMP brought new areas under cultivation, including the northern portion of System B, where a majority of the host population for the first time were Tamil-speaking Hindu and Muslim villagers. Selection of these 45 households was done on an opportunistic basis, meaning that households were incorporated that were available at the time and that met criteria for selection. For example, during the 1979-81 period, we actively sought out evacuees, whereas in 1989, we added two Muslim and two Hindu households. Most were selected because they happened to be available at home when their homelots were visited.

Respondents in the sample were also asked to give information about other households (reference groups) who were in the same irrigation turnout or came from the same community of origin (village in the case of hosts, evacuees, and spontaneous settlers; and electorate in the case of government-sponsored settlers). Thus, respondents provided information not only about their own households, but also about others as well.

In addition, community interviews were conducted when neighbors and relatives came to the sample household during or following an interview. The sample also included seven key informants.

Such an opportunistic sample is clearly biased. As Table 2.1 demonstrates, a disproportionate number of households are evacuees. Because of specific interest in how evacuees cope with compulsory relocation in connection with large-scale development projects, several such households were selected before the study became longitudinal. Two of the three households that had been interviewed prior to 1981 were therefore included in the larger 1981 sample in order to provide some continuity back to 1979. Another bias relates to the disproportionate number of wealthier settlers, a bias that is apt to cause problems to be underestimated rather than overestimated. In the AMP case, however, there is no evidence that such biases have led to faulty conclusions. Where the evaluator is looking for evidence of major problems and major impacts, it makes little difference whether the percentage who have been unable to move beyond subsistence, or more specifically, have been unable to pay back their bank loans, is 60 percent or 75 percent.

Substantive Issues and Research Instruments

From the very beginning, an attempt was made to question *both* adult male and female members of each household about a wide range of topics. The selection of topics was largely based on a series of formal questionnaires that the Institute for Development Anthropology had formulated for a multi-year, AID-funded global evaluation that began in 1979 concerning the experience with land settlement in the tropics and sub-tropics (Scudder, 1981 and 1984). Selected specifically for the study of rainfed and irrigated settlement projects, these topics dealt with the broad issue of land settlement "success"—success being defined in terms of regional development resulting from increased productivity, increased disposable income and living standards, and associated multiplier effects. Other than getting more detail (including increasingly quantitative data) little change has been made over the years in topics selected for the Mahaweli study, presumably because those topics were derived from previous analysis of a world-wide sample of over 100 settlement projects.

Without jeopardizing their utility for comparative international analysis, the wording of questions was adapted to Sri Lankan conditions. During the first interview, fairly detailed information on household history prior to incorporation within the AMP was collected, including the agricultural and employment experiences of the household head since the completion of schooling. Other information was gathered on the nature of the AMP resource base and the various components of the household production system (homelot, field allotment and water conveyance system, livestock, and such off-farm activities as wage labor, carpentry and masonry, and business enterprises) and associated problems; costs of production; nature of housing, household furnishings, and such equipment as sewing machines, plows, and carts; local organizations, including water user associations; social services; health; and relationships with government officials.

A one-page wealth index was also created (Table 2.2) dealing with five major topics relating to living standards, as demonstrated primarily by a visual inspection of each household's homelot. Supplemented by a few questions, this enabled a rapid assessment of changes in living standards to be made as they related to housing, household furnishings, production gear, fuel and lighting, and domestic water supplies and waste disposal. In the absence of detailed quantitative information, such a wealth index can provide, within a five- to ten-minute period, rankings on a scale of 1 to 5 for each of the five variables.

While questions were taken from formal questionnaires, answers were not written down on a schedule in the 1979-85 period. Rather, the evaluators carried with them a list of questions to be asked, the answers to which were written down in notebooks during the interview. Each interview was typed up that evening or within the next few days if possible. This procedure is not recommended, since there was a tendency to skip various questions, especially after lengthy digressions to follow up on interesting issues mentioned by household members. While such open-ended information is invaluable, it should not be collected at the expense of a core of key questions on which comparative and longitudinal analysis is to be based. Fortunately, one of the benefits of repeated interviews is that many omissions can be subsequently corrected.

In 1989, a detailed interview form was used for three reasons. The first was to correct for the deficiencies of not using such a form in the past. The second was because of the need to gather information for a four-year period rather than a single year, since AID funding was unavailable for the 1986-88 period. The third reason was the desire of the evaluators to gather more quantitative data on income and expenditures to make possible the type of analysis presented in Table 2.3.

Looking to the future, a more efficient mechanism is needed for recording information in the field. While the complexity of the data gathered and the importance of open-ended questioning preclude coding material in the field, for 1991, the evaluators planned to use a laptop personal computer during each interview for entering new data directly on files that contain time-series data on each household.

Table 2.2. Wealth Index

Category	Ranking
A. Nature of housing	
1. Tile or other improved roofing and over five rooms	5
2. Tile, etc. roofing, 4-5 rooms	4
3. Tile, etc. roofing, 1-3 rooms	3
4. Thatch or cadjan roofing, over 2 rooms	2
5. Thatch, etc. roofing, 2 rooms or fewer	1
B. Nature of domestic water supplies and sanitation facilities	
1. Improved (concrete) well/piped water supply and water-sealed toilet	5
2. Improved well, etc. or water-sealed toilet, etc.	3
3. Improved well and unimproved sanitation	1
C. Home furnishings	
1. Five major items of furniture such as glassed-in cupboard, large wall clock, television, settee set, spring bed, radio/cassette player	5
2. Three or four major furnishings	4
3. One or two major furnishings	3
4. No major furnishings, but cane or simple wooden furniture and a small radio	2
5. Small radio or cane/wooden chairs, etc. only	1
D. Farm equipment/transport/boutique/mill	
1. Tractor/truck, boutique, and/or grinding mill	5
2. Motorcycle/water pump plus 2 trained buffalo/oxen	4
3. Motorcycle/water pump or 2 trained buffalo/oxen	3
4. Bicycle only or dairy cows, commercial pigs, etc.	2
5. No bicycle, hand tools only	1
E. Appliances/lighting	
1. Kerosene or other type refridgerator, stove, and one other major appliance	5
2. One or two major appliances	4
3. No major appliances, but working petromax (pressure) lamp or electric lighting	3
4. Parrafin wick lamp only	2
5. Candles only	1

Note: Items used should be adapted to each project situation.

Table 2.3 Household Expenditures for Basic Needs, 1988-89
(average for a 12-month period in rupees)

Need	Expenditure
Food (33 households)	20,449
Production for paddy (17 households)	18,558
Clothing (family of five) (37 households)	4,400
Travel (37 households)	946
Social and ritual (38 households)	943
Medical (39 households)	800
Minor household (pots, pans, etc.) (35 households)	470
Total	46,566

Note: October 1989 exchange rate: SL Rs 39.69 = US$1.0.

Nature of the Interviews

While the basis of each interview at the household level was a series of pre-determined questions for comparative and longitudinal analysis, the answers invariably raised interesting issues that were then explored through open-ended questioning. As an example, questions about health indicated a relatively high level of stress associated with AMP settlement, as revealed by suspicions and accusations of sorcery with regard to relatives and neighbors, and by high rates of suicide within the reference groups of sample households. Through open-ended questioning, more detail was elicited on both subjects. Fears associated with the communal strife that has stricken Sri Lanka during the 1980s were also explored in detail, along with actions based on those fears. Although no pre-determined balance between structured and unstructured questioning was set, perhaps 25 percent of the information gathered came from unstructured interviewing.

Data Collection

Selecting Households

Selection was always opportunistic. In the field, the survey team traveled by car. Opportunity sampling was used not only to select households, but also to check out any activities of interest. In the latter case, unannounced side trips into offices and projects sign-posted along the way were made in order to learn about their activities from participants and managers. In one or more towns in each system, censuses were taken of the number and type of business enterprises, with conversations often leading to re-visits to the same business in later years. Similarly, frequent stops were made to query individuals and groups about their activities as seen from the road.

In some cases, the households of individuals interviewed during roadside stops were incorporated in the sample. For example, two households of government-sponsored settlers were selected after interviews were carried out with the worker/settler group to which each household head belonged. (In the AMP, once household heads were selected as settlers, they preceded their families and worked in government-constituted groups to assist with the construction of the water conveyance system. They also cooperated in building temporary housing on their homelots.)

In another case, a household of spontaneous settlers—first interviewed because they had a small roadside boutique—were added in order to see if subsequently they were incorporated within the project (they were and have been interviewed during each visit since 1979). Conversations with a Hindu family in 1979 led to their subsequent incorporation into the sample in 1989. In other cases, government officials were asked where settlers meeting certain criteria might be found. Then, in the village mentioned, a household would be picked in which members were present and who met those criteria.

Interviewing Household Members

To interview household members, the research team simply arrived unannounced. In most cases, the interview then proceeded. If it was clear that the time of arrival was inconvenient, then a specific time to return was arranged. To date, interviews have never been refused—another benefit of sequential visits. While the evaluators may be perceived at times as a nuisance, especially by wealthier settlers involved in many activities, after a number of years their presence was taken for granted. Indeed, in 1989, after a three-year absence, the research team was warmly welcomed in a majority of cases, not so much as friends but as influential outsiders who were familiar with the difficult lives of settler households.

Though the questions are written out in English, interviewing is always done in the vernacular. Flexibility is needed in working out the particulars of the interviewing process. Where research assistants do most of the interviewing, a formal questionnaire should be used with questions translated into the vernacular on the form. In the Mahaweli case, practically all interviewing has been done in the presence of the two senior investigators. Two procedures dominate. In one, the team splits up. While the Sri Lankan works alone, his expatriate colleague works with a research assistant. In the other, the two work together, with one asking the questions in the vernacular and the other writing the answers in English. Although the second procedure takes longer, owing to the need for translation, it actively involves both team members in the research. This partnership has proved to be synergistic, resulting in a more probing interview than would otherwise be the case. On occasion, the research team has also invited a colleague with special skills such as agricultural economics or regional planning, or with Tamil-language competence, to join them for a few days to conduct interviews.

The time required for interviewing each household has gradually increased from about an hour to between two to three hours. Given the intensity of each interview, when travel time is included along with community interviews and interviews with officials, two interviews per day tend to be the maximum that is possible. In collecting data, the presence of a number of household members is preferred, but not visitors from other households. In cases where it is not tactful to ask visitors to leave, a household interview is changed to a community interview.

While 60-90 minutes appear to be the optimal length for an interview, in only two cases did greater length require splitting the interview between two or more visits. Both related to wealthier settlers, the complexity of whose affairs in relationship to other households required both more tact (due to an understandable unwillingness to discuss income) and more time, including evening visits.

Over the years, to increase familiarity with household activities and conditions, an effort has been made to visit members of each household at their home, in their one-hectare allotment, and at any non-farm enterprises. Visits to fields are especially important to help assess frequent complaints of settlers about the inadequacy of land preparation (especially leveling) and delivery of irrigation waters. Such visits also provide an opportunity to discuss water management with a number of cultivators in the irrigation turnouts to which each household belongs.

Starting in 1989, a decision was made to begin interviewing more widely in the kinship networks to which household members belong. Previously, this had been done on an *ad hoc* basis. When a household head has died between visits, he or she is replaced with the deceased's nominated heir. Should that person be the head of a new household, information continues to be gathered about the whereabouts and activities of other members of the original parental household. In other instances, where a household happened to be absent at the time of a visit, relatives living nearby are interviewed. While this broadening of networks has increased the number of people associated with each household, prior to 1989, such interviewing was done more to maintain continuity than to provide new types of information. That approach changed in 1989.

All Mahaweli households maintain ties of various sorts with people who live outside the project. Especially in the case of evacuees and government-sponsored settlers who did not live in the Mahaweli systems prior to the AMP, these ties involve economic transfers of wealth to the various AMP systems and from those systems to outside persons and investments. The research team had been aware of such transfers for some time. However, the decision to expand interviewing in all cases in which major sources of capital came from non-Mahaweli relatives (in the form of loans, and remittances and other types of gifts), or where AMP settlers made major investments outside of the Mahaweli scheme, was made when one evacuee household moved back to the sending area in order to concentrate on business operations there. While the nearby household of his mother was substituted during 1989, in the future, the original household head (who has been interviewed since 1979) will also be interviewed in his new home.

Such "network" interviewing is important, not just to better understand the production system of sample households, but also to better understand the flow of resources into and out of the Mahaweli systems. For example, as households try to move beyond subsistence during the early years of settlement, resource flows from without—in terms of labor, loans, gifts, plow animals, and agricultural equipment—tend to predominate. Such assistance may be essential for survival as a Mahaweli settler. In one case, a government-selected household experiencing family health problems that required them to mortgage their land would have lost that land without a major gift from a non-Mahaweli relative.

On the other hand, as settler households improve their living standards, they diversify their economic activities, not just within, but without the settlement areas. This is especially the case with evacuees and selectees who may diversify into agricultural and non-farm activities in the area of origin where parents, brothers, sons, or other relatives still live. To better understand the nature of multiplier effects associated with such projects as the AMP, these resource flows began to be assessed for the first time in 1990 and 1991.

Assisting Household Members

During the first ten years of the study, visits brought no direct benefits to sample households other than prints of color photographs, which it was hoped would reduce the risk of informant "burnout."

Though benefits should be kept to the minimum to avoid introducing yet another bias, during 1989, the research team decided to help six families solve some immediate problems. In three cases of extreme poverty and misfortune, households have been given enough capital to purchase the necessary farm inputs for the next cropping season or to cover the expenses of a child about to sit for the secondary school graduation examinations. In three other instances, special problems (such as totally inadequate land preparation on the part of the government, or foot-dragging in providing homelots to married sons of settlers who want loans for widening the production base of their extended family) have been brought to the attention of senior MASL officials.

Confidentiality

Except in the few cases in which household members request that information be given to Mahaweli officials, the contents of all interviews are kept confidential. While it probably is not possible to hide the identities of households involved in repeated interviews, in this case, there is no evidence that AMP officials have tried to learn their identity, or if they have, that they have paid special attention to them.

Other Types of Data

By the time the formal interview has ended and the wealth index completed, more often than not neighbors and other visitors have arrived so that most interviews end with a "community" discussion of various issues of interest to the people and to the research team. "Community" discussions are also held in irrigation tracts when household members are visited in their fields. Such interviews provide an opportunity to check reference group information provided by sample households, as well as to obtain other types of data, such as the proportion of households unable to repay seasonal loans and problems with land preparation, irrigation water delivery, schools, and health facilities. Table 2.4 provides an example of the data that could be interpreted through interviews.

While in the field, household and community interviews are mixed with other data-collection activities. As with interviews with settler households, the approach used in such data collection is repeated interviews with the same officials, the same business people, and the same researchers. Generally speaking, the purpose of these other data is to enable the research team to elicit a wider range of opinion on settler perception of problems, to assess opportunities available to the entire settler population, and to assess constraints to the realization of those

Table 2.4 Loans to Mahaweli Settlers and Repayment Rates
(SL Rs)

Season	Bank of Ceylon System B area (approximately 7,500 families)		Hatton's Bank System H-5 area (approximately 5,000 families)	
	Loans given	Repayment	Loans given	Repayment
Yala 1985	623	558 (90%)	861	91%
Maha 1985/86	1,322	1,051 (80%)	2,040	92%
Yala 1986	1,273	930 (73%)	798	91%
Maha 1986/87	2,502	1,860 (74%)	1,130	95%
Yala 1987	2,305	1,350 (59%)	418	99%
Maha 1987/88	2,249	1,044 (46%)	1,124	79%
Yala 1988	1,076	647 (60%)	434	97%
Maha 1988/89	943	628 (60%)	446	97%
Yala 1989	990	Collection still under way	No cultivation	
Maha 1989/90	No data yet	No data yet	867	

Source: Scudder and Vimaladharma (1989, Appendix 4).

opportunities. Under opportunities, the research team assesses the implications of special MASL and donor projects that are designed to diversify income-earning possibilities for settlers and the children of settlers, and to increase—through water user associations, dairy societies, and other producer organizations—the involvement of settlers in project management.

Under constraints, the researchers are particularly interested in institutional weaknesses of the Mahaweli agencies, including poor relationships between settlers and officials, and in settler indebtedness, health, conflict, and a wide range of other factors (such as poor land preparation, inadequate irrigation, increased weed growth in paddy fields, and disease in chillies) that interfere with the efforts of settlers to improve their living standards.

Analysis

Analysis of the impacts of the Accelerated Mahaweli Programme on the lives and livelihoods of several hundred thousand settlers is based in large part on the time series data collected from sample households. Analysis of other project-related impacts and problems is based on complementary information gathered during sequential interviews with government officials, with private sector bankers, equipment providers and other business people, and with researchers. Analysis of the wealth index, for example, shows the extent to which living standards have improved, stayed the same, or deteriorated in regard to the criteria assessed. The formal interview provides a much wider range of information for comparative, longitudinal analysis. Repeated visits with Hatton's National Bank in H System, and with the Ford dealer in the same system, provide time series data on the proportion of settlers taking out credit, on repayment rates (see Table 2.4), and on purchase of equipment. Sequential visits to the same towns make it easier to assess the impact of settler purchasing power on the number and kinds of business enterprises, and on changes in their inventories. Because the same research team has been collaborating for over ten years, their familiarity with the data has enabled them to draft a final report toward the end of each three- to seven-week survey within a three-day period.

Problems Arising from Methodology

Skepticism among Government/Donors

When evaluations in 1983, 1984, and 1985 concluded that the potential of the AMP settlement component was not being realized due to a number of planning, implementation, management, and maintenance deficiencies, the initial reaction of government officials was to dispute their accuracy because of the nature of the methodology. At that time, the general impression in government and donor circles was that the AMP was achieving its goals; hence, any studies that reached opposite conclusions were received with skepticism. The fact that none of the conclusions reached has subsequently been shown to be wrong has increased the acceptability of the two investigators' evaluations, although discomfort over the nature of the methodology remains. Ways of dealing with this problem are discussed in the last section of this case study.

Interruptions

While repeated interviews are the most important component of the methodology, they are also the most difficult to ensure because of the risk of interruptions in, or termination of, a long-term study. Interruption or termination can occur for a number of reasons, such as loss of interest by the investigators, outbreak of hostilities, or withdrawal of support by either the government or the funding agency.

Though the Mahaweli research has benefited from the collaboration of the same investigators over a ten-year period, their withdrawal at some point needs to be anticipated. One way to ensure a degree of continuity is to institutionalize the study within a local research institution. To this end, another researcher has been periodically invited to joint the team from the government-affiliated Agrarian Research and Training Institute (ARTI), a research institution that has the capacity to continue the study.

Serious communal strife in Sri Lanka since the mid-1980s has been a constraint. For example, it kept Vimaladharma from re-establishing contact with a majority of sample households for nearly a year following AID's agreement to renew funding in August 1988. The researchers were able to re-interview members of all 33 previously selected households (or, in three cases, close kin or neighbors). Another 12 households were added in October-November 1989.

As with communal strife, there is no way that the investigators can guard against withdrawal of government and donor support. In the case of the AMP, while individuals in the Mahaweli agencies disagreed at times with study conclusions, and while some officials resented any criticism of what was the country's largest and most important development program, there is no indication that government officials requested AID to stop funding. When funds were stopped between 1986 and the end of 1988, this was due more to an in-house memo on the effectiveness of AID's role than to objections to the 1985 Mahaweli report.

Time Constraints

In planning evaluations to be based on repeated interviewing of the same households, it is *crucial* that enough time (and hence, enough funding) be allocated for data collection, management, and analysis. In Mahaweli, time constraints have been due largely to the busy schedules of the research team, resulting in insufficient time for data collection, and virtually no time for data management and analysis following completion of fieldwork and report writing, or preceding the next field trip. As a result, both in the field and during report-writing, more often than not they have had to work a 12-hour day, 7 days a week, and then, having submitted their report, de-emphasize any further data analysis.

Data Management and Analysis

Long-term studies present serious data management and analysis problems as the amount of time series data piles up. In Mahaweli, the research team initially did not pay enough attention to such problems, with the result that their evaluations have relied too much on their memories of the histories of the sample households, complemented by checking those memories against past notes, interviews, and wealth criteria, as opposed to detailed analysis of the time series data itself.

Though most household interviews through 1985 have been typed up, because of time constraints, the information is only now being organized to facilitate more systematic analysis and further data collection, management, and analysis. Two efforts are under way. First, files are being prepared on each household that presents the data in a historical format that covers, for each interview, information obtained on ten topics. During future interviews, laptop computers will be used to enter new information directly on the file. The ten topics are: (1) household history before incorporation within the AMP and updated details on household members; (2) activities, and income and expenditures relating to the one-hectare allotment, and to livestock, since the last interview; (3) water management, including the performance of water user associations at the turnout level of the irrigation system; (4) community-based organizations such as social welfare, religious, and more economically-oriented institutions; (5) description of the homelot, including housing and household furnishings; (6) other sources of income; (7) community dynamics (including information on such topics as numbers of community members who have draft and dairy animals and tractors; who have sought work in the Middle East, Singapore, or elsewhere outside Sri Lanka; who have committed suicide; and so on); (8) problems; (9) plans; and (10) experiences with government institutions (especially Mahaweli agencies, schools, and medical facilities). Second, data are being coded on 68 variables, by interview year, for computer analysis.

Findings and Recommendations

Findings

The most important finding of the surveys, and the one that initially created the most controversy within the Mahaweli agencies, was the 1983 conclusion that the potential of the AMP—in terms of major goals for the settlement component—was "not being realized" (Scudder and Vimaladharma 1983, p. 38). Although more detailed micro-studies dealing with a portion of System H had pointed up specific problems at an earlier date (Lund 1978 and Siriwardena 1981), the 1983 report was apparently the first to suggest serious deficiencies throughout the project. The major problem was that net income was insufficient to generate major multiplier effects in terms of enterprise development and employment generation. While production goals were being met in terms of paddy yields, for many settlers the income received was insufficient or barely sufficient to cover costs of production.

The 1984 report emphasized ongoing poverty as the major AMP constraint. That conclusion was based primarily on interviews in System H (the oldest Mahaweli settlement area) that "living standards of seven of our 16 sample households (44 percent) appear to have deteriorated, while those of another three families have stagnated at a poverty level" (Scudder and Vimaladharma 1984, p. 5). Further interviewing in all three AMP systems during 1985 led to the conclusion that "the double-cropping of paddy of a 2.5-acre holding will not advance the large majority of Mahaweli settler households beyond a subsistence level, even after the correction of land preparation and irrigation system defects." (Scudder and Vimaladharma 1985, p. 8).

The failure of a paddy-dominated farming system to replace wage income lost when contractors moved on after completion of physical infrastructure was a major reason behind drops in living standards, as were government miscalculations concerning the rapidity with which the "second-generation problems" would arise. This has hastened the illegal subdivision of holdings to accommodate children as they married, with those cultivating subdivided holdings more apt to emphasize paddy production for food security, as opposed to the cultivation of higher-value crops (Wanigaratne 1984). The 1985 report also emphasized deteriorating relationships between settlers and AMP officials, due in part to increasing politicalization of the project. This included appointment of lower-level Mahaweli officials as the presidents of what were supposed to be separate, settler-run water user and community development associations.

As noted in the 1985 report, another finding dealt with what appeared to be an exceptionally high suicide rate among evacuees and government-sponsored settlers. The research team suggested that this was due to insufficient attention paid to settler welfare, including insufficient awareness of the inevitable stress that accompanies the colonization of new lands (suicide rates being lower among host-population settlers). As with others, this finding received support in a later, more systematic analysis in which the conclusion stated, "The early phase of new Mahaweli settlements is characterized by an exceptionally high suicide rate." (Silva and Kumara, no date, but incorporating data through 1987).

The 1985 report also noted that Tamil-speaking Hindu settlers were not being incorporated within the AMP according to their proportion in the national population, and that a significant proportion of host-population, Tamil-speaking Hindus were being passed over in System B.

Contrary to stated government policy, this trend reinforced the belief among many Tamil-speakers and their supporters that the AMP was being used as a mechanism both to increase the proportion of Singala-speakers in an area in which Tamil-speakers were in the majority and to displace some of the latter from their lands. The research team stated a concern that a continuation of such actions would lead to increased communal strife at the expense of both Singala-speaking selectees and Tamil-speaking hosts. This indeed was the case in May 1987 and February 1989.

Recommendations

Derived from the comments of settlers and individual Mahaweli officials, as well as from the analysis of the research team, each report has included a broad of range suggestions and recommendations. Some focused more specifically on the production system, such as recommendations dealing with correction of land preparation and irrigation system defects, with weed growth, and with diseases of chillies. Others dealt more broadly with the settler population, including its social welfare, and with the composition of the settler population. Still others dealt with institutional and regional planning issues.

During the 1983-89 period, report recommendations emphasized the need for diversification at the household and community level (with special emphasis on higher-value crops, livestock production, fisheries, and a range of non-farm activities) as the "best" way to raise living standards, to increase demand for locally-provided goods and services, and to increase non-farm enterprises and employment opportunities. A gradual handing over of management responsibilities to appropriate settler organizations was also emphasized. Such recommendations have contributed to the formulation and implementation of a number of major policy changes. AID's Scope of Work for the 1989 evaluation noted that the series of Mahaweli reports "have been extensively used by MASL, USAID, and other donors in revising policies and projects related to the AMP."

Earlier reports emphasized the importance of upgrading existing towns rather than developing, at great financial cost, new towns in the center of the irrigation command areas that had been planned as if they existed in a vacuum. As for the balance between Singala- and Hindu-speaking settlers, the 1989 report included two recommendations. The first was that "The Mahaweli family of agencies should stop settling poor people in zones where they are at risk because of conflicting land claims" between ethnic communities. The second was that the Mahaweli agencies and the donors should proceed at the earliest possible time with the development of the right bank of System B. Right bank development was considered to be an important part of a national reconciliation effort currently under way, since that was the area reserved for the settlement of Tamil-speakers. The research team emphasized its development and its settlement by Tamil-speakers, since both the government and the donors appeared to be de-emphasizing their earlier commitment to proceed.

Utility of the Methodology for Other Uses

During the ten-year period during which this interview methodology has evolved, lessons have been learned that should improve its utility for other users.

Sampling

While the investigators believe that a methodology based on repeated interviews with a relatively small number of households has proven merit as a major, low-cost evaluation technique, how the sample is stratified and proportioned between different strata should be done with more care than in the AMP case. Provided it is carried out in time, a pre-project benchmark study could provide valuable information for sample selection. Furthermore, use of key informants, reference groups, and community interviews should be more systematically incorporated within the methodology from the start. The key component of such a methodology, however, should continue to be repeated interviews with a small number of carefully-selected households, complemented by information gathered from and on the local leaders, reference groups, and communities with which these households identify.

Data Collection

Where repeated interviews are carried out on relatively small numbers of households, the amount of data collected can easily become explosive. Though flexibility is crucial in order to add questions as new issues are identified and to drop questions that were misconceived or are no longer relevant, researchers should attempt at the start to identify "core" data to be collected. They should also decide which questions need to be asked of every household during every interview versus questions that need be answered by only a proportion of the households.

Quantitative data cannot be collected from every household simply because of the time required. For example, to record in detail expenses for double cropping in one year and income received requires well over an hour, leaving insufficient time to deal with other questions. The AMP research team has tried to solve this problem by relying on a small number of informants (say 5-6) to provide detailed information on agricultural expenditures, while other informants are asked to give a detailed accounting of expenditures on foodstuffs, clothes, school and household expenditures, and so on. If the information given is quite similar (as it was for costs of production) or can be easily fitted into two or three settler categories (as was the case with food consumption), then composite costs (and incomes) can be suggested, as in the 1989 report (Table 2.3).

Data Management

Managing time series data collected on small samples of 30 to 50 households is nonetheless a daunting task, the importance and duration of which was seriously underestimated by the research team. More than any other factor, poor data management has threatened the extraction of full value from the research completed to date. Regardless of where their interests lie, evaluators who plan to utilize methodologies based on sequential interviews should work out their data management systems before initiating the first set of interviews. If this had been done in the Mahaweli case, not only would analysis have improved, but more comprehensive data on a somewhat smaller set of variables would have been collected from the start to the benefit of both policy and academic analysis.

Complementary Means for Checking Results

An ongoing evaluation utilizing repeated interviews with a relatively small number of households should preferably be institutionalized outside of the planning and implementing agencies. However, those agencies should also have their own monitoring capability, including the ability to assess the conclusions and recommendations arising from repeated household interviews (and complementary data collection), and to carry out special surveys as needed. Greater encouragement also should be given to universities, and especially to masters and doctoral candidates, to carry out low-cost, intensive research in project areas. If properly integrated (with degree candidates given financial incentives to research certain critical issues in more depth), these two types of investigation can complement each other in ways that offset each others' weaknesses. With the exception of an initial benchmark survey, large surveys based on random sampling are not recommended. This is because repeat surveys are rarely, if ever, undertaken because of the time and money required, while several years usually pass before the results of the initial survey become available.

References

Johnston, Bruce, and Peter Kilby. 1975. *Agricultural and Structural Transformation: Economic Strategies in Late-Developing Countries*. New York: Oxford University Press.

Lund, R. 1978. "A Survey on Women's Working and Living Conditions in a Mahaweli Settlement Area: With Special Emphasis on Household Budgets and Household Surplus." Study Papers. Research Department, Peoples Bank. Colombo, Sri Lanka.

Mellor, John W. 1986. In J.P. Lewis and V. Kallab, eds., *Development Strategies Reconsidered*. New Brunswick, New Jersey: Transaction Books for the Overseas Development Council.

Scudder, Thayer. 1979. "Evaluatory Report on Mission to Sri Lankan Settlement Areas: A Discussion of Some Basic Issues." Evaluation report. USAID/Colombo. (photocopy)

_____. 1980. "The Accelerated Mahaweli Programme (AMP) and Dry Zone Development: Some Aspects of Settlement." Evaluation report. USAID/Colombo. (photocopy)

_____. 1981a. "The Accelerated Mahaweli Programme (AMP) and Dry Zone Development: Some Aspects of Settlement. Report Number Three." IDA Working Paper No. 14. Binghamton, New York: Institute for Development Anthropology for USAID.

_____. 1981b. "The Development Potential of New Lands Settlement in the Tropics and Subtropics: A Global State-of-the-Art Evaluation with Special Emphasis on Policy Implications." Binghamton, New York: Institute for Development Anthropology for USAID.

_____. 1984. "The Development Potential of New Lands Settlement in the Tropics and Subtropics: A Global State-of-the-Art Evaluation with Special Emphasis on Policy Implications." (executive summary). USAID Program Evaluation Discussion Paper No. 21. Washington, D.C.: U.S. Agency for International Development.

_____. 1985. "A Sociological Framework for the Analysis of Land Settlements." In Michael M. Cernea, ed., *Putting People First: Sociological Variables in Rural Development*. New York: Oxford University Press for the World Bank, pp. 121–153.

Scudder, Thayer, and Kapila P. Vimaladharma. 1984. "The Accelerated Mahaweli Programme (AMP) and Dry Zone Development: Report Number Four." IDA Working Paper No. 23. Binghamton, New York: Institute for Development Anthropology for USAID.

_____. 1985. "The Accelerated Mahaweli Programme (AMP) and Dry Zone Development: Report Number Five." IDA Working Paper No. 24. Binghamton, New York: Institute for Development Anthropology for USAID.

_____. 1986. "The Accelerated Mahaweli Programme (AMP) and Dry Zone Development: Report Number Six." IDA Working Paper No. 25. Binghamton, New York: Institute for Development Anthropology for USAID.

_____. 1989. "The Accelerated Mahaweli Programme (AMP) and Dry Zone Development: Report Number Seven." Binghamton, New York: Institute for Development Anthropology for USAID.

Silva, K. Tudor, and W.D.N.R. Pushpa Kumara. No date. "Suicide and Sexual Anomie in a New Settlement in Sri Lanka." In Padmasiri de Silva, ed., *Suicide in Sri Lanka.* Proceedings of a workshop held at the Institute of Fundamental Studies, Kandy, Sri Lanka, pp. 51-64.

Wanigaratne, Rangit Dissanayake. 1984. "Subsistence Maintenance and Agricultural Transformation on the Frontier in Sri Lanka: The Kaltota Irrigated Settlement Project." Unpublished Ph.D. dissertation. University of Wisconsin, Madison, Wisconsin.

Appendix: Annual Evaluation of the Settlement Component of the Accelerated Mahaweli Programme

1989 INTERVIEW FORM FOR OLD SETTLER HOUSEHOLDS

Name of Interviewer   Date of Interview

Name of Settler   Location/Village Name

Block   System

Adult Members of Household Present at Interview

SOCIAL CHANGE AND CONTINUITY

1. Changes in household structure since 1985 interview (births, including those of married children; deaths; marriages; divorces; and in- and out-movement of people—marrying out of children, for example, or marrying in of childrens' spouses, or arrival or departure of other relatives. Note: where new sons-in-law have moved in, note background, in terms of place of origin and land status).

LAND AND YIELDS

2. Changes in access to land since 1985 interview (including clearing of new land; leasing in or out of land, and reasons involved; sharing of land with children or son-in-laws; involvement in *bettma*, etc.)

3. Changes in character of allotment since 1985 (including further land preparation; changes for the better or the worse in the water conveyance system; weed growth; inadequacy of water supplies; waterlogging; etc.)

4. Yields since 1984/85 Maha:

	Paddy in bushels	Chillies	Other Crops (Bombay onions, etc.)
1985 Yala			
1985/86 Maha			
1986 Yala			
1986/87 Maha			
1987 Yala			
1987/88 Maha			
1988 Yala			

5. Changes in the character of the homelot (coconuts now fruiting; status of other perennial and annual crops)

6. Current ownership of livestock and type of ownership

	Number	Origin (purchase; ande; birth if purchase, date and price)
Buffalo		
Draft cattle		
Dairy cattle		

7. Credit dependence

Date and amount of last bank loan

Amount and type of indebtedness (bank; relative or friend; mudalali; etc.)

INCOME AND EXPENSES FOR AGRICULTURE

8. Costs of production for main allotment (inputs; hired labor; hired equipment; etc.)

	1987/88 Maha	1988 Yala (or 1987 Yala if 1988 harvest not complete)
Seed		
Land preparation		
Transplanting		
Weeding		
Harvesting		
Transport		
Fertilizer		
Herbicides		
Insecticides		
Other expenses (specify)		
Total		

Note: Type of "equipment" should be noted under land preparation: buffalo; neat cattle; two-wheel tractor; etc. Labor costs should note number of man-days involved; wages (including cash, food, or other compensation); and whether type of labor is daily, seasonal, or permanent.

9. Costs of production for crops grown for sale on homelot

10. Income from main allotment
    (bushels/kilos sold;
    price per kg;
    and incomes from sales)

11. Net income from main allotment

12. Income (if any) from the homelot during last 12 months

13. Sale of livestock during last 12 months

14. Income from livestock (hiring out; dairy; etc.) during last 12 months (if recollection poor, try at least to record estimated income during an average week or month)

15. Income from wage labor during last 12 months (including wage labor of resident children and in-laws)

16. Income from special skills such as carpentry, masonry, etc. during last 12 months (if recollection poor, try at least to record estimated income during an average week or month)

17. Income from boutiques and other commercial ventures such as dairying or fish ponds during last 12 months (again, try at least to obtain estimate for an average week or month)

18. Other sources of income

OTHER EXPENSES

19. If paddy supplies exhausted, when did the family begin purchasing paddy? Costs per week?

20. Costs per week for fish (# of purchases per week and price) and other protein

21. Costs per week for bread and other carbohydrates (other than paddy)

22. Costs per week for:

    Vegetables/fruits/nuts
    Milk/cheese/yoghurt/curd
    Tea, sugar, etc.
    Curry ingredients
    Cooking oil
    Cigarettes, betel, liquor
    Soft drinks
    Soap and detergents
    Fuel

23. Estimated expenses for clothes during past 12 months

24. Estimated expenses for minor household purchases during the past month (major purchases listed separately under PROPERTY category)

25. Travel expenses during past 12 months, including home visitation, travel for health needs, and pilgrimage

26. Medical expenses during past 12 months (or last major medical expenses if can't summarize)

27. Recreational expenses (cinema, etc.) during the past month

28. Special occasion expenses (weddings, funerals, etc.) over past 12 months

29. Other (gifts, un-repaid loans, etc.)

PROPERTY AND RESOURCES

30. Major property obtained since 1985 interview (tractor, trailer, pump, TV, sewing machine, and other major household furnishings; etc.)

    Type of Item   Date Purchased   Price

31. Status of major property acquired before 1985 (especially as to whether tractors, pumps, TVs, etc., are still operational)

32. Changes in housing since 1985 interview (note type of improvements or deterioration)

HEALTH AND SANITATION

33. Changes in toilet facilities since 1985 interview (note type of improvement or deterioration)

34. Changes in domestic water supply since 1985 interview (note type of improvement or deterioration)

35. Incidence of malaria among household members during past 12 months

36. Hospitalization among household members during past 12 months

37. Conflicts with family members, relatives, and neighbors since 1985 interview and status of previous conflicts (including suspicions of sorcery)

38. Other health problems

TRAVEL

39. Date of last "home visit"

40. Number of "home visits" during the last 12 months

41. Date and location of last pilgrimage

TURNOUT AND OTHER COMMUNITY ORGANIZATIONS

42. Status of turnout group (including its functions and effectiveness; whether or not turnout leader is a farmer or unit manager; extent of conflicts over water delivery; maintenance; and turnout heterogeneity, especially where members come from different electorates, etc.)

43. Status of hamlet association

44. Status of temple, welfare, and other religious and social organizations

MEA AND MASL RELATIONSHIPS

45. Participation in MEA and other Mahaweli courses

46. Relationship with and assessment of unit manager and other Mahaweli officials

OPEN-ENDED QUESTIONS

47. How has your situation changed since 1985 interviews?

48. How has your household benefited from Mahaweli?

49. What are your major problems at this time?

50. What are your plans for the future?

51. In what ways has Mahaweli met your expectations at the time you first became a settler?

52. In what ways has Mahaweli failed to meet those expectations?

COMMUNITY CHARACTERISTICS

(State here what the nature of the community is. For example, 59 Bowatanne people, 100 Kotmale evacuees, 120 selectees from Kandy, 12 turnout members, etc.)

53. Number of community households with two-wheel tractors

54. Number of community households with boutiques

55. Number of community households benefiting from special Mahaweli programs (here specify number from dairying, fish ponds, special projects, etc.)

56. Number (proportion) of households that have mortgaged/leased out:

    (a) part of their land (and reasons for such mortgaging/leasing)

    (b) all of their land (and reasons for such mortgaging/leasing)

57. Number of households that have returned to area of origin

58. Number of households from which family members have gone:

    (a) to the Middle East

    (b) taken jobs that require them to reside outside the community

59. Number of suicides within the community since 1985 interview

60. Respondent's assessment of the proportion of community members who have raised their living standards since 1985 interview; who have "stood still"; and who have "gone downhill."

3

Use of Group Interviews in Evaluating an Area Development Project

Krishna Kumar

*In this chapter, Krishna Kumar illustrates the use of community/
group interviews for the evaluation of an area development project
in Malawi. The case study outlines the planning and conduct of
group interviews and gives examples of the type of information and
data that were generated by them. Finally, it presents a few lessons
derived from this effort about the conduct of group interviews in
development settings.*

*In this project, farmers' clubs were being used as the sole me-
dium to provide short-term loans to farmers for purchasing recommended agricultural inputs. Under the leadership of the author, the
evaluation team undertook group interviews with the members of
eight farmers' clubs. The selection of these clubs took into consideration their size, age, accessibility, and different ecological zones.
The interviews took the form of public meetings in which the team
members asked questions on the basis of a carefully-prepared interview guide. The team made every effort to ensure the participation
of all those present in the meeting. As the chapter indicates, the
team was able to gather considerable information through group
interviews, which, with the data generated by the review of project
records and key informant interviews, formed the basis for the
evaluation.*

*Kumar also identifies a few problems with his methodology that
might have undermined the validity and reliability of the findings.
First, although every effort was made to solicit advice from a number of experts about the selection of the clubs for group interviews,
it was quite possible that the selection process was biased, in that
the project management and government officials recommended
clubs that had performed well. Second, the club members were
generally reluctant to reveal any information that seemed critical of
the government and project authorities. Finally, there was a ten-*

dency among club leaders to dominate discussions. On the basis of his experience in Malawi, the author suggests several measures that can help future investigators in generating relevant and objective data through community/group interviews.

THE DOWA WEST AREA DEVELOPMENT PROJECT was one of the earliest initiatives implemented under a national rural development program introduced by the Malawi Government. It was designed and implemented as an integrated rural development project with two key objectives: (1) to increase the incomes of 9,300 smallholder farmers through the sale of an increased surplus of cash crops and an incremental increase in livestock production; and (2) to improve the living conditions of these farmers and their families through expanded and better water supplies, health facilities, community development services, and energy conservation.

The project was funded by the International Fund for Agricultural Development and supervised by the World Bank, and began functioning in late 1981 under the auspices of the Malawi Ministry of Agriculture. It focused on provision of agricultural credit, extension services, research on crop storage and milling, storage capacity, roads, drinking water, and health services. The project established precise targets in each of these areas, to be accomplished over a six-year period.

A midterm evaluation of the project was conducted in 1984 by a three-member team led by the author. The team remained in the field for three weeks of field research and spent another two weeks preparing the draft evaluation.

One of the several substantive areas that the evaluation team studied was the growth and contribution of farmers' clubs to agricultural development.

The farmers' club movement started in Malawi in 1974, five years before the Dowa West project was formulated (1979). The country's extension service promoted farmers' clubs to encourage cooperation in agricultural operations, particularly in strip cropping and the purchase of agricultural inputs in bulk quantities. At least 36 clubs were functioning in the project area by the end of 1979. However, the real momentum for their growth came from the project itself, as is evident from Table 3.1.

A club usually encompassed one or more villages, depending on the size of the local population. Although the club sizes ranged from 10 to 100 members, most had a membership of between 20 to 40. Nearly a quarter of their members were women.

The Dowa West project relied exclusively on the clubs for the delivery of seasonal agricultural credit for the purchase of seeds, fertilizers,

Table 3.1. Cumulative Numbers and Membership of Farmers' Clubs, Dowa
West Area, 1981–84

Year	No. of farmers' clubs	No. of male members	No. of female members
1981-82	61	1,770	501
1982-83	265	8,090	904
1983-84	403	11,279	2,268

and other inputs. Project records indicated that they were especially
successful in this regard; the amount of credit channeled through them
to the target populations increased seven-fold within two years. This
exceeded the optimistic projections included in the project appraisal report. In addition, the clubs also provided midterm credit for farm
equipment such as ridgers, plows, ox-carts, and oxen.

At the time of the midterm evaluation, extension work was also
largely organized around the clubs. Club members regularly attended
extension meetings, demonstrations, and training courses, and they also
cooperated in agricultural operations.

Research Methodology

The basic research method used by the evaluation team was group interviews with farmers' club members, involving the use of direct probing
techniques to gather information from several individuals in a group
session.

The evaluation team had only one week to examine the workings of
the clubs and assess their project contribution. This time constraint was
further compounded by logistical problems; the clubs were scattered all
over the project area and were not always accessible by automobile.
Also, more time was needed than was available to alert clubs about the
evaluation team's impending visit, so that their members would be
available to be interviewed.

After a careful review of the available documentation and in-depth
interviews with key project staff, government officials, and other experts, the team decided to conduct some initial group interviews with
the members of a few clubs to gain first-hand information about their
activities, achievements, and problems. In this particular case, group
interviews took the form of a meeting of the club members in which
questions on relevant topics were posed and answers received.

Planning of Group Interviews

The evaluation team recognized the need for careful planning at the outset, and developed an interview guide, a protocol for team members, and a list of the clubs to be visited initially.

The Interview Guide

The evaluation team decided that the interviews should focus on a limited range of topics that could easily be answered in a group setting. With fewer questions, the interviewers would have more time to pursue leads in-depth before moving on to other items. Moreover, a shorter agenda would enable the participants to express themselves freely and in a relaxed atmosphere. While there was a general agreement on this issue, the evaluation team members differed on what subject areas the guide should cover. After considerable discussion, agreement was eventually reached on the topics to be explored.

The evaluation team also debated whether the interview guide should list questions or just the topics. The advantage of merely listing topics is that interviewers are able to frame questions spontaneously, thereby "tailoring" them by following the flow of discussion and considering the general background of the participants. On the other hand, predetermined questions keep the discussions focused. They also reduce the risk that the participants will not understand what is asked, which can occur when the questions are framed on the spur of the moment. After considerable discussion, the team decided to list the questions in the interview guide, but not to restrict team members to their use. They agreed that the interviewers should feel free to add questions that arose naturally during the discussion or to change the sequence of questions. For example, if a club official made an interesting point while introducing the evaluation team, the team member could use the comment as a starting point for the interview.

Some excerpts from the interview guide are shown in Box 3.1.

Interview Protocol

The evaluation team also developed an interview protocol by formulating the following three ground rules to guide its members during the interview. These ground rules proved extremely useful in ensuring the interviews proceeded smoothly.

First, the team leader was to introduce all members, explain the objectives of the evaluation, and ask questions about the origin and organization of the club. He was allotted 20 to 25 minutes for this purpose. The

Box 3.1   Excerpts from the Interview Guide for Dowa West Farmers' Club Members

1. Origin and Initiative
    -   Why did you join the club?
    -   Who organized the first meeting?
    -   Did you know other members well before joining the club?
    -   Did you receive any help or assistance from extension workers or other government officials in organizing it?
    -   How did you frame the rules and regulations?
2. Organization and Activities
    -   What is the total number of members in the club?
    -   Do you have women members who are the heads of households? If so, how many?
    -   Do you still welcome new members?
    -   Have members dropped out of the club? If so, how many and why?
    -   Some people tell us that if credit is not available, many members will lose interest in the club. What is your assessment?
    -   How many times does your club meet in a month?
    -   How many persons attend these meetings?
3. Credit and Supply of Inputs
    -   Do you get the amount of credit you generally need from the club each year? If not, why not?
    -   How many of you present would like to have a larger amount of seasonal credit?
    -   Do you have problems in obtaining credit vouchers on time? If so, what are they?
    -   If you do not get loans from the club, what other sources of credit are available to you?
    -   Did the club face difficulty in getting repayments from the members in the past? If so why?
    -   What do you do to persuade all members to make the prompt repayments?
4. Benefit Assessment
    -   How many of you also purchase fertilizers and other inputs for cash?
    -   How many of you were using fertilizers before joining the club?
    -   Do you think that the availability of inputs through the club has contributed to an increase in your maize production?
    -   Do you think that your income has increased as a result of participation in the club?

other two members were given 15 to 20 minutes each to ask questions on credit and input supply and impact assessment. After all the team members had covered the items listed in the interview guide, they had 20 minutes to pursue unlisted issues.

Second, all members were to take elaborate notes to be compared and developed the same evening.

Third, team members were not to interrupt one another and were to resist the temptation to help out a colleague by trying to interpret a participant's response. Such an action was permissible only when a team member misunderstood the respondent.

Club Selection Process

The evaluation team originally planned to hold group interviews with ten clubs. However, because of logistical and time constraints, it completed only eight interviews.

To select these clubs, the team consulted several well-informed persons, including the project staff, and requested that each of them list 15 clubs for group interviews. These persons suggested about 30 names, from which 10 were selected. This took into consideration factors such as size, ecological zones in which clubs were located, year of origin, and accessibility.

On the whole, the selection process was not entirely satisfactory because of inherent bias. It is likely that the project management and government officials suggested the clubs that had good performance records. In addition, as mentioned above, the clubs located in remote areas were generally excluded because of transportation problems. Also, the team had to be content with a very small sample.

Conducting Group Interviews

The duration of an interview ranged between 1 1/2 and 2 hours. Participation levels were very good. An overwhelming number of members attended each of the meetings, and in two cases every member of the club was present. In no instance were more than three members absent out of memberships ranging in size from 25 to 30. (Obviously, since all members of a club resided either in the same village or adjoining villages, it was not inconvenient for them to attend.)

Initial Introductions

Because the club members were not accustomed to interacting with people from different cultures, the evaluation team members tried to put them at ease by initiating individual conversations prior to the start of the interview. The team members also introduced themselves as interested individuals, and not as representatives of an international organization. They gave their country of origin and family backgrounds, and mentioned their earlier visits to Malawi.

Where possible, the group sat in a semi-circle to keep the atmosphere informal.

At the beginning of a meeting, the club chairman/secretary welcomed the team. The team leader then introduced his colleagues and stressed that the purpose of their visit was to learn and to know the views, opinions, and suggestions of the club members. He stated that they would like to hear from each person present, and encouraged anyone with a divergent view or thought to express it freely. He also mentioned that team members would be delighted to answer any questions.

Probing Techniques Used

A question-and-answer session began after the team leader made his introductory remarks. In most instances, the evaluation team started with questions about the size of the club, the year of its inception, and its present activities. Because of their simplicity and non-controversial nature, such questions helped to establish an initial rapport between the evaluation team and the club members. The members easily answered them and felt a bit more confident and better prepared to answer more difficult questions.

The evaluation team generally asked most of the questions listed in the interview guide. However, the sequence of the questions changed depending on the flow of the conversation. Moreover, team members asked many additional questions not listed in the guide.

In the interests of obtaining more useful information, the team members tried to adopt, though not always successfully, a posture of "sophisticated naiveté," by conveying the impression that while they knew about farmers' clubs, they lacked an in-depth knowledge and understanding of them. Using this approach, team members were often able to obtain more details through remarks such as "You know that I am not very familiar with farming practices in this part of the country, so you will have to tell me the agricultural activities in which you have helped each other."

For probing purposes, queries based on "what," "when," "where," "which," and "how" were used frequently. The evaluation team tried to seek as many specific details as possible. For example, one issue of prime interest to the evaluation team was the 100-percent repayment rate for seasonal credit. The team members usually asked several questions on that topic, for example: "Do you know any member who was in financial difficulty and therefore could not make the repayment in time?" "What will people do if a member is unable to repay the loan?" "Was there any time when, in your club or elsewhere, people had to exert pressure on a member to repay?" However, team members were careful not to make the participants feel that they were being cross-examined. To this end, they asked probing questions in a highly informal way.

Obtaining Balanced Participation

One problem that the evaluation team constantly faced was that a few club members often tried to dominate the session. Such persons tended to be club officers, village or community leaders, and in some cases, party functionaries. Constraining them required considerable tact and interpersonal skills on the part of the evaluation team.

The team used two strategies to ensure that participants contributed equally to the discussions. First, team members addressed questions to individual participants. For example, a team member would turn to a reticent participant and say, "I would very much like to hear what you have to say about this issue." Such a remark often succeeded in evoking some response from the participant. In many instances, the same question was asked of several persons. For example, the question, "Why did you join the club?" was typically addressed to many participants in a meeting.

Second, the evaluation team took polls on selected questions. For example, participants were asked, "Those of you who did receive the amount of seasonal credit you really needed this year, please raise hands." This strategy enabled the team to get an indication of the opinions or experiences of participants, even when they were reluctant to speak.

However, the evaluation team was not entirely successful in obtaining the participation of women in all of the group interviews. Because of their low social status and prevailing socio-cultural barriers, many women preferred to remain silent spectators. One strategy that partially worked in some situations was a judicious sense of humor, samples of which are shown in Box 3.2.

Controlling Group Pressure

The evaluation team was also concerned about group pressures that might inhibit dissenting participants from expressing their views on a particular subject. There were several reasons for such a concern. In Malawi society, great value is attached to consensus. People are not

---

Box 3.2 Encouraging Women to Participate in Group Interviews

To encourage the participation of women in the group interview, the team leader included the following in his introductory remarks:

> When I was coming here, my boss called me and told me that he was interested in knowing the views of all the people in a meeting; he would not make his decisions on the basis of the opinions of a few individuals. In fact, to tell you the truth, he promised me a raise if I succeeded; otherwise he might even fire me. So .please promise me that all of you will participate in discussions. If you don't, you will have to give me a piece of land so that I can join you. (Loud laughter)

The team leader then turned to women participants, who usually sat separately, and added:

> But this is not the only problem that I have. My wife has heard a lot about you and your participation in farmers' clubs. She wants to know more about what you have been doing, what your experiences have been, and what can be done to improve your participation. If my boss gets angry, he can only fire me, but if my wife gets upset, I might be in greater trouble.

These remarks gave the team leader an excuse to humorously probe the participants. Whenever some people were not participating, he would simply say, "Oh, my friends, you seem to be forgetting my problem." Club members would laugh and respond to his questions.

---

supposed to differ, at least in public, with their elders, leaders, government officials, or others holding higher status. Moreover, club members were subsistence farmers who were not very articulate. Thus, it was reasonable to anticipate that they would agree to a view expressed by another person simply to extricate themselves from the uncomfortable position of answering a question in public.

To minimize such group pressure, the evaluation team took the following three steps.

First, whenever the team members saw that an idea was being generally adopted without any discussion or disagreement, they would specifically ask for other ideas, explanations, or recommendations. For example, in several cases, the initial response of the participants to the question, "Why did you join the club?" was that they wanted to cooperate with one another. Confronted with this reply, the team members pressed for additional reasons, and often the participants then said that they also wanted credit to purchase agricultural inputs. Pressed further, some of them said that extension workers had explained the advantages of forming a club and indicated that, as club members, farmers could easily gain access to extension services.

Second, the team members would pursue one response with mention of another idea or explanation. For example, in response to the question concerning why all club members regularly repaid their loans, many of the respondents would say that it was in their own interest to do so; otherwise, they would not get credit in the future. The team members typically would then ask, "Do you think that the defaulters would be concerned about their relationship with other members?" (In the project area, a club is responsible for all the credit advanced to its members, and if one member defaults, the entire club is barred from further credit.) In many cases, respondents would answer affirmatively and then go on to explain the social ostracism that a defaulting member would encounter in the local community.

Finally, team members tried to observe the non-verbal behavior of the participants. If a member felt that some persons looked skeptical or doubtful, he would look at them, and say something like, "What about you? You might have a different view." Such remarks often encouraged participants to express dissenting views.

Recording Group Interviews

All team members took notes during the interviews, which they then compared at the end of the day. This helped them to fill in the information gaps and avoid potential sources of error.

The evaluation team then prepared a short summary of each group interview, outlining the information obtained, the team's impressions, and implications of the information for the evaluation. Such summaries proved very useful during the preparation of the evaluation report.

One unintended advantage of the preparation of the interview summaries was that this exercise provided useful insights and ideas that could be explored in future interviews. For example, in the first group interview, the evaluation team learned that the extension staff had helped in drafting the constitution of the club. The team pursued this lead in the remaining interviews and found that this was the accepted practice.

Major Findings and Conclusions

As indicated earlier, group interviews were not the only sources of data for the evaluation. The team members also reviewed the available literature and conducted in-depth interviews with several key informants. Moreover, they had access to the quarterly reports of clubs, which were often prepared with considerable precision and care. It is therefore difficult to isolate the information and insights gained through group interviews from those from other sources of data. However, there is little doubt that the group interviews were extremely valuable in generating the following information.

Profiles of Club Membership

The group interviews revealed that practically all of the club members were smallholders. An overwhelming majority of them owned and cultivated between 2 to 3 hectares of land. Rarely did the team find a member who owned and cultivated more than 4 hectares.

An earlier study had indicated that very tiny smallholders, that is, those cultivating less than 1 hectare, were underrepresented in the clubs. Although such smallholders constituted 36.1 percent of the farming population, they represented only 11.2 percent of club memberships. Group interviews, however, provided a plausible explanation for such low representation, revealing that a high proportion of these smallholders worked on estates or took employment in nearby towns, and were therefore only part-time farmers. Moreover, some of them were economically or physically too handicapped to work effectively in the clubs. In either case, they often did not meet the membership criteria.

Club Leadership

The group interviews revealed that club leadership was generally provided by the farmers who had been exposed to outside influences. These included farmers who had previously worked in mines or on estates, literate individuals, and party functionaries. (Only one legal political party existed in the country at the time this project was undertaken.) The village headman was invariably a prominent member. On the whole, club leadership represented a blending of traditional as well as modern authority structures, which contributed to its legitimacy in public eyes.

All the senior officials of the clubs were men.

Distribution of Credit

The most important function of the clubs was to provide credit to their members for agricultural inputs. Even the non-funded clubs survived in the hope that they, too, would ultimately receive credit. (Many clubs had remained unfunded because of the shortage of funds at the national level. The evaluation team found that the current momentum for the growth of clubs might be arrested unless additional funds were made available for seasonal loans.)

Credit was provided in kind and not cash. Seasonal credit was meant for the purchase of seeds, fertilizers, and other inputs, which were supplied by a parastatal organization. Medium-term credit was meant for farm implements such as ridgers, ploughs, ox-carts, and oxen.

Available documentation suggested that the clubs had a policy of distributing seasonal credit equally among their members, irrespective of the size of their holdings. However, interviews indicated that this policy was not uniformly implemented and that members could sometimes make informal arrangements with one another to get around it.

Group interviews also revealed that the amount of credit advanced to clubs was not sufficient to meet members' requirements. On average, members received enough credit to buy only a single package for maize, even though they needed two.

Agricultural Cooperation

The government viewed agricultural cooperation as the prime justification for establishing the clubs. All the members of a club were supposed to engage in group farming, or at least cooperate with one another in agricultural operations. However, group interviews indicated that despite the stated policy, only limited cooperation existed among the clubs' members. The examples of cooperation most often cited included bringing inputs from the parastatal organization, assisting in soil preparation, and helping members during illness or other emergencies. A few clubs owned common plots that were jointly cultivated by their members.

Role of Agricultural Extension

The role of extension staff has been most crucial in the formation and functioning of the clubs. The field assistants (grassroots extension workers) have worked very closely with farmers to establish new clubs and assisted them in framing appropriate rules and procedures. Once a club is formed, field assistants have provided assistance to maintain accounts and obtain credit. They have also supervised the supply and use of inputs by the members.

The field assistants have tried to make the clubs a focal point for extension activities by establishing "demonstration gardens" and organizing meetings and discussions. Attendance at such meetings was virtually mandatory. Group interviews revealed that club members were not very enthusiastic about extension services, in part because the extension staff focused primarily on maize. Once the members had used the recommended technical package or improvised on it, they had nothing to gain from attending more meetings or visiting the demonstration farms.

Repayment of Credit

The most remarkable achievement of the clubs was the 100-percent loan recovery rate. An obvious reason for this was that loan recovery was the collective responsibility of the club; credit was given to a club and not to individual members. Since a defaulting club was not eligible for further credit, all members had a vested interest in assuring that the loans were repaid on time.

The interviews revealed the intense pressure brought to bear by the clubs on potential defaulters. In one case, a member who delayed his repayment was visited by club members and virtually coerced into making instant payment. Such group pressure undoubtedly works because the members belong to closely-knit communities.

Overall Achievement

The group interviews lent some credence to the project management's assertion that the clubs had contributed to increased agricultural production. In all the clubs, participants stated that because of their involvement their maize production had increased and their standard of living had improved. Three reasons were typically given for this. First, there was a universal shortage of credit in the project area, and without the clubs it would not have been possible for most of the members to raise resources for the purchase of needed inputs. Second, as a result of their participation in the clubs, members also received significant extension advice. However, as previously noted, several members indicated that the extension workers focused primarily on maize, and in many cases had nothing to add to what farmers already had learned. Third, club membership contributed to a continual pressure to improve agricultural production and productivity.

Lessons in Conducting Group Interviews

The project team learned several lessons about planning and conducting group interviews, and these are described below.

Preparation of a Structured Interview Guide

As mentioned earlier, the evaluation team discussed whether the interview guide should simply list issues and topics alone or provide precise questions, and eventually opted for the latter. However, the team members argued that interviewers should enjoy considerable freedom to explore issues not listed in the guide.

Following this course during the interviews proved eminently practical. One advantage of this was that posing the same questions in all the interviews generated comparable data, facilitating the eventual analysis. Another important advantage was that the structured interview guide saved time, because the interviewers did not have to construct questions on the spur of the moment. After one or two group interviews, team members had almost memorized the questionnaire, and their questioning looked quite spontaneous.

The flexibility the interview guide provided enabled the team members to explore new issues and ideas that had not come to mind at the time of its preparation. Thus, the list of questions was constantly being revised. For example, the team had not initially realized the important role of field assistants in framing the clubs' constitutions and providing overall supervision and guidance. Once this fact was revealed, the team members began posing questions about it in subsequent interviews.

To sum up, it is suggested that the best interview guide design lists specific questions for group interviews, but allows the interviewers considerable flexibility.

Determining Optimum Group Size

In starting out, the evaluation team paid little attention to the issue of group size, and assumed without making inquiries that no more than 60 to 70 percent of club members would attend the interview sessions. As indicated earlier, this assumption proved to be wrong. Thus, the size of group meetings ranged between 25 to 31 persons, although one meeting was composed of more than 50 people. However, the evaluation team found that it was difficult to effectively manage a group interview with more than 30 individuals.

It is recommended that investigators carefully consider the probable size of groups to be interviewed and have contingency plans. For example, if the number of participants is over 30, the group should be divided into two or more subgroups.

Generating Quantitative Data

The evaluation team also found that group interviews can also generate quantitative data or information. Although such data, being purely nominal, have obvious limitations in terms of possible analysis, they can still be of value for rational decision-making. On several issues—such as the number of seasonal loans provided by the club, the effects of club participation on agricultural production, and the problems facing the members—the evaluation team took polls and thus gathered some quantitative data.

The data generated by such polls can be aggregated and analyzed either by treating individual respondents as separate cases, or treating each group as a separate case.

Effects of Group Inhibitions on Veracity of Information

It is very important that interviewers not take all respondents' comments in group meetings at face value. Many people, particularly in totalitarian societies, feel constrained in expressing themselves freely particularly in groups in which individuals in positions of authority are present. The information thus obtained on sensitive topics must be cross-checked with other sources of data.

As an example, the evaluation team often felt that club members were extremely reluctant to reveal any information that was critical or might be construed as critical of the government or the project authorities. Some participants appeared to go out of their way to make positive comments about the extension staff, local leaders, and the government.

As another example, most of the club members indicated that there was no discrimination against women, though considerable anecdotal evidence exists that women smallholders were universally discouraged from joining the clubs. Also, the members did not reveal that many farmers who had initially used the recommended variety of maize were discarding it at the time of the interviews, and that production remained stagnant on many farms.

Post-Meeting Conversations

Usually, post-meeting conversations are extremely useful for obtaining information that some participants might not like to share in public, and it is recommended that such conversations be an integral part of the group interview process.

Because of time constraints, the evaluation team could not arrange for such conversations in most instances. However, when this was possible, many issues were clarified and insightful information obtained. For example, in one such post-meeting conversation, a club member mentioned that many farmers did not find the recommended technical package entirely satisfactory. This was later confirmed by many key informants. Another participant complained that "demonstration gardens" did not serve any useful purpose, as most of the farmers knew about the recommended technical package and its strengths and limitations.

4

A Commodity Systems Assessment Methodology Workshop: Improving Agricultural Production and Marketing

R.J. Haggerty and J.E. Armstrong

In this chapter, Haggerty and Armstrong describe a variant of the group interviews technique, in which a workshop format is used to generate information and recommendations. Haggerty and his associates were asked to determine ways to improve the production and marketing system for ginger in the Rapti Zone of Nepal. Practically no published material was available on the subject, and the project did not have time and resources to mount a comprehensive study. Under these conditions, they employed what is known as "Commodity Systems Assessment Methodology" (CSAM), in which a series of questionnaires are used to generate information in a workshop setting.

Haggerty and his associates organized a five-day workshop of 40 participants, including ginger farmers, merchants, agricultural experts, project staff, and concerned government officials. The participants were divided into four groups and held 36 group sessions which focused on different dimensions of the system. At the end of each session, group leaders filled in structured questionnaires drawn from the data, information, and ideas generated during the discussions. The findings of various groups were synthesized in the final report. By tapping the experiences and opinions of the major actors involved in the production and marketing of ginger, the team was not only able to generate a reasonable body of knowledge that could be further tested and refined, but also able to produce a set of recommendations that were used by the program managers and the Nepalese government.

The methodology used by Haggerty and Armstrong is essentially qualitative in nature and is suitable for analyzing a broad range of problems in a commodity system. However, it can only be used to assess a specific commodity in a limited geographic area. Extreme care is also needed in selecting participants, refining questionnaires, moderating discussions and filling out the questionnaires. Otherwise, the discussions may be misleading.

THE PURPOSE OF THIS STUDY was to determine ways to improve the production and marketing system for ginger in the Rapti region of western Nepal. USAID/Nepal contracted with a U.S. institution to collaborate with a Nepalese consulting firm to conduct the study.

The U.S. and Nepalese·contractors were charged with conducting a workshop in the Rapti Zone to analyze the production, post-harvest handling, marketing, infrastructure, and government/private sector inputs and outputs for ginger, using the Commodity Systems Assessment Methodology (CSAM, La Gra, 1990). The workshop, held April 24–28, 1989, had the following objectives:

- provide a rapid, low cost analysis of production and marketing of ginger in the Rapti Zone;
- identify problem areas in the system, and propose interventions to alleviate them;
- improve communication and coordination among the members of the ginger commodity system; and
- train Nepalese technical assistance personnel in the use of the CSAM.

Two U.S. consultants each spent a total of 18 days in Nepal to complete the assignment.

Country and Program Setting

The Rapti Zone, located in western Nepal, has very few roads in the region, and most movement of people and goods is via backcountry footpaths. The workshop took place in Dang District, which lies partly in the Gangetic plain. The zone's four other districts (Pyuthan, Salyan, Rolpa, and Rukum) are situated in mountainous regions.

The USAID/His Majesty's Government (HMG)-funded Rapti Development Project was initiated in 1980 for the economic and social development of the people in the Rapti Zone. The first phase of the project, ending in 1987, achieved significant progress in infrastructure development, in availability of services to the rural people, in natural resources management, and institutional development.

The project continues efforts to improve crop, livestock, and forestry production through a decentralized and highly participatory approach involving local government entities, farmers, and private entrepreneurs. Programs are aimed at the fulfillment of the basic needs of the people in

the region. USAID/Nepal seeks to assist HMG in improving crop production, post-harvest handling and processing, and marketing of a variety of agricultural products in the Rapti region. USAID/Nepal
determined that there was a serious lack of information available about
the production and marketing of ginger, an important cash crop in the
region. To facilitate improvements in the commodity system, the application of participatory and qualitative assessment techniques was
needed.

Research Design and Rationale

The Commodity Systems Assessment Methodology (CSAM) is a rapid,
low-cost data collection method involving elements of group interview
and focus group discussion methodologies. The CSAM was developed
by the Postharvest Institute for Perishables (PIP) at the University of
Idaho in the United States under the leadership of Jerry La Gra, a marketing specialist working for the Inter-American Institute for Cooperation on Agriculture (La Gra, 1990). It was designed to provide scientists
and decision-makers concerned with post-harvest problems a methodological tool for collecting field data on magnitudes and causes of post-
harvest losses, primarily with perishable commodities. The information
obtained with CSAM is used to design economically viable solutions or
to recommend priority areas in which additional information is required
to analyze and resolve post-harvest problems. CSAM was also designed
to develop a local capacity in the host country for applying the methodology without expatriate assistance.

CSAM is based on the premise that examination of perceived problems cannot take place without considering the commodity system in
which the problems exist, including the participants in the system. Because a commodity system is influenced by the agronomic and physi-
ological features of the particular commodity, by weather conditions,
other geographical variables, and the socio-political-economic environment, the system of necessity encompasses all the participants involved
in the planning, financing, production, processing, marketing, and support services of a particular commodity, including a diversity of public
and private institutions and marketing intermediaries. Figure 4.1 illustrates the generic categories of activity in a commodity system used in
CSAM. An assessment of problems in a commodity system requires
input from an interdisciplinary group of people familiar with different
aspects of the system in question.

The CSAM assumes, in general, that the various participants in a
commodity system familiar with different aspects of the system know
how well it is functioning. These people have insights about what the

problems are and their root causes, and can generally propose solutions. Further, CSAM assumes that a group of system participants can establish priorities for their problems, recognize commonalities, and propose specific solutions or improvements that will benefit the whole system. The CSAM approach is therefore interdisciplinary in nature and draws upon the knowledge of local people. Each application of CSAM must be commodity-specific and geographically limited.

CSAM is applied in a workshop setting in order to achieve objectives that are clear to all participants. The methodology requires discussion groups to complete a set of about 30 questionnaires representing functional components of the commodity system. The components, shown in Figure 4.1, are presented in a circle format. The center part of the circle is divided in half, identifying those components that fall into pre-harvest versus post-harvest stages. Each half-circle is further sub-divided to indicate whether the components deal with pre-production (planning, policies, and institutions), production, post-harvest handling, or marketing. The components are addressed in chronological order, from pre-production planning to marketing.

Each one of the components is potentially important, because the decisions or actions occurring at that point may affect production, productivity, quality, or cost of the product. However, not all the components are relevant for every commodity system. In such cases, the irrelevant components are eliminated from discussion. The list of questions that guide the discussion on each component should be modified in accordance with the commodity and the circumstances of the commodity system.

CSAM is conducted in three phases: collection of background information, problem identification, and solution identification. To complete all three phases, CSAM utilizes—as previously stated—a group discussion method in a workshop setting. Depending on the situation, for example, if the size of the group is large, there may be more than one discussion group operating simultaneously. CSAM discussions are not completely open-ended. In all three phases, discussions are directed toward objectives of which the participants are made fully aware.

The main purpose of the background information collection phase of the workshop is to generate information that describes the commodity system in question. This is accomplished by having the discussion group answer about 30 structured questionnaires. If there are several groups in the workshop, each discussion group answers the same series of questions from each structured questionnaire. Because not all group members are knowledgeable about all aspects of the commodity system, answering the questions requires input from group members who are familiar with these different aspects. To be able to fill out the question-

Figure 4.1 Principal Components for a Commodity Systems Assessment

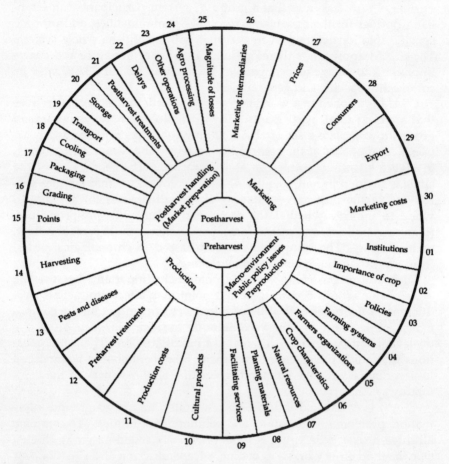

Source: La Gra et al. (1987, p. 9).

naires as a group, consensus within the group needs to be reached. The resulting interchange of ideas and perspectives highlights the secondary purpose of this phase of the CSAM workshop. That is, the group discussions enhance communication among diverse members of a commodity system who might not otherwise have the opportunity to view the system from someone else's perspective.

Once the commodity system has been described in this manner, the discussions move into their second phase, which is to identify perceived problems in the commodity system and to assign priorities to the problems identified, in terms of their importance. Producing such a priority list of problems usually requires extensive discussion among members of the group.

The third phase of the CSAM workshop builds on the outcome of the second. During this phase, the groups must identify possible solutions to the problems previously identified. The solutions must be realistic and serve as the basis for recommendations to authorities for intervention or further research.

Each discussion group requires a moderator to guide the discussion and ensure that the questionnaires are answered and the group completes its task in each session. At least one observer is present to assess the non-verbal reactions of the group(s), and to observe group dynamics for discussions with the moderator(s) and other workshop leaders after each session. In discussions by workshop leaders after each session, the observer(s) and moderator(s) compare their views concerning what they heard and observed during the group sessions and determine the most appropriate actions for subsequent sessions. These monitoring discussions between sessions also are a validity and reliability check of the process.

In a workshop in which several discussion groups answer the same questionnaires, it is necessary to pool the results and summarize them into one set of responses. A report is also written at the conclusion of the workshop. The report summarizes the results of the group sessions (that is, description of the system: production, post-harvest handling, and marketing practices; constraints identified in the system; and suggested solutions to those constraints), incorporating the moderator's interpretation of group findings. The report serves as a document to help stimulate the recommended next action by the appropriate organization.

In contrast to the traditional group interview method, CSAM uses a group of moderators who are referred to as the "coordinating committee." Ideally, this committee consists of host country specialists who are knowledgeable about or familiar with policies and planning, finance, production, post-harvest, marketing, and support services aspects of the commodity and geographical location in question. The coordinating committee usually includes a U.S. consultant whose role doubles as overall CSAM workshop moderator and trainer of CSAM. It is a goal of the developers of CSAM that, following a CSAM workshop, other members of the coordinating committee should be able to conduct similar workshops for data gathering without outside assistance.

The coordinating committee works together to plan the CSAM workshop, prepares all logistical arrangements for the workshop, modifies the questionnaires in advance to ensure their appropriateness to the situation, moderates group discussions, conducts monitoring discussions after each group session with a group observer, pools and summarizes responses to questionnaires, and prepares the final report.

Nepal CSAM Ginger Workshop: Planning and Questionnaire Preparation

Prior to the Nepal CSAM ginger workshop, the Nepalese contractor, in coordination with the U.S. contractor, identified key people to serve as the Coordinating Committee and over 30 individuals as workshop participants. The Nepalese contractor had several years of experience working in the Rapti region and had become acquainted with many farmers, merchants, and extension personnel in the area, in the context of previous Rapti Development Project activities. Many of these individuals were invited to participate in the workshop. The Coordinating Committee included:

- a planning and policy specialist (USAID/Nepal)
- a planning and policy specialist (Nepalese contractor)
- a marketing specialist (Nepalese contractor)
- a production specialist (National Agricultural Research and Services Center)
- a production and post-harvest specialist (Nepalese contractor)
- a marketing specialist (U.S. contractor)
- a post-harvest specialist (U.S. contractor)

Upon arrival of the U.S. team, the final technical plan for the workshop was developed by the Coordinating Committee (CC). In lengthy sessions of the CC in Kathmandu, and with secondary information on ginger gathered by the Nepalese contractor, the CSAM questionnaires were modified to address the known characteristics of the ginger production/marketing system.

This workshop was designed to include as participants small-scale farmers and local marketing agents with limited formal education. (In previous applications of CSAM, all workshop participants were educated to at least the high school level, and most held bachelor or graduate degrees.) It was therefore anticipated that illiteracy or language differences would exist. In the interests of saving time and expense, it was decided to prepare the questionnaires in English, with the language gap being bridged by English/Nepali-speaking moderators, who would translate the questions orally in Nepali and complete the questionnaires in English.

The preparation of the questionnaires among the CC resulted in the elimination of the "cooling" component, one of the aforementioned 30 components, which was felt to be irrelevant since precooling is an unnecessary step in ginger processing and is not carried out in the Rapti Zone. There were also numerous changes in wording to tailor the questions to the ginger commodity system.

CSAM questionnaires are designed to foster discussion, as well as to obtain valid, useful, and objective information. The questionnaires are structured to generate descriptive information and do not focus much on the gathering of quantitative information. Questions probe for information by asking "who, what, when, where, why, and how." Some of these are open-ended questions intended to elicit comments and observations from the participants in the discussion groups. Samples of all CSAM questionnaires are found in La Gra's 1990 document, and can be obtained at the address noted in the references. A sample of the CSAM questionnaire designed for the present study is shown in Box 4.1.

In previous CSAM workshops, the questionnaires were developed to deal with the commodity system in the order of a discussion of pre-production components, and continuing through production, post-harvest handling, and marketing. However, because this workshop involved farmers who might be uncomfortable and reluctant to speak out, it was decided to start with the production component with which they would feel most familiar. The CC felt this would ensure continued active participation.

Furthermore, to ensure there was sufficient time available for discussion on all components and a sequence that would maximize active participation, the component questionnaires were clustered into 9 blocks containing a total of 29 components. Each of these blocks then served as the basis for one discussion session. The CC felt this approach would be less likely to overwhelm the participants with thick bundles of papers and questions. The block descriptions and daily schedule are shown in the appendix to this case study.

As a matter of protocol, once the questionnaires had been revised and the tentative schedule for the workshop developed, the material was presented to appropriate government officials for review and comment. Planned workshop activities were also discussed with representatives from these agencies. Each of these individuals was invited to attend a final seminar after the workshop to be presented in Kathmandu.

The final workshop planning took place in Tulsipur. The Nepalese contractor produced stenciled Nepali translations of the workshop schedule, opening statements, and block descriptions. Meetings were held with the representatives of USAID/Nepal and the Rapti Project Coordinator's Office (PCO) to discuss details of workshop implementation. Participant certificates were prepared. The Rapti Project Coordinator's Office volunteered the participation of some of its personnel, all of whom spoke and read English, but who knew little about ginger production and marketing. The CC intended to take advantage of the volunteers' language skills to enhance communications by including them in group discussions.

It was determined that one member of each discussion group would be a volunteer from the Rapti Project Coordinator's Office with English language skills who would act as discussion group moderator and recorder. The moderators translated the questions orally in Nepali for the discussion group and filled out the questionnaires in English.

In a departure from previous CSAM applications, it was decided that one Nepalese member of the CC would join each discussion group as a "CSAM trainee" to observe the process, rather than function as moderator. Each trainee would function as an observer in order to learn about the application of CSAM for future use on other commodity systems. The trainees were made responsible for assessing the process of information collection, group communication, and evaluating the appropriateness of the questions. The trainees were to have minimal participation in the discussions and were to rotate to a different discussion group each session.

The CC planned to hold monitoring discussions between sessions and at day's end to determine what changes, if any, were to be made for the next session and/or day. In this way, the trainees would have their understanding of CSAM reinforced and would develop their ability to apply the methodology.

Workshop Implementation and Problems Encountered

Approximately 40 participants attended the workshop, which was held at the conference hall at the Rapti Project Coordinator's Office complex in Tulsipur. Among these were 15 merchants and 12 farmers, including one woman farmer. The mix of participating farmers and merchants represented enterprises ranging from small to above-average size, and from below-average to above-average prosperity. The remainder of the participants were government agents and staff from the Rapti Project Coordinator's Office. All workshop participants were acquainted with one or more of the Nepalese people working for the Nepalese contractor. The workshop was completed in five days.

Opening Activities

After an opening ceremony was held, four discussion groups were formed. Each participant was assigned to a discussion group by one Nepalese member of the CC. Each discussion group was formed so as

Box 4.1   Sample CSAM Questionnaire for Marketing Ginger, Rapti Region

STORAGE

NAME OF DATA COLLECTOR: TEL:

TITLE: INSTITUTION:

1. Identify the points in the post-harvest system where storage takes place.

	Yes	No	Duration of Storage (Days)
• on the farm	( )	( )	
• rural collecting point	( )	( )	
• regional collecting point	( )	( )	
• packinghouse	( )	( )	
• retail market	( )	( )	
• wholesale market	( )	( )	
• agro-industry	( )	( )	
• supermarket	( )	( )	
• export warehouses	( )	( )	
• container terminal (export)	( )	( )	
• government marketing board	( )	( )	
• import warehouses	( )	( )	
• other	( )	( )	

2. For each instance of storage identified, provide the following information:

a) Type of storage (from 1 above):

b) Who is responsible for the storage? farmer ( ), middleman ( ), gov't ( ), wholesaler ( ), retailer ( ), processor ( ), other ( )

c) What is the purpose of storage? await shipping ( ), await better market price ( ), maintain quality ( ), assemble larger volumes ( ), other ( )

d) Describe the storage facilities and equipment.

e) How long after harvest does the product normally go into storage (hours and days)?

continued on next page

Box 4.1 (continued)

f) How long is the holding period?

g) At what degree of ripeness/maturity is the product when it is normally placed into storage?

h) How does the quality of produce change during the storage period?

i) Is air temperature controlled in the storage environment? yes ( ) no ( ) Explain:

j) What is the range of air temperature in the storage environment?

k) Is humidity controlled in the storage environment? yes ( ) no ( ) Explain:

l) What is the range of relative humidity in the storage environment?

m) Is the atmosphere in the storage facility modified ( ), or controlled ( )? Describe:

n) Is the product normally stored by itself ( ), or with other produce ( )? If with other produce, specify what kind:

o) Describe the type of container in which the product is packaged during storage.

p) Who owns the storage facilities?

q) Who operates the storage facilities?

r) What is the cost of holding the produce?

s) Is the storage facility operated efficiently? yes ( ) no ( ) If no, explain:

3. Summarize storage problems that may affect post-harvest losses.

1.
2.
3.

4. Observations:

to contain about ten members, representing a mix of farmers, merchants, extension agents, financiers, and researchers. In the end, the general makeup of the discussion groups was typically two farmers, two merchants, two bankers, one moderator (recording results in English), and one observer (a member of the CC learning how to use CSAM). One CC member (from the U.S. contractor) acted as overall observer of all four discussion groups, without participating in any group discussions.

A group solidarity exercise was conducted by all the discussion groups. Each of the four discussion groups created a slogan for their individual group. This exercise was initiated and led by the Training Coordinator (a Nepalese) from the Rapti Project Coordinator's Office. Each discussion group's slogan was presented to all other discussion groups and the members were introduced. This exercise seemed to reduce nervousness among the participants and helped prepare them for the interactive nature of the workshop. The final workshop schedule was negotiated with the whole group and settled quickly.

Collecting Background Information

Over the course of the first three days, the discussion group participants conducted the background information collection phase of the workshop. During this phase, all four groups held nine simultaneous discussion sessions, corresponding to the nine blocks of component questionnaires, and answered the structured questionnaires. In this way, a total of 36 group discussion sessions were held during this initial phase.

"Block 1—The Importance of Ginger" was conducted as the initial task. It served as an introduction to the CSAM approach of information-gathering through active discussion and the completion of the questionnaire. The discussion groups were led through this block by the Nepali-speaking workshop moderator. A printed explanation, in Nepali, of the block objectives was distributed to all the participants at the beginning of each session. The Nepali-speaking workshop facilitator introduced all four groups to each block by reading out loud a definition of the block's components and the objectives of the session's discussions. All four discussion groups then simultaneously discussed the topic and completed the component questionnaire for this initial block. Members of each discussion group sat in a circle to facilitate open discussion.

Introduction and functioning of all subsequent discussion sessions during the first phase followed the same procedure as Block 1. One set of questionnaires was given to each group moderator, who filled out the questionnaires with input from the discussion group.

At the end of each discussion session, each discussion group reported to all the others, calling for questions and comments. At the end of the first workshop session (Block 1) each discussion group moderator reported his group's results to all the other groups. In the monitoring discussion held after this initial session, the CC concluded that this mode of operation limited the involvement of farmers and merchants. Thereafter, the moderators recorded results and another group member did the reporting. The introductory session's discussion went well.

At the conclusion of each discussion session, one U.S. CC member summarized the results of all four group questionnaires into one set of responses and entered these into a portable computer. The other U.S. CC member documented observations made during all sessions for inclusion in description and analysis of the CSAM workshop process for the final report.

Problem Identification

On the fourth day, the problem-identification phase of the workshop began. The tasks were organized as follows: each individual participant identified as many problems as possible; each discussion group collected these problems and presented 10 to 20 of them to the other discussion groups; and in rotation, each group presented its top priority problem to be tackled in the Phase Three exercise (solutions to problems). Excluding duplications, the discussion groups presented problems until 15 had been selected.

The discussion groups were then briefed by the CC on approaches to solving problems and were encouraged to develop solutions they themselves could accomplish as well as ones requiring outside help. Judging by the energetic, boisterous activity of the second and third workshop phases, the creative task of problem identification was a welcome change from the first phase task of completing questionnaires. The difference in language was not a constraint to satisfactory completion of the tasks.

Solution Identification

Continuing on into the fourth and fifth days, the groups developed solutions to the problems identified—the third phase of the CSAM workshop. As stated, the participants were encouraged to identify solutions that they themselves could accomplish rather than just solutions that someone else might provide for them. Each group's solutions to the problems were presented to all workshop participants on poster paper and the other groups contributed comments on ways to improve the solutions. The discussion on these was very vigorous.

Problems Encountered

"Block 2—Production" took a long time to complete. The main problem arose in trying to balance completion of the questionnaire with open, full discussion among the focus group members. There was lengthy discussion during this session, and it progressed slowly. Concern arose that all the blocks would not be finished in time for the workshop to proceed on schedule. Consideration was given to eliminating another component or two. However, the CC instead encouraged the moderators, under the supervision of the observers, to be slightly more pro-active in guiding the discussion group to complete its task.

The CC determined from the first session that the sessions covering problem identification and solution proposals would require all of days 4 and 5. As it turned out, the groups moved much faster on day 2. None of the components had to be eliminated, and they were rapidly summarized and entered into the computer.

The discussion groups, in general, seemed to work quite effectively. Part of the problem with one group which lacked vitality was that the moderator assigned to that group had other commitments and wasn't diligent in attendance.

The group that included the one female participant made efforts to enhance her active involvement in the discussions. Her opinion was sought by the moderator in a non-threatening way. The efforts had little success. Although the woman attended every session diligently and paid attention, she made very little verbal contribution to the discussions.

The exchange of views among the individual discussion group members appeared to be very good. This was especially true between merchants and farmers. Though it was anticipated they might be mutually antagonistic, they had consistently active, amicable interaction in the discussion groups. Caution was taken by the moderators to ensure that the merchants did not feel proprietary information was being sought from them. (The information provided by the merchants in fact may not have been the most accurate, in the interests of protecting their businesses.) In all cases, the group moderators made conscious efforts to balance participation and involve all members to the maximum extent possible.

The information generated was comprehensive, even if it was not absolutely consistent among the groups in every detail. Enough geographic diversity exists, even in the relatively small Rapti region, to account for some differences in practices from area to area. In general, however, there was remarkable consistency among groups in the information generated.

By the end of day 3 when the questionnaires were completed, discussion group participants appeared tired. Three days of continuous questions and discussions about production and marketing had become tiresome. It was evident that all participants had a broader and deeper understanding of the production and marketing system under study. However, one member of the CC pointed out that, without reinforcement in the near future, the participants would have lost what they had gained.

Group members were confused about a format to be used for presentation of solutions and treated the first round of proposal development as an experiment for fashioning a workable format. The CC encouraged the groups not to take time in developing a format, but to concentrate on the following items: problems to be solved, actions needed, identification of who would act, and description of how the solution would be accomplished. With that information, the CC was later able to formulate more specific project profiles. The sessions on solution development were a more tedious process for the participants than problem identification had been. However, when individual groups presented their solutions, the discussions became very animated.

Findings

Phase I—Database Generation on Ginger Production and Marketing

With the active participation of more than 40 individuals, the CSAM workshop developed a new, larger information base on ginger production and marketing in the Rapti region. The information generated provided more specific details about ginger production, processing, and marketing in the Rapti region than existed in any secondary source in Kathmandu at that time. Post-harvest losses were found to be small in quantitative terms, but significant in terms of lower prices earned for the lower-quality ginger produced.

Phase II—Significant Problems Identified

Using the background information, the participants identified 15 significant problems they felt needed to be addressed. These problems included:

- monopsony power of India and Indian merchants
- lack of price information
- lack of plant protection materials and techniques
- no improved varieties available
- use of traditional practices due to lack of new production technology available
- no knowledge of alternative ginger products
- lack of coordination among support services and organizations
- no organization or institutional support for private sector development
- no organization or institutional support for improving production/ marketing skills
- lack of drying technology
- lack of knowledge about relationships between soil, ginger varieties, and fiber development
- no knowledge of consumer or market needs
- lack of storage and packing materials and facilities
- lack of commercial ginger industry (processing and transformation)
- lack of credit facilities

Phase III—Identification of Solutions to Ginger System Problems

To resolve the identified problems, it was suggested that the following activities be undertaken to intervene in the system: creation of a ginger research site in Salyan; development of improved ginger market assembly points; international market and consumer research; processing improvements and industrial development; and packaging technology improvement.

Accomplishments

This application of CSAM produced good-quality descriptive information in a short time and at relatively low cost.

Enhancement of Communication

The workshop also achieved the other significant objectives of increasing dialogue between producers and traders, and developing and improving the capacity of local personnel to conduct activities like CSAM. It was suggested that additional CSAM workshops be conducted in the Rapti region for other important crops such as apples and vegetable seeds.

Development of CSAM Skills

The U.S. team felt strongly that the workshop was a success and that the CSAM, as modified to study ginger in Nepal, was an appropriate and effective tool. However, as stated above, some further modification could be made in the format for completing the questionnaires that would result in a less tedious operation for the participants and would stimulate more discussion. The main strength of the workshop was that it effectively provided a forum to improve communications among farmers, merchants, and facilitating services personnel, especially between farmers and merchants.

The information gathered was very comprehensive, although not as detailed as it might have been, since not all the questions were answered. However, with the information gathered by the Nepalese contractor before the workshop, a very complete picture resulted.

The problems identified and the solutions developed by the participants were well-focused and structured. Certainly, all the participants broadened and deepened their understanding of all aspects of ginger production and marketing in the Rapti Zone.

Four of the farmers in the group said they now considered forming an association to strengthen their marketing position. Whether this kind of enthusiasm will endure depends on adequate follow-up to the workshop. There is certainly an interest in continuing application and modification of CSAM, thus, the U.S. team felt that the training objective of the workshop was clearly met.

The members of the CC from the Nepalese contractor, the National Agricultural Research and Services Center, and USAID/Nepal demonstrated a firm command of how to apply the CSAM and recognize its strengths and weaknesses. One shortcoming, however, was that the recorders/moderators working in the discussion groups had received no prior exposure or training in CSAM. Their role in the functioning of the groups was critical, and they did a good job. However, their effectiveness would have been improved if they had studied the questionnaires in advance or had some orientation to CSAM. This would have cleared up some of the ambiguities and vagueness experienced on the first day, and better information might have been the result.

Suggestions for Potential Users of this Methodology

Guidelines

A portable computer and printer were essential to the timely preparation and modification of the questionnaires. A small Toshiba 1100 Plus was brought by the U.S. contractor, since it was known to be compatible with the equipment of the Nepalese contractor. The report editing would have been almost impossible without this type of on-site word processing capability.

Fundamental to the success of the workshop was the effective management provided by one of the Nepalese members of the CC working for the Nepalese contractor. Not only was he an excellent overall moderator and facilitator, he also made all logistical arrangements flow smoothly. Perhaps his most critical contribution was to effectively select and encourage participation by the farmers and merchants. It is clear that such an effective local organizer will be critical to success in future work with the CSAM.

The workshop was also a success because the participants took it seriously and were fully committed to it. The PCO staff was very supportive and worked enthusiastically.

Limitations

Some caution about the limitations of the CSAM should be noted. First, the CSAM is most appropriately used to assess a specific commodity in a limited geographical area. Covering a very large geographical area makes it more difficult to accurately describe a commodity system. The process becomes more cumbersome and the information less reliable.

Second, the CSAM is probably better-suited to identification of problems internal to the functioning of a commodity system than it is for identification of problems in government policy and institutional inputs. Farmers are not likely to be well-informed about detailed aspects of national policies. It is also likely that the dynamics of group discussions would be impaired if high-ranking government officials joined groups with local farmers and merchants. The person of lower social status would probably feel inhibited and not contribute effectively to the group discussion. The result would be unbalanced group discussions and, perhaps, less reliable information.

Third, it is critical that questionnaires be tailored for each application of the CSAM. If the right questions are not asked, then the information generated has limited utility. However, modifications in the component discussions are needed to stimulate more discussion and break the tedium of answering questionnaires. Appropriately refined questionnaires are essential to the successful application of CSAM. It would also be prudent to consider limiting the number of questions and/or questionnaires for groups of individuals who may be less-educated.

Users of CSAM should not be overly concerned with quantifying post-harvest losses in a commodity system. The CSAM is really intended for analyzing a broad scope of problems in a commodity system. Even if post-harvest losses are specifically being addressed, the CSAM is not designed for quantifying these losses in detail, but rather, for establishing their magnitude, the causes, and the economic and technological possibility of reducing them.

CSAM discussion group moderators should have adequate previous exposure to or training in its application and its questionnaires to effectively guide and stimulate discussions.

The application of the CSAM requires an interdisciplinary or team approach. It is highly unlikely that one person will have all the knowledge to properly identify the problems related to pre-production, production, harvest, post-harvest, and marketing that make up any commodity system.

Furthermore, application of the CSAM is not limited to perishable crop commodity systems. The CSAM could conceivably be applied to grains, seeds, and marine or freshwater fish. It would be useful to test the CSAM in conducting rapid, low-cost assessments of these types of commodity systems.

Applications

The CSAM will prove useful to short-term consultants and decision-makers interested in rapid appraisals and development from a commodity system perspective.

The CSAM manual (La Gra, 1990) can be used in a workshop environment to train professionals in the commodity systems approach, either from a theoretical point of view, or as an applied, in-service case study (specific commodity) form of training. In the first instance, the trainees may be of the same or of different disciplines. When the case study approach is used, the trainees should include persons with expertise in economics, agronomy, social sciences, food technology, post-harvest activities, and marketing.

The CSAM manual will also prove useful to ministries of agriculture, marketing boards, corporations, research institutes, and other national institutions interested in the systematic improvement of production, post-harvest handling, and marketing within existing commodity systems. At the regional or national level, the methodology will be valuable in the identification of agricultural development projects. It will be of particular value in the execution of rapid appraisal exercises, using interdisciplinary teams of national specialists.

References

Greenbaum, T.L. 1988. *The Practical Handbook and Guide to Focus Group Research.* (ISBN No. 0-669-14775-3). Lexington, MA: D.C. Heath Company.

Honadale, G. 1982. "Rapid Reconnaissance for Development Administration: Mapping and Moulding Organizational Landscapes." *World Development* 10(8):633-649.

La Gra, J. 1990. *A Commodity Systems Assessment Methodology for Problem and Project Identification.* Moscow, Idaho: Postharvest Institute for Perishables, University of Idaho.

La Gra, Jerry, Leong Poo Chow, and Robert J. Haggerty. 1987. *A Postharvest Methodology: Commodity Systems Approach for the Identification of Inefficiencies in Food Systems.* Moscow, Idaho: Postharvest Institute for Perishables, University of Idaho.

McCullough, J. and R. Haggerty. 1989. *An Application of a Commodity System Assessment Methodology to Improve the Functioning of the Production and Marketing System for Ginger in the Rapti Region of Nepal.* GTS Report No. 104. Moscow, Idaho: Postharvest Institute for Perishables, University of Idaho.

McCullough, J., and H. Murray. 1988. *Approaches for Improving Marketing and Reducing Postharvest Loss of Agricultural Products from the Rapti District of Nepal.* GTS Report No. 101. Moscow, Idaho: Postharvest Institute for Perishables, University of Idaho.

Appendix: Block Descriptions

The blocks discussed in the workshop included the following:

Block 1—Commodity Importance (Day 1)

Relative Importance of Crop to be Studied	Component 01

Block 2—Production (Day 1)

Farming Systems	Component 02
Characteristics of the Commodity	Component 03
Natural Resource Constraints	Component 04
Availability of Seeds and Planting Materials	Component 05
Facilitating Services	Component 06
Farmers' Cultural Practices	Component 07
Theoretical and Actual Costs of Production	Component 08

Block 3—Harvesting and Pest Controls (Day 1)

Pre-harvest Treatments	Component 09
Pests and Diseases that Affect Product Quality	Component 10
Harvest of Commodity	Component 11

Block 4—Post-Harvest System (Day 2)

Identification of Points in Post-Harvest System	Component 12

Block 5—Handling and Processing (Day 2)

Selection, Grading, Classification, and Inspection of Horticultural Produce	Component 13
Packaging of Horticultural Produce	Component 14
Post-Harvest Chemical and Physical Treatments	Component 15
Other Operations	Component 16
Agro-Processing of Horticultural Crops	Component 17

Block 6—Post-Harvest Losses (Day 2)

Magnitude of Post-Harvest Losses	Component 18

Block 7—Transport and Storage (Day 3)

Transport of Commodity   Component 19
Storage of Horticultural Produce   Component 20
Delays or Waiting   Component 21

Block 8—Marketing (Day 3)

Intermediaries in Marketing   Component 22
Market Price Information   Component 23
Consumers   Component 24
Exportation of Horticultural Produce   Component 25
Marketing Costs of Horticultural Crops   Component 26

Block 9—Policy and Institutions (Day 3)

Institutions Relevant to the Commodity System   Component 27
Policies   Component 28
Farmers' Organizations   Component 29

5

Using Focus Groups to Develop and Promote an Improved Weaning Food Product

Cecilia Cabañero-Verzosa, Cecile M. Johnston,
and Olabode Kayode

As discussed in Chapter 1, the focus group discussion has emerged as one of the innovative information-gathering methods being used in development settings. In this chapter, Cabañero-Verzosa, Johnston, and Kayode illustrate the use of this method to assess mothers' reactions to an improved variety of weaning food designed to improve infant nutrition and develop effective communication strategies to market the weaning food as part of a health intervention effort in Nigeria.

This chapter describes the various steps—the composition of focus groups, locations of discussions, selection of participants, discussion guides, group discussions, and data analysis—involved in the implementation of this component of a larger research project. More important, it also discusses a few changes that the investigators made in the standard focus group methodology to make it more suitable for a developing country setting. For example, permission of the village chief was sought to interview female participants for focus groups. "Pre-" and "post-" focus groups were also conducted. First, mothers were taught an improved recipe for a commonly-used weaning food in a focus group context. Later, after the mothers had tried the recipe at home for some time, their preferences and suggestions were discussed in another set of focus groups.

The focus groups generated useful information about both product-related and communication-related questions, which was ultimately used in the final decision-making related to the more widespread introduction of the nutritionally-improved weaning food. For example, the groups indicated that roasted cowpea flour was most acceptable to mothers as a fortifying ingredient; that mothers could easily prepare the improved food; and that an addi-

*tional preparation step—the addition of malt flour—was acceptable
to mothers. The focus groups also suggested that the improved
weaning food could be better marketed as a food for a healthy child,
rather than as a "medicinal" food for a sick one, and that the additional ingredients to be added in the old variety should be sold
separately so that mothers could fortify the food themselves.*

IN NIGERIA, as in other developing countries, poor nutrition often pre-
disposes young children to diarrhea and other childhood illnesses.
When the Dietary Management of Diarrhea (DMD) Project[1] got underway in Nigeria, the team uncovered a pattern of feeding during the
weaning period that seemed to exacerbate infant susceptibility to diseases, including diarrhea.

Traditionally, Nigerian infants begin the weaning process at four to
six months. Their first weaning food, called *EKO*, is a very watery
concoction made from a maize or guinea corn pap called *ogi*. Infants are
given *EKO* daily and are introduced to more nutritious solid foods only
at a much later date. In fact, the research data indicate that at 12 months
of age only half the children are consuming solid foods as part of their
regular diets.

Families also take *ogi* as a daily breakfast and snack food. The mixture often contains as much as 70 percent water and, needless to say, is
not very nutritious. It can also be a carrier of the water bacteria that
cause diarrhea.

Project Overview

This paper describes how focus groups were used in conjunction with
quantitative research techniques to develop and promote a new, en-
riched weaning food to Nigerian mothers as a means of improving both
the nutritional and health status of their babies. The chapter provides
background on the use and mechanics of focus groups as a rapid appraisal method, and explains how the group discussions for the present
project were planned. The chapter then discusses the specific focus
group methodology used in this project and the analysis of results, and
finally highlights how the study results were used.

The Intervention

A DMD Project team of medical and public health professionals and
social scientists reasoned that *EKO* could be fortified to create a new
weaning food that would help to improve the nutritional status of these
children. Cowpea flour, red palm oil, and sugar were eventually chosen

as fortifying ingredients—items that are all readily available in the community and provide the required nutrients for weaning-age children. The new product came to be known as *EKO ILERA*, or "*EKO* for Health". The fortified *EKO ILERA* is much more nutritionally sound than the traditional watery *EKO*.[2]

The improved weaning food was introduced in two local government areas, Asa and Oyun, in the Kwara state of Nigeria. This area offers a good mix of urban and rural communities and is comprised mostly of the Yoruba ethnic group. This environment provided a homogeneous audience for the project's communication component and for its research component as well.

During the last stage of the intervention, health care workers at each of 12 sites trained 10 mother leaders who in turn were each responsible for training 10 neighbors in the preparation and feeding of the new *EKO ILERA*. Training materials included flipcharts, flyers, and product samples. Mothers were taught how to prepare the new *EKO ILERA* during cooking demonstrations held in the community and in public places like the markets. In all, approximately 1,200 mothers from Kwara State were trained during the intervention.

The Research Issues

This project was based on research related to two basic areas of decision-making. The first were product decisions dealing with the specific composition and mixing of the *EKO ILERA*. The second dealt with the nature of communication support needed to effectively encourage the acceptance of *EKO ILERA* among mothers.

The four sets of product-related questions that had to be answered were:
- Is fortification of the traditional *ogi* acceptable to mothers and *EKO* sellers? What fortifying ingredients are acceptable? Why?
- Can mothers learn the recipe? Can they teach others?
- What product characteristics are important to mothers? Is the addition of malt flour to maintain the desired liquid consistency an additional step in the cooking process that would be tolerated?
- Will mothers prepare the new *EKO ILERA* at home?
The communications-related questions included such issues as:
- What communication strategy is appropriate? Is there an audience other than mothers? What benefit can be identified for the target audience—the mother—and for the ultimate beneficiary—the child?
- What materials will be effective in teaching the mothers to use *EKO ILERA*?
Focus groups were the research vehicle used to answer these questions. The qualitative, exploratory nature of focus groups seemed ideal

for examining reactions to a new product that deviated from traditional methods. Because group discussions lend themselves to probing and uncovering perceptions, attitudes, and feelings, it was believed useful for gauging mothers' impressions about a new food. Because *EKO ILERA* deviated from conventional practices, focus groups were an ideal format to informally explore possible resistance and to learn what appeals might prove persuasive to the Nigerian mothers.

However, the focus groups were only part of an overall research program of the DMD Project that included in-depth interviews, ethnographic assessments, observational studies, cost monitoring, clinical studies, and surveys. The focus groups, with their opportunities for group dynamics and consensus-building, functioned very effectively as a complement to these other types of research. While the more quantitative studies were objective, definitive, descriptive, and measurement-oriented, the focus groups were subjective, exploratory, and interpretive.

To summarize, in addition to the focus groups, the following research studies were undertaken in the effort to effectively introduce the new weaning food to Nigerian families:

- *Ethnographic Studies.* Key informants provided information on infant feeding, diarrhea taxonomy, and household feeding and treatment patterns during diarrheal episodes.
  At the time that the project team was trying to reach a decision on whether to fortify an existing watery pap used as weaning food, or to introduce solid foods earlier, ethnographic interviews were also conducted to assess which option mothers would find more acceptable.
- *Surveys.* A representative sample of 2,655 mothers of children less than 3 years of age provided information on child feeding practices and provided anthropometric assessments of targeted children.
- *Food Price Monitoring.* Quarterly market surveys were carried out in both urban and rural markets to establish the cheapest sources of energy and protein.
- *Longitudinal Household Treatment Studies.* Laduba, a rural village near the city of Ilorin, was chosen as the site for conducting dietary intake studies and diarrheal epidemiology among 45 children aged 5 to 30 months.
- *Recipe Trials.* Recipe trials provided mothers with first-hand experience in the preparation of the new food. A list of possible ingredients for fortification was compiled. Mothers were invited to focus group discussions and cooking demonstrations to determine the acceptability of these fortifying options and the food preparation procedures. A second set of recipe trials occurred at the individual homes of mothers who volunteered to try two recipes that affected the liquid consistency of *EKO*.

- *Clinical Trials.*   Clinical trials assessed the acceptability, safety, and nutritional quality of the maize-cowpea weaning diet in children with acute diarrhea.   A total of 60 children aged 6 to 24 months were randomly treated with either the DMD candidate diet or a commercial soy protein isolate, lactose-free infant formula immediately following rehydration therapy.

Focus Group Planning

Focus group interviews offer a means of obtaining in-depth information on a specific topic through a discussion group. The underlying premise is that people who share common experiences, problems, or concerns are willing to reveal them in a group atmosphere. Focus group interviews are not simply individual interviews conducted in a group setting; the moderator does not ask the same question of all respondents. Rather, focus group interviews represent a situation in which the participants are stimulated to talk with each other on the chosen topic under the guidance of a moderator. The primary role of the moderator is to promote group discussion.

Focus groups can be carried out in developing country settings, but because developing country conditions often present constraints, researchers must take steps to ensure the quality of the research data. These quality assurance steps may include ensuring that: the recruitment process brings qualified participants into the discussions; the moderator functions as a facilitator rather than as an authority figure on the issue under discussion; and the results of group discussions are adequately recorded and analyzed by someone who has a clear understanding of the goals of the research.

There are other, indirect advantages to using focus groups as a research tool in developing countries. They provide a mechanism through which the researcher and the community cooperate in the solution of the community's problem. Focus groups also provide a means for researchers to work with the project beneficiary—the community itself—in all phases of project work from identifying issues, to developing and testing solutions, to preparing communication materials, and finally, to introducing an intervention.

To explore the questions concerning product and communication strategies vis-à-vis the new weaning food, four sets of focus groups were conducted as indicated in Box 5.1.

The first set of focus groups was held with two different audiences: mothers, and women who were active in the cottage industry of making and selling *EKO*. These initial groups were exploratory in scope. With mothers, the discussions turned to feeding practices with *EKO* and reac-

Box 5.1 The Use of Focus Groups in Developing the Product and the Communications Effort

Question Area	Focus Groups To Respond
Product Questions	
Is fortification of EKO acceptable?	Initial groups—mothers Initial groups—*EKO* sellers
Can mothers learn recipe, then teach others?	Recipe trial groups
Is the use of malt flour acceptable?	Pre- and post-groups with in-home product use test
Will mothers prepare new EKO at home?	Post-groups with in-home test
Communications Questions	
What communication strategy will work?	Initial groups—mothers Initial groups—*EKO* sellers Materials pre-testing groups
What materials will be effective teaching aids?	Materials pre-testing groups

tions to the addition of fortifying ingredients. Among *EKO* sellers, the groups examined cooking procedures and selling practices. With regard to the seller groups, there was keen interest as to whether these women could serve as agents for making a fortified version of their product or participate in the intervention in some other way. As a second goal, these initial groups examined possible messages and communication strategies for the intervention.

The second set of focus groups was conducted with mothers in conjunction with recipe trials. Several fortifying options and cooking procedures were illustrated during the recipe demonstrations. The focus groups provided a format for testing mothers' reactions to the new ingredients and the resulting products.

A third set of pre- and post-focus groups wrapped, like bookends, around an in-home product use test. The test took place in four communities and determined preference for two recipes that affected the liquid consistency of *EKO*. One recipe included malt; the second had no malt. The discussions were held at a central location within each community, and mothers discussed their perceptions of the two pap products.

Finally, focus groups with mothers were used in pre-testing graphic materials. A flipchart describing the food, the ingredients, and the cooking process was developed, along with a scaled-down version in a flyer that mothers could take home. Focus groups gauged reactions to the print materials and also proved useful for finalizing the product name and the final positioning of the new, fortified *EKO* as a weaning food.

Methodology

Group Composition and Size

In general, each group discussion included six to ten individuals. Group members were homogeneous with respect to two different characteristics: nursing mothers who currently gave their children traditional *EKO*, or *EKO* sellers who made and marketed the product in their communities.

Group Locations

All group discussions were held in the community. Often the village leader offered his residence as a venue for the group discussions. His home was often centrally located for participants and usually had a quiet, inside room for the discussion. Because of the wide discrepancy in maternal behavior patterns between urban and rural areas, it was important to hold groups in both venues.

Table 5.1 summarizes the composition, size, and locations for the four sets of focus groups.

Participant Recruitment

Recruiting mothers in Nigeria for focus groups posed some unique challenges. The interviewing staff usually arrived in the village a week or so in advance of the focus groups. Nigerian women are often discouraged from talking to strangers, so permission to interview them was first obtained from the village leader. Only then could interviewers visit the mothers to invite them to participate in a group discussion.

To determine whether a woman qualified, potential candidates were contacted in person and then led through a structured sequence of questions. As previously stated, depending on the specific focus group, the

Table 5.1 Composition and Location of the Focus Groups

Groups		Members	No. of groups	No. of members	Rural locations	Urban Locations
(I)	Initial	Nursing mothers aged 20–40	7	88	Alapa Ballah Otte	Alanamu Baboko Erin-Ile Offa
(I)	Initial	EKO sellers aged 30–50	6	51	Ballah Oke-Oye Otte	Alanamu Baboko Erin-Ile
(II)	Recipe trials	Mothers	8	apx. 60	Alapa Ballah Oke-Oye Otte	Alanamu Baboko Erin-Ile Offa
(III)	Pre-in-home	Mothers aged 15–40	4	apx. 40	Oke-Oye Otte	Alanamu Baboko
(III)	Post-in-home	Mothers aged 15–40	4	apx. 40	Oke-Oye Otte	Alanamu Baboko
(IV)	Material pre-test	Mothers	apx. 12	apx. 100	Oke-Oye Otte	Alanamu Baboko

women had to meet certain criteria, such as currently nursing a child and feeding the child the traditional pap, or being in the business of making and selling *EKO*. An example of such a screening questionnaire appears in Box 5.2.

The Focus Group Team

The focus group team consisted of three individuals: a lead moderator, a moderator's assistant, and a marketing specialist. The moderator (and observers and note-takers who also attended each focus group) were recruited largely from the corps of field researchers and supervisors who had worked on the baseline DMD research projects. With few exceptions, none had previous experience with the focus group research technique. Training for the staff included organized sessions and role-playing.

The lead moderator was a woman who had previously conducted individual interviews for the quantitative surveys and the ethnographic studies for the DMD project. She knew the Yoruba language and culture and had the interpersonal skills of a good moderator. She could put people at ease, offer unconditional positive regard, withhold her own opinions, and encourage discussion. This person received on-the-

Box 5.2 Focus Group Screening Guide

Good morning/good evening.

We are from the University of Ilorin. We are in your village to meet with some mothers to discuss child care. We met your village chief and he has agreed to our talking with you. May we ask you a few questions?

DATE: VILLAGE
                                   Urban____ Rural____

HOUSEHOLD NAME:

CHILD'S NAME:

AGE OF YOUNGEST CHILD: _____less than 3 years of age

                                _____more than 3 years of age

IS CHILD CURRENTLY BEING FED *OGI/EKO*?

                                _____YES

                                _____NO

Note to interviewer: OGI is a paste made from fermented and sieved maize or guinea corn. A pap called *EKO* is prepared by adding some of the *ogi* paste to boiling water until it thickens. If the mother has a child less than three years of age who is currently fed *ogi/eko*, please invite the mother to a meeting to be held:

                                Date_____

                                Time_____

                                Place_____

Otherwise, thank her for talking with you today.

job training that included organized sessions with role-playing and specific advice on topic sequencing and probing. She also received written guidelines on moderator techniques and had a chance to try out her techniques in pilot groups held as a pre-test for the topic guide.

The lead moderator was assisted by a professor of health education from the University of Ilorin. He was the field manager for the communications component of the DMD project and was well-versed in the rationale for the focus groups. He attended the groups as an observer and prepared summary reports following each one.

The marketing specialist, a U.S.-based consultant, also joined the local team during the focus groups. This person worked with the U.S.-based multi-disciplinary DMD team that prepared the discussion guide prior to the site visit.

Discussion Guides

Discussion guides for the four sets of focus groups were drafted in the United States by the marketing consultant, with input from the multi-disciplinary group. The guide relied on input from baseline data and other ongoing research. This discussion guide was then pre-tested and revised in Nigeria prior to conducting the actual focus groups. (The moderator was also trained during this pre-test.) The first two focus groups in each set were used as a pilot. If it proved that major changes were needed in the discussion guide, the research team was prepared to delete these first two pilot groups from the overall analysis.

Excerpts from one of the focus group guides are shown in Box 5.3.

Conducting Focus Groups

In general, a focus group moderator leads participants through a sequence of topics that reflects an inverted pyramid. Very general behavioral and attitudinal issues are discussed first. These are followed by topics of ever-increasing specificity, from child-rearing practices, to reactions, to concept statements, and preferences among product options. For the DMD Project, in the first set of groups, mothers began by discussing the food and methods of feeding for children under three. The discussion moved on to sources of *ogi* and reasons for use. Eventually, the conversation was guided to reactions to a list of possible additives. Mothers completed the session by talking about credible sources of new information.

Whenever possible, the focus groups were held indoors, with participants seated in chairs in a circle. Although the home of the village leader was often pressed into service for this purpose, on other occasions, the group discussions were held outdoors in some communal living space. All sessions were audio-taped.

Analysis of Results

When focus groups are conducted in the United States, the moderator usually prepares the final report. This approach poses a problem in

Box 5.3 Focus Group Discussion Guide for Mothers: Pre-In-Home Product Test

PART ONE: RESEARCH PLAN

Objectives

To determine overall consumer preference among three recipe variations:

Ingredients/recipes

A. *Ogi* cooked with palm oil and roasted cowpea flour
B. Above with malt flour added before serving
C. *Ogi* cooked with palm oil and roasted cowpea flour, with malt flour mixture re-boiled before serving

Methodology

The products will be tested in the home by mothers who have children between the ages of six and eighteen months who are fed *ogi*. Four sites, two urban and two rural, will be chosen and up to ten mothers will participate in each group, for a total sample of 40 mothers.

Mothers will be taught the recipes in focus group discussions, to be held in a central location within their village or urban neighborhood. For the recipes containing malt, mothers will be permitted to choose the method of preparation they prefer; that is, whether to add the cowpea flour while cooking the pap, or to add the cowpea flour along with the malt after the cooked pap has cooled somewhat.

Mothers will be given sufficient supplies of roasted cowpea flour and malt to last for ten days. They will test malted fortified *ogi* for five days and unmalted fortified *ogi* for five days. The order of testing will be varied between locations as follows:

	Malted F/Ogi	*Unmalted F/Ogi*
Urban 1	1st 5 days	2nd 5 days
Urban 2	2nd 5 days	1st 5 days
Rural 1	1st 5 days	2nd 5 days
Rural 2	2nd 5 days	1st 5 days

Mothers will each be given a cup and spoon at the start of the testing period for this product in order to encourage the desired behavior of spoon-feeding.

continued on next page

Box 5.3 (continued)

Observers will be assigned to each test site in order to record data about in-home preparation and feeding practices of the test products, and to answer any questions the mothers may have. At the end of the testing period, the observers will complete an individual questionnaire with each mother before the final focus group discussion is held.

A final focus group discussion (FGD) will be held with all participating mothers in each test location to determine overall product preference, method of preparation and feeding, quantity and frequency of feeding, and intent on the part of the mothers to adopt the new recipe.

Below is an example of a focus group discussion guide used for both the recipe-teaching and materials-testing FGDs.

PART TWO: MODERATOR'S GUIDE (sample)

I. *Introduction*

 A. Introduce team, purpose of visit.

 B. *Positioning*—We want to know what you think about a new way of making *ogi* to help make your baby strong to cope with diarrhea and other diseases. We are working on several ingredients and we want you to try the recipes in your home and tell us about your experience with them.

II. *Present Ingredients* (Rotate order)

 A. Present roasted cowpea flour and explain how it is prepared. Ask:
 • Have you ever seen it in this form?
 • Have you ever used it?
 • What might it be used for?
 • Is it available in the market?
 • What do you think about adding it to *ogi*?

 B. Present malt flour and explain how it is prepared. Ask the same questions as above.

III. *Demonstrate Recipes** (Rotate order)

 A. Get reactions to preparation steps/time/ingredients

 B. Reactions to appearance/consistency of finished *ogi*

 C. Taste of the finished *ogi*

continued on next page

Box 5.3 (continued)

D. Overall impressions:
- Would they give it to their child/family?
- Would they add/omit anything?
- Is this recipe better/worse/about the same as previous ones tried?

* Prepare a large enough quantity so that enough remains after tasting in order to make a comparison of the three recipes.

IV. *Volunteer Recipe Demonstration*

A. Ask for a volunteer to choose one of the recipes and prepare it.

B. Why did she choose that recipe?

C. Reaction to preparation steps/time.

D. Reaction of volunteer and group to finished product.

E. How can she teach another mother to prepare the recipe.

F. Problems expected.

V. *Overall Preferences*

A. Rank overall preferences. Reasons.

B. Of the first preferences:

- Is it liked a lot/a little/not much?
- Is it for baby/family?
- Problems expected.

VI. *Product Test Instruction*

A. Introduce observer who will come to their homes.

B. Instruct which recipe to try first.

C. Distribute ingredients, cups, and spoons.

D. Thank mothers for participating.

developing countries, however, since few trained moderators are available who know both the language and culture and who are sufficiently conversant with social marketing principles to understand how the focus groups can affect the program. Often, moderators are trained on-site from among health workers or interviewers. Consequently, the task of preparing the analysis gets divided among several persons.

In this Nigerian project, a data plan was drafted prior to each set of focus groups. It clearly delineated what types of information were needed and how they would affect the program. As soon as possible after each focus group, the staff of moderator, observers, and note-takers met to discuss and concur on the key findings. A short summary report was prepared by a professor of health education after each group discussion. A report guide for this purpose is shown in Box 5.4.

Labor-intensive tape transcriptions, often completed by two independent listeners, were *not* undertaken for these groups due to cost and time considerations. Although the group discussions were taped, the team referred to the tapes mainly to clarify points discussed.

Findings

Product/Product Use Features

Fortification. The first round of focus groups revealed some key points on how to go about fortifying the traditional *EKO*. The *EKO* sellers were reluctant to tamper with their successful recipe formulas unless there was a large-scale mass media campaign to support the introduction of the new food. *EKO* sellers were therefore eliminated as possible agents of change during the DMD research phase. Mothers, on the other hand, were already quite used to fortifying the pap themselves after purchase to sweeten it or add variety. For *EKO ILERA*, then, it was concluded that mothers accepted the concept of fortification and should be responsible for fortifying the *ogi* themselves.

Preferrred ingredients were uncovered during focus groups held at the recipe trials. Of the four possible fortifying ingredients, roasted cowpea flour emerged the winner for several reasons. Cowpea, a common household item, was readily available at the market and was affordable to villagers. The final roasted-cowpea *EKO* looked similar to high-status infant foods like *Cerelac, Nan,* and *Similac.* Finally, mothers believed that by drying and roasting the cowpea flour, its shelf life could be extended from two to eight weeks.

Learning and Teaching the Recipe. Recipe-teaching trials showed that mothers could definitely learn the recipe and teach this newly-learned skill to other mothers. However, the teaching of a new recipe meant

Box 5.4 Focus Group Report Guide: Mothers' Groups

I. *Introduction*

Comment on place/date/group (the mothers)/moderator. Comment on composition of group, e.g., older/younger members, total number, changes during the course of the FGD, and special circumstances that may have affected the group, e.g. outside distractions, etc.

II. *Current Feeding Habits*

Summarize mothers' description of child feeding practices. Describe the age of weaning; foods given; frequency of feeding. Probe their reasons for believing that current feeding practices are desirable. Determine their concept of the healthy child and the relationship between feeding and the child's health.

III. *Ogi Preferences*

Summarize their overall preference. Identify the reasons for their choice. Describe in detail food preparation and feeding of the various recipes. Probe their concept of the "cost" of the new recipe, in terms of monetary cost and other factors, including psychological resistance to change and time needed to prepare and feed the new weaning food. Describe mode of feeding, frequency, food handling, and food storage practices. Identify any negative perceptions about the recipe.

IV. *Ogi Additives*

Summarize answers and probe whether these additives are also good for children with diarrhea.

V. *Concept Test* (where applicable)

Comment on reaction to concept(s) tested. The concepts introduced were:
  A. This new *ogi* will make your baby light and active, because it contains cowpea, which makes your baby strong. With this new ogi, your baby will be better able to cope with illness.
  B. This new *ogi* will make your baby light and active, because instead of taking too much water, the baby can take more *ogi*. With this new *ogi*, your baby will be stronger after being ill with diarrhea.
Specifically comment on overall reaction (positive/negative), believability, and what was liked or disliked.

continued on next page

Box 5.4 *(continued)*

VI. *Solid Food Introduction*

Summarize mothers' practices regarding the feeding of solids. Probe beliefs about the feeding of solids during the first year of life.

VII. *Sources of Information*

Describe sources of information about child care, specially feeding. Who are credible authorities?

VIII. *Implications/Forward Action*

Indicate decisions made by the debriefing team as a result of the FGD regarding need (or no need) for additional FGDs, changes necessary in the moderator's guide, and changes/new concepts to be tested in future FGDs.

---

that mothers would need to remember to add new ingredients or modify the traditional cooking process. The accompanying focus groups provided a chance to clarify a few issues, including the following: that the additional ingredients used in the new *EKO ILERA* are readily available; that the food is easy to prepare; and that the cooking process entailed adding malt flour to make the *EKO* thin.

Product Characteristics. The *ogi* of cowpea flour, red palm oil, and sugar had a very thick consistency. The DMD team was concerned that this would make the product unacceptable to mothers, most of whom practiced hand-feeding and force-feeding. The thick consistency would require spoon-feeding. Since hand-feeding is a deeply entrenched practice, the DMD team decided that it would be beyond the time and financial resources of the project to promote a new fortified food and a new feeding mode at the same time. The nutritionists experimented with a unique solution commonplace in the beer industry, the addition of malt flour, which gave the final product a thin consistency.

This product modification meant an additional ingredient in the recipe, and also an additional step in the cooking process. Furthermore, it meant teaching mothers how to sprout, dry, and grind maize or guinea corn to produce malt flour. This product modification was introduced to mothers in the third round of focus groups. An in-home product use test was preceded and followed by focus groups, which attempted to determine the acceptability, convenience, and feasibility of this additional step.

During the in-home test, mothers prepared the cowpea-fortified *EKO* two ways: with malt and without malt. As expressed in the post-focus groups, the malt recipe was well received by mothers. Reports that it produced healthy, strong babies, stopped diarrhea, and helped babies sleep and play well were commonplace.

Preparation at Home. During the at-home trials, mothers were given enough malt and cowpea flour to cook the new *ogi* in their homes for ten days. They were visited daily by DMD staff to observe whether the food was prepared and how it was cooked, as well as to provide assistance for any problems they encountered. At the post-focus group, a drawback was identified. Would the addition of malt prior to serving invite contamination? This problem was eventually solved by a nutritionist who suggested additional reboiling after adding the malt. On this basis, the DMD team felt convinced that mothers could prepare the product effectively in their homes.

Focus groups had been useful in moving a new product from concept stage to final form. Mothers had supplied input on acceptability, preferred ingredients, texture, and ease of preparation.

Communications

Developing a Communications Strategy. The initial groups developed the communication strategy in three critical ways: they suggested positioning *EKO ILERA* as a weaning food; they recommended mothers rather than *EKO* sellers as the target audience; and they isolated a message for the campaign.

At the outset, the project faced a dilemma, in terms of how to position *EKO ILERA*—as a food for diarrhea or as a weaning food. Focus groups with both *EKO* sellers and mothers supported the weaning food strategy. According to sellers, attempts to make *EKO* "medicinal" by adding ingredients for a child with diarrhea were old-fashioned and likely to detract from *EKO*'s use as a family food. Positioning *EKO ILERA* as a weaning food was judged to be consistent with mothers' beliefs and behaviors, while maintaining the status of *EKO* as a food for the whole family.

A second issue that was unresolved prior to the focus groups was what role the *EKO* sellers would play in distributing the fortified pap. Could they, for example, revamp their cooking procedure, add the fortifying ingredient, and then market the product through their usual channels? The focus groups argued against this tactic. *EKO* sellers were reluctant to tamper with their successful recipes or to add any ingredients that would detract from *EKO*'s status as a general family food. It was further discovered that mothers already are quite used to fortifying the pap themselves. Consequently, it made sense to exclude *EKO* sellers from the intervention and to make fortification the job of the mother.

Lastly, the communication strategy required a promised benefit of the new weaning food to encourage full participation of the target audience. The mothers welcomed a concept statement that promised that fortified *EKO* would strengthen a child to cope better with childhood diseases. The "healthy baby" promise, as portrayed in the name *EKO ILERA*, became a message of the final intervention.

Pre-Testing of Communication Materials. The final contribution of the focus groups was the refinement of communication materials. The program planned to use a flipchart for teaching and a flyer that mothers could take home with them. Three versions were tested for comprehension in focus groups with nursing mothers. When mothers were able to enumerate the ingredients and follow the cooking process, the materials were printed and used in the intervention.

Notes

1. The Dietary Management Project was funded by USAID between 1985 and 1989 for the purpose of developing practical methods for either reducing or eliminating the adverse nutritional effects of diarrhea in children. The project was carried out in Nigeria and Peru. The HEALTHCOM Project, also funded over five years by USAID, provided technical assistance to DMD in the development and pre-testing of training materials.
2. *EKO*, a traditional weaning food, a maize or guinea corn pap, was fortified with toasted cowpea flour, red palm oil, sugar, and malt. The energy density of this recipe was 85 kcal/100 gram wet weight, a considerable increase over the traditional *EKO* of 25 kcal/100 gram. The protein density supplied by the recipe was 2.2 grams/100 gram wet weight, compared to only 0.8 grams/100 grams for traditional *EKO*.

6

Rapid Appraisal Methods in a Diagnostic Assessment of Vegetable Seed Marketing

John S. Holtzman

John S. Holtzman presents the methodology and findings of a rapid appraisal study on vegetable seed marketing in Nepal. In this investigation, he and his associates relied heavily on key informant interviews with seed growers, farmers' organizations, traders, distributors, and vegetable growers. They prepared structured interview guides for interviewing different categories of informants. In addition, they conducted direct observation of vegetable seed production, processing and sales, as well as group interviews with farmers and seed dealers. As the chapter indicates, the investigators succeeded in obtaining a wide range of information, insights, and recommendations from the study.

The author discusses several shortcomings of the methodology and makes practical recommendations for the future. One suggestion is to temper the enthusiasm of investigators to seek out more progressive farmers, traders, and processors instead of the typical participant in the food system. Another is to undertake a systematic analysis of the secondary data to cross-check findings and conclusions of the interviews. Such an analysis should be done in advance and independently of the rapid appraisal exercise. Still another recommendation that Holtzman makes concerns the interdisciplinary composition of the research team in which economists work closely with agricultural or commodity marketing specialists.

THIS CASE STUDY is based on rapid appraisal (RA) field work as applied to agricultural marketing research. The field work was carried out in Nepal by the author in collaboration with Nepalese analysts during June-July 1989. This activity built upon the findings of a collaborating group of analysts who carried out an earlier, related rapid appraisal in October-November 1988. The latter paid special attention to a remote production zone not visited in the June-July 1989 effort.

Both rapid appraisal exercises were diagnostic assessments of public sector programs and private sector efforts in the production and marketing of vegetable seed, and were designed to identify opportunities for investment by USAID/Nepal in that country's vegetable seed subsystem. USAID/Nepal was especially interested in the emerging *private* vegetable seed industry in Nepal and the constraints faced by private actors in a subsystem historically dominated by public entities.

Based on the findings of the later (1989) RA exercise and its recommendations for pilot innovations in vegetable seed handling and processing, USAID/Nepal decided to incorporate a vegetable seed subsystem improvement component into an agro-enterprise project that it designed the following year.

Background: RA in Agricultural Marketing Research

The first objective of a rapid appraisal in agricultural marketing research is to provide a snapshot of how the current marketing system is organized, how it operates, and how it is performing in accordance with criteria such as technical efficiency, operational efficiency, pricing efficiency, progressiveness, equity, and wholesomeness/nutritional quality of the food supplied to consumers. The assessment of performance relative to such qualitative and quantitative norms provides the basis for problem identification and diagnosis. The experience of the analyst comes into play in assigning priorities to problem areas for further in-depth applied research.

In addition to providing an accurate snapshot of the current situation, a marketing rapid appraisal should focus on examining forces for change and improved productivity, as well as on identifying successful and creative participants in the food system who are willing to take risks and experiment with new technology, production and management methods, and institutional arrangements. This examination of the dynamic evolution of marketing systems requires analysts to seek out some participants who are progressive and searching for ways in which they can improve productivity through better organization, management, information, and technology.

Purpose and Scope of Marketing RA Exercise

A long-term objective of the government of Nepal and donors such as USAID is to increase domestic production of vegetable seed in order to substitute for imports from India and other countries, and to export selected vegetable seed varieties (especially open-pollinated temperate types) that can be produced competitively by Nepalese small farmers.

With this objective in mind, from mid-1988 to April 1990, the Agricultural Marketing Improvement Strategies Project (AMIS), with funding from the Bureau for Research and Development of AID/Washington and USAID/Nepal, participated in an assessment of the vegetable seed subsystem in Nepal. The assessment focused primarily on the fledgling but vibrant private vegetable seed industry, and on policy, regulatory, institutional, technological, and management constraints on its emergence.

The two discrete rapid appraisal studies carried out by AMIS in collaboration with Nepalese analysts in October-November 1988 and in June-July 1989 were related to two USAID/Nepal-funded activities. One of these was a longer-term applied research program on agricultural marketing. The other was an area development project in the Rapti Zone of Midwestern Region (The Rapti Zone Development Project), which began in the early 1980s.

The applied research program began with an exploratory trip to Nepal by the RA team leader in August-September 1988. During this period, the key study objectives were identified, the research program was designed, study implementation responsibilities were assigned, and a timetable for completion of different tasks was elaborated. Given resource limitations and the difficulties inherent in managing formal surveys in remote vegetable seed production zones of Nepal, rapid appraisal was chosen as the data-gathering method.

Figure 6.1 depicts schematically how rapid appraisal can be used in an applied research program, and the linkages among the activities of RA, applied research, policy analysis, and monitoring and evaluation of policy reform or other interventions in technology, management, institutions, and organizations.

The Rapti Zone Development Project has focused increasingly in recent years on promoting production of high-value cash crops by small farmers. The high value-to-weight (and volume) ratio of vegetable seed, plus excellent isolated growing conditions in remote rural areas of the Rapti Zone, make vegetable seed an excellent potential source of cash income for smallholders.

In addition to the two RAs in Nepal, the AMIS Project carried out two related RA market surveys on behalf of USAID/Nepal and the Nepalese government in Bangladesh (October-November 1988) and in Thailand (January 1990). These surveys were designed to inform Nepalese private vegetable seed companies, public sector agencies mandated to promote exports (the Nepal Trade Promotion Centre), and USAID/Nepal of supply and demand conditions for temperate types of vegetable seed, and potential export opportunities for Nepal in Bangladesh and Thailand.

Description of Field-Based RA Methods

Rapid appraisal of the vegetable seed subsystem in Nepal relied heavily on key informant interviews with selected farmers, wholesale traders, retail seed dealers, public officials, extension agents, and knowledgeable observers. The RA team also visited farmers' fields, vegetable seed processing facilities, and seed dealers' shops. An important part of the larger applied research program, however, was assembly and tabulation of extensive secondary data on vegetable seed production, marketing, and prices, which had to be compiled from numerous sources and sev-

Figure 6.1 Schematic Overview of Rapid Appraisal and Applied Research Linkages

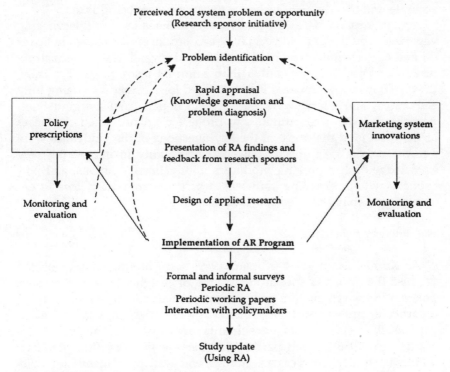

Note: Unbroken lines indicate flow of applied research activities. Broken lines indicate feedback loops. Boxed off items are project outputs.

eral agencies. Bringing together such a large volume of secondary data into one paper (Holtzman and Munankami, 1990) took several months. These data were presented primarily as annexes and used to supplement and complement the findings of the field studies.

Developing Structured Informal Interview Guidelines

Approximately one week was devoted to developing and refining structured informal interview guidelines to be used in the key informant interviews of the field work. This was a team effort, in which the expatriate consultant and chief Nepalese investigator drafted the guidelines, which were then critiqued by the Nepalese agro-input specialist who had participated in the October-November 1988 RA effort (Chilton and Shrestha, 1989). This individual had carried out numerous interviews with producers, public officials, and dealers during this earlier field work, and his technical knowledge of vegetable seed production methods and the Nepalese seed industry enabled him to verify that the technical content of the structured informal interview guidelines was accurate and that the right technical questions were being asked.

Actual questions from the interview guidelines used in interviewing vegetable seed traders and vegetable seed producers are shown in Boxes 6.1 and 6.2. The interview guidelines were designed to serve as a structured checklist, however, rather than a formal instrument. Typically, the questions were prepared in abbreviated form rather than being fully elaborated, and interviewers were free to depart from the guidelines, particularly when opportunities to probe for unanticipated responses arose—provided that most of the key questions in the guidelines were addressed. This approach allowed for flexibility in uncovering new knowledge and in probing producers' motivations, opinions, and perceptions, while providing sufficient structure across interviews to ensure comparability of interview findings.

Selecting Key Informants

As Kumar has argued (Kumar, 1989), key informants are selected because they possess special knowledge or insights by virtue of their position in the economy or government, or their experience in studying a particular problem or topic. In food systems research, key informants can be characterized as participants or knowledgeable observers (Holtzman, 1986). Such participants include farmers, first handlers, wholesale traders, processors, storage and transport agents, and distributors who are actively and productively engaged in commodity subsystems.

Box 6.1 Informal Interview Guidelines: Vegetable Seed Traders

Location

1. Brief history of involvement in trade

   • Date and place it began

   • Initial product mix and change over time

2. Description of business

   • Collect seed from farmers?

   • Sell seed to other traders, exporters?

   • Sell seed purchased from other traders, firms at retail level?

   • Itinerant collection/sale?

   • Collection/sale from fixed place of business (shop)?

3. Seed purchases during last two crop seasons
   (winter and summer)

   Seed type   Quantity   Price   Seller type   Location

4. Use of contracts

   Seed   Location   # Farmers   Quantity   Price   Delivery

   Inputs   Type   Quantity   Credit?

5. Do you offer premiums/discounts for quality differentials? If so, describe.

6. Do you provide extension/supervision services? Describe number of visits (per crop) and types of extension input.

7. Do you hire your own extension/supervision agents to provide supervision? If so, describe their training/experience. How long are they in your employ? How much do you pay them? Are they effective in working with local farmers? How do you supervise them?

continued on next page

Box 6.1 (continued)

8. Non-contract purchases: Do you use spot markets or purchase directly from the farm gate?

   Location   # Sellers   Seed Type   Quantity   Price   Quality

9. Seed sales during the last crop season

   Seed Type   Quantity   Price   Buyer Type   Location   Credit

10. Sales potential: Could sales be expanded? Do some potential customers go unsatisfied? Are there shortages of particular types of seed (varieties, hybrids)?

11. Describe any promotional efforts.

12. Processing: Do you clean, sort, and grade vegetable seed?

   Location   Type/Technology   Cost   Observations

13. How do you package seed for wholesale and retail sale?

   • Wholesale: types, costs, and effectiveness of packaging.

   • Retail: types, costs, and effectiveness of packaging.

   • Repackaging? Costs, methods.

14. Storage

   Seed Type   Location   Method   Period   Cost   Losses

15. Have you experimented with improved storage methods? If so, describe and discuss whether you were satisfied with the results.

16. Transport: methods, costs of transporting to different locations, losses. Have you experimented with improved packaging or bagging to reduce losses in transport? If so, describe.

17. Relationships with suppliers: Who, where, length of relationship, volume commitments, price negotiation, mode of shipment and packaging. Are you satisfied with the relationships? Have you ever considered alternative suppliers?

continued on next page

Box 6.1 (continued)

18. Buyer types and relationships: farmers, other traders, retail seed dealers, Agricultural Input Corporation (AIC). Informal contracts, long-standing relationships. Percentage distribution of sales by buyer type, prices received, other services rendered.

19. Feedback, if any, from buyers/growers about seed quality, purity, germination rates.

20. Marketing costs and margins

   • Most covered above. Note other costs.

   • Trade license or export fees.

   • Handling costs not included in above costs.

   • Informal fees, payments.

21. Place trader's problems in rank order and ask him to propose solutions.

22. Perceptions/opinions of roles of AIC and Vegetable Development Division (VDD) in their areas. How could their services be improved? Does the AIC floor price for vegetable seed impose a constraint? Are private traders able to use AIC facilities (cleaning, storage)? Does AIC provide extension to growers?

23. Describe export/import operations (including cross-border trade with India):

   • Buyers/sellers (are they established?).

   • Costs of exports/imports.

   • Communications with importers and knowledge of prices in export markets.

   • Export/import share in total seed business.

   • Problems.

24. Note opinions/perceptions of farmer organizations specializing in vegetable seed production and marketing. Do traders intend to organize farmers? Are there advantages to working through farmer organizations rather than with individual farmers?

Box 6.2 Informal Interview Guidelines: Vegetable Seed Producers

1. Basic farm data

   - Farm size

   - Laborers' availability (full-time, seasonal)

   - Principal crops by season

2. Vegetable seed production history

   - When did commercial production begin?

   - Describe how it happened: AIC or trader contract?

   - What have been the changes in area cultivated and crop mix over time?

3. Vegetable seed crop mix, 1988-89 and 1987-88

   Year   Crop   Area   Production   Quantity Sold   Sales Price

4. Input use (including hired labor) for 1989 and 1988 seed crop

   Availability   Crop   Price   Source   Quantity   Quality   Timely?

   Application

   - Observations about problems

5. Production practices and production problems:

   - Preparing seed bed

   - Transplanting

   - Rouging

   - Irrigating, controlling pests

   - Harvesting

continued on next page

Box 6.2 (continued)

6. Post-harvest handling practices and problems

    • Harvesting methods

    • Drying

    • Transport to storage place

    • Sorting/grading/cleaning

    • Storage methods (packaging)

7. Contracts

    • Inputs provided

    Crop   Input   Cost   Credit Date   Delivery Date   Application

    • Production supervision: number and timing of visits, information conveyed, assessment of value of information conveyed.

    • Output supplied

    Crop   Quantity   Price   Delivery Date   Place   Post-harvest Reqs.

    • Grower observations on advantages/disadvantages of contracts

        - Quality, timely availability, usefulness of inputs

        - Quality, timely availability, usefulness of extension

        - Fairness of price

        - Timely payment

        - Provision of inputs on credit

    • Recommended changes for future

8. Sales not on contract

    Crop   Location   Date   Buyer   Quantity   Prices   Credit?

continued on next page

Box 6.2 (continued)

9. Intentions for 1990

    Crop   Area   Contract   Inputs   Output   Price

10. Evaluation of Agricultural Input Corporation (AIC) and Vegetable Development Division (VDD)

    *   AIC: contract price, quality/availability/timeliness of inputs

    *   VDD

11. Use of revenues from vegetable seed sales. Projected use of 1990 revenues.

12. Importance of revenue from vegetable seed sales relative to other enterprises:

    *   Grains: quantity sold, sales revenue

    *   Seasonal labor

    *   Livestock sales

    *   Fruit and vegetable sales

13. Perception/opinion of farmer organizations (FOs)

    *   Feasible?

    *   Desirable? Perceived advantages.

    *   How best to organize?

    *   Who would manage?

    *   Role of such FOs.

    *   Could FOs effectively manage improved harvesting and processing equipment?

    *   Contracts between traders and FOs? Perceived advantages and disadvantages.

The Nepal vegetable seed RA team concentrated initially on interviews with key informants representative of different scales of operation and types of technology and economic organization. These key informants included vegetable seed growers, wholesale seed traders, retail seed dealers, officials of the Vegetable Development Division of the Nepal Ministry of Agriculture (VDD) and of the government-sponsored Agricultural Inputs Corporation (AIC), extension agents, and selected horticultural producers who use Nepalese vegetable seed. In order to gain valuable contextual information, the team also interviewed knowledgeable observers, who included expatriate advisors, representatives of donor agencies, and local analysts who were not associated with the government.

An important secondary task of the RA team was to seek out as key informants selected progressive individuals in the vegetable seed subsystem, who provided assessments of experiments in progress and indications of how the subsystem was evolving in a dynamic sense.

An example of such a "progressive informant" is a large-volume wholesaler or processor who is experimenting with formal or informal contracts with first handlers or producer groups. Another example of progressive informants is producers or producer groups who are experimenting with alternative institutional arrangements (such as producing under contract to a wholesaler or processor), new harvesting and post-harvest handling or processing technology, and improved organizational forms (such as farmer marketing groups for achieving scale economies in input supply or commodity storage and transport).

Conducting the Interviews and Recording Findings

The Nepalese senior analyst took the lead in most of the interviews. He opened with a brief explanation of the purpose of the inquiry, including mention of the auspices under which the study was being conducted. No mention was made of explicit project or program assistance to informants. (As a general rule, interviewers should avoid promising projects or credit programs, even if the RA is being conducted as a feasibility study for an anticipated intervention.)

Interviews with farmers and most shopkeepers were conducted in Nepali. Government officials and formal sector seed traders were usually fluent enough in English so that these interviews could be conducted in English. In interviews carried out in Nepali, the junior Nepalese analyst typically translated questions and responses for the benefit of the expatriate analyst. He was able to do this simultaneously in most cases, or after questions had been asked or answered in other cases. Since the team had developed the interview guidelines before the RA field work began, only brief reference needed to be made to the questions posed to the various respondents.

The two RA team members other than the senior Nepalese analyst—one a junior Nepalese analyst and the other an expatriate— took shorthand notes during the interview in cases in which the respondent did not appear to be intimidated by note-taking. When respondents appeared uncomfortable, however, or in fields, shops, or marketplaces where note-taking was cumbersome, the analysts recorded interview findings as shortly as possible after the interview was concluded. In this way, little of the detail of the interview was lost.

Write-Up of Results

The expatriate analyst drafted much of the report and left the collaborating local analysts with a working draft of most of the report. This provided an adequate base that the local analysts could expand, modify, and refine.

Presenting RA Findings

The draft RA report was disseminated three months after field work was completed. Although this was a longer-than-desirable delay, it was acceptable, given the effort required in tabulating and analyzing secondary data that were used in the body of the report and in most of the 17 annexes. Despite the delay, key findings of the field research were presented to USAID/Nepal after the expatriate analyst had drafted much of the report, and before he left Nepal. A two-hour briefing was held within ten days of completion of the field work.

A very desirable technique of RA studies of agricultural marketing systems is for study sponsors to disseminate the final report widely to interested public and private sector parties and convene a follow-up workshop to discuss its policy and program implications. If an expatriate analyst or two participates in the field work, this may require bringing her/him back, albeit at considerable expense. The expense may be well worth it, however, if the RA findings are intended to effect policy reform, regulatory streamlining, or interventions in technology, institutional arrangements, or management. Without a final workshop among RA team members and interested local parties, a RA report risks collecting dust, as have so many short-term studies in developing countries.

Five months after the field work was completed by the two agricultural economists (Holtzman and Munankami), the senior Nepalese analyst (Munankami) and the expatriate vegetable seed specialist (Chilton, who had participated in the first field study in late 1988) presented the findings of both the first and second rapid appraisals to a broad public and private audience. Both analysts served as subject matter resource specialists at a national workshop on private agro-enterprise development held in Kathmandu in November–December 1989.

Problems and Possibilities for Improvement

Potential Bias in Informant Selection

Rapid appraisal is often criticized as being plagued by bias in informant selection and because of its inability to generate precise, statistically valid estimates. This issue is discussed above, where it is argued that analysts examining agricultural marketing systems need to purposively seek out key informants with special knowledge, insights into system organization and operation, and a willingness to take risks and experiment in order to improve their productivity and system performance. The enthusiasm with which rapid appraisers seek out the most progressive and skillful farmers, traders, and processors, however, needs to be tempered with interviews with less progressive yet more typical participants in the food system. Knowledge of new technology, management, and marketing methods and institutional arrangements has to be balanced with an appreciation of constraints facing a broad range of participants. Knowledge of what is possible and new ways of doing things does offer insight into those constraints that need to be dealt with and those facilitating factors that must be strengthened in order to achieve higher levels of productivity.

As a general rule, rapid appraisers need to interview as many key informants as possible at critical stages of commodity subsystems in order to obtain as objective and unbiased an understanding as feasible under time and resource constraints. Skillful cross-checking of responses within individual interviews, across interviews with participants at the same stage of the food system, and across interviews with participants at different stages of the food system can help to identify misinformation and atypical behavior, practices, and opinions. In assessments of constraints (rank ordering) and in opinion and perception questions, respondents at different stages of the commodity subsystem cannot be expected to agree. Moreover, different interpretations of constraints may not be readily reconcilable. This reflects parochial perspectives and different perceptions of problems and opportunities. Reports with divergent results, however, can provide fertile ground for design of further applied research.

Organizational and Coordination Limitations on Research

The difficult terrain and dispersion of vegetable seed production sites in Nepal made national geographic coverage impossible. Under these circumstances, the RA field research was made more manageable by restricting the effort geographically to a given region. (However, coverage can be expanded by using multiple teams in different vehicles.) The RA exercise in Nepal used one team to cover several areas of the Terai and lower Hills. The earlier field work done in August-September 1988 by the two vegetable seed specialists was focused on one remote production region in the mid-Hills. However, it would have been better had the field work of both teams of analysts been carried out simultaneously and had report writing been coordinated so that a single draft report was produced. Furthermore, one or more additional teams could have strengthened the RA and given it a more comprehensive geographical scope.

Composition of RA Teams

The field work of both the June-July 1989 and October-November 1988 exercises was conducted by teams comprised of analysts with similar training and disciplinary expertise. The first RA was carried out by analysts trained in agronomy and experienced in seed husbandry and trade. The second was conducted by two agricultural economists and an economist. However, it would have been better if at least one seed specialist and one economist had collaborated on each interviewing team. This would have provided better balance on technical, agricultural, and economic issues.

Resource, Time, and Geographical Obstacles to Widening the Scope of Study

Nepal poses very difficult problems for researchers wishing to penetrate deeply into rural areas.

The team that performed the June-July 1989 study did not trek much off the road to visit farmers. This was due partly to a geographic focus on the Terai and lower Hills, where more farms are readily accessible to roadways. It also resulted from a focus more on seed marketers than producers. However, the earlier (October-November 1988) study focused more on producers and on government officials and extension agents working in isolated areas. For this effort, analysts were required to trek long distances to visit isolated villages suitable for vegetable seed production. In this sense, the two studies were complementary. Still, more field research in more remote production zones would have strengthened the entire rapid appraisal effort, but time and resource limitations restricted this type of field work.[1]

Greater Participation by Junior Analysts

In the Nepal RA, team size was constrained by the fact that sufficient funds were not available for rental of a larger or a second vehicle. For this reason, only one junior analyst participated in the field work, which was unfortunate, since RA can be professionally broadening for young professionals who need field experience under the supervision of experienced senior analysts.

Key Findings and Resulting Measures

The results of the two RA exercises became the basis for a recommendation by the AMIS Project for the establishment of an agri-business strengthening project, which would also contain a vegetable seed component. USAID/Nepal acted on this recommendation and designed the pilot innovation during the first half of 1990 (Chilton, 1990). Because the RA exercises had identified vegetable seed handling and processing as key constraints that lowered the quality of Nepalese seed in both domestic and foreign markets (particularly Bangladesh), a key feature of this project focuses on experiments with improved seed harvesting, handling, processing, and testing technology. In large part, these can be adapted from other South Asian economies such as Thailand and Taiwan (China).

A second constraint identified during the RA studies was the poor organization of the private vegetable seed industry in Nepal during a period when opportunities were emerging for the private sector (at the same time that assistance provided by public agencies is being scaled back). The AMIS Project therefore recommended that the recently formed Nepal Seedsman Association be strengthened through USAID/Nepal assistance to identify and screen improved technology for vegetable seed harvesting and processing, represent interests of the private seed industry in public fora and in national seed legislation, and conduct domestic and foreign market research.

Finally, limited Nepalese knowledge of other South Asian markets for vegetable seed was also identified as a key constraint. As a result, USAID/Nepal plans to fund marketing studies by private entrepreneurs and selected public officials (principally in the Trade Promotion Centre) in nearby South Asian countries. The AMIS Project has already carried out reconnaissance studies of the vegetable seed subsectors in Bangladesh (Zaman, 1989) and Thailand (Welsh and Kayastha, 1990) to begin this process.

USAID/Nepal has also funded an Agro-Enterprise and Technology Systems Project to provide support to agro-enterprises in Nepal. This is the contractual mechanism for implementing pilot innovations in vegetable seed technology, for strengthening industry organization and representation, and for conducting foreign market intelligence.

Suggestions for Users of RA in Agricultural Marketing Research

Several lessons emerged from the rapid appraisal studies and from the reconnaissance surveys in Bangladesh and Thailand. Some of these are broadly significant for agricultural marketing research in general, while others are quite specific to rapid appraisal methods for field research.

Nepalese Agricultural Marketing in an International Trade Context

One important lesson was the need to examine vegetable seed marketing and trade in a regional (South Asian) context.

Although Nepal has exported modest quantities of radish seed to Bangladesh, it faces stiff competition from Japanese, Korean, and Taiwanese competitors in that market. The competing suppliers export top quality seed having very high germination rates and purity to Bangladesh in attractive packaging (that is, tins). The Nepalese exporters ship a lower quality, albeit slightly cheaper, product to Bangladesh, but they need to upgrade seed handling, processing, packaging, storage, and shipping practices in order to improve their competitiveness.

The Thai market also offers limited possibilities for Nepal in the short term. However, Thailand imports approximately 60 percent of the vegetable seed sold commercially from New Zealand, Australia, the United States, Taiwan (China), China, Japan, and other economies. In addition, a local vegetable seed industry has emerged in the highlands of northeast Thailand.

The lessons of the vegetable seed RAs, as well as many other recent agricultural marketing studies, are that the international marketplace and world supply and demand conditions cannot be overlooked, even by small, landlocked, isolated countries such as Nepal. An examination of world production and international trade suppliers, flows, prices, and practices needs to be built into many agricultural marketing studies that may seem at first glance to be solely domestic studies. As world markets become increasingly integrated during the 1990s, this will become an even higher priority.

Secondary Data Collection and Analysis

Compilation and tabulation of data on the vegetable seed subsystem was carried out independently of the RA field studies. These secondary data were integrated, however, into the final RA and proved to be a valuable complement. Unfortunately, the data were not available to the researchers before the field work was undertaken. Even in those studies where this is the case, it usually makes sense to provide resources for local agencies or firms to compile, tabulate, and analyze available secondary (and perhaps selected primary) data. Building a commodity subsystem data base can prove useful for analysts and policy-makers in future work. In cases in which secondary data are readily available, this material can be examined before field work begins in order to provide better knowledge about historical patterns and current supply-and-demand conditions. Key analytical findings can then be integrated into the RA report.

Looking at secondary data forces analysts to take a longer-term historical perspective. If data cannot be obtained before arriving in-country, allocating some time for gathering and analyzing available secondary data before beginning the field work is strongly recommended. It also pays to make some effort to obtain data that may appear inaccessible on first try. If necessary, analysts are advised to hire people to copy numbers out of abstracts when they are not available on computer diskettes. Sometimes an incentive payment in the form of a consulting contract to "owners" of public data may be necessary.[2]

Devising Guidelines for Structured, Informal Interviews

Before beginning field work and during exploratory pre-testing, the investment of considerable time in developing workable, structured, informal interview guidelines will usually have a high payoff. For the most part, this process will follow the literature review and analysis of initially available secondary data. In addition to basic factual questions, interview guidelines should address issues, knowledge gaps, and themes that emerge from the literature review and data analysis. It is also strongly recommended that private sector marketing agents, particularly wholesale traders and importers/exporters, be queried about their perceptions of policy and regulatory barriers, system constraints, and untapped, under-exploited, or emerging opportunities.

It is strongly recommended that a written guide be prepared, although analysts will not always be able to consult it when interviewing informants, who may fear misuse of the information, or who may only provide accurate information if the interview is conducted confidentially (without recording precise responses). Preparing a written guide forces one to think in terms of the best sequence of questions or streams of questions based on the likely alternative responses to key questions early in the interview. A guide also assists later in recording information, which should be done as soon as possible after an interview is completed. After interviews are concluded, or at the end of each working day, discussions of interview findings with colleagues participating in the RA are strongly encouraged in order to compare interpretations of what informants reported.

The informal interview guidelines may be attached to the RA report as an annex.

It should be noted that, in all likelihood, an analyst will only rarely be able to ask any one informant all the questions in the guidelines. What will emerge, however, is a composite understanding of the activities and perceptions of different actors in the marketing system.

Conducting interviews with a minimum of 25-30 participants at each major stage of the marketing system is recommended. This sample size is large enough to permit statistical analysis of some variables if deemed necessary. In many studies, however, fewer interviews will likely be carried out per informant group due to time, resource, and logistical constraints. Since the objective of the RA is to sharpen problem identification and diagnosis, rather than to do statistical analysis of findings from typically non-random samples, smaller sample sizes need not cause undue concern. When precise information is required for certain key variables at a particular stage of the marketing system, the RA team should consider conducting a mini-survey, in which the sample would be a minimum of 30 respondents (Kumar, 1990).

Interviews with key informants should be conducted in private, preferably in quiet settings. When key informants are contacted at marketplaces or in their fields, interviews may be brief (less than 30 minutes, and as short as 5-10 minutes in some cases). Follow-up interviews away from where the informants are doing business may be scheduled for a later time, though this may prove difficult in RA.

Effective interviewing of key informants requires tact and diplomacy, sensitivity to the respondent's perceptions and needs, persistence in adhering as closely as possible to the structured informal interview guidelines, and the ability to think on one's feet and to follow up either vague or stimulating unanticipated responses with skillfully sequenced, probing questions. While some analysts have the personality traits, intellect, and predisposition to become excellent key informant interviewers with relatively little training, most analysts will have to develop effective informal interviewing skills through training methods such as role-playing, exploratory practice interviews with informants, and on-the-job in collaboration with an experienced interviewer.

In recording key findings after an interview is completed, the team participants in an RA exercise should collectively recall specific responses and, where necessary, discuss their implications. In the case of some respondents, what they do not say or the way in which they respond to particular questions can be as illuminating as what they actually say. Since the interpretation of subtle nuances is more of an art than a science, it is useful for team members to discuss their interpretations of interview findings shortly after an interview is concluded, rather than to wait until a later date, such as the time when findings are being written up.

Visiting Foreign Terminal Markets

Agricultural marketing research usually requires site visits to farms and markets, and interviews in production zones, marketplaces at higher levels of the distribution system, and in terminal markets. As donor interest in crop diversification and export promotion increases, however, the terminal market is often in a second country or in several other countries. In these cases, the analyst is well-advised to go to at least one of those other markets. This is well worth the extra trouble and expense, because one gains a more complete, first-hand picture of the competing export suppliers to this market, recent changes in market share (and reasons underlying changes), and intermediate or end-user (processor, consumer) perceptions of the quality, availability, price, reliability, and timeliness of delivery of the product under study relative to the competition.

In the June-July 1989 RA study, the participating analysts did not visit foreign markets at the time of the field work or shortly thereafter. However, based on their existing knowledge and on subsequent visits, market profiles of the Bangladesh and Thai vegetable seed subsystems were later prepared by the expatriate vegetable seed specialist who had participated in the earlier RA (Chilton and Shrestha, 1989) and by the Nepalese agricultural economist who collaborated with the author. These foreign market profiles were part of the broader research program managed and coordinated by USAID/Nepal and AMIS. They provided useful and timely information that was incorporated into the design of the USAID/Nepal agri-business strengthening project.

Report Writing

To retain their crispness and policy relevance, RA findings need to be captured on paper as soon after completion of the field work as possible. If write-up drags on for six months to a year, production and marketing conditions, as well as selected policies and regulations, may change. Expatriate analysts are strongly encouraged to write up their sections of the report, or at least detailed notes of key findings before leaving the country.

It is preferable for report-writing to be divided up among all of the participating analysts. When analysts have different disciplinary skills, they should of course be asked to write up findings in their area of expertise. In most cases, however, a chief writer and editor will need to be designated. This person will have the authority to edit sections written by other analysts, as well as the responsibility for organizing and integrating individual sections into the final report. In some instances, an outside consultant (who is typically an expatriate) may be able to play this role most effectively, since she or he has no other responsibilities in that country. In an earlier exercise in Liberia, the author did not play this role and local analysts were left with the task of drafting most of the RA report. This led to delays in producing the report, minimal editing, and unevenness in the draft that could have been avoided in large part had the author and other participating expatriate analysts played a more active role in report production.

Briefing the Client

Briefing the study sponsor soon after completion of RA field work is strongly encouraged for several reasons. First and foremost, RA is driven by client needs and timetables. A key advantage of RA is that it generates timely and policy relevant output at relatively low cost. Second, timely discussions of RA findings allow the sponsor an opportunity to shape the final report and raise questions for selective follow-up research. The seminars give the sponsor the chance to challenge preliminary findings, which at the least force the RA team to consider alternative interpretations and to be careful not to state their preliminary findings too definitively. Tentative findings, depending on their importance as an input into policy-making or program planning and monitoring, may require further, more focused, applied research.

Third, requiring the RA team to present findings early on disciplines them to record their findings as shortly as possible after completion of field work. This is pragmatic, in that it discourages procrastination and enables analysts to capture findings when they are fresh. Obviously, the team needs enough time (10 to 14 days) to prepare an adequate draft report or at least a detailed outline for presentation. Shorter deadlines may create more problems than they solve if they induce a poorly organized, uneven draft. After the seminar with the RA sponsor and a week or so of distance from the draft report, the RA team can begin to finalize the report from a better perspective.

Team Composition and the Value of Junior Analysts

RA teams can be as large as four or five people and mixed in composition, in terms of age, experience, and disciplinary expertise. However, RA can be an especially good training exercise for junior analysts, who typically have had little field experience. A junior analyst can learn a great deal in a short time by working with a skilled senior interviewer and analyst. The former can observe the interviewing techniques, questions asked and their sequence, and methods of probing for further information used by senior analysts. They can also learn from discussing RA findings and interpreting informants' responses with senior analysts. Junior staff may also add a fresh perspective to senior researchers who may have done many similar exercises and lack spontaneity or originality.

Interview teams of three or four are workable, although some intimacy is sacrificed when more than two analysts work together. In larger interviewing teams, one or two junior analysts are typically paired with one or two senior investigators. As the RA progresses and junior analysts master interviewing techniques and fully understand the objectives of the RA exercise, teams can be split into smaller units to maximize geographic and informant coverage, as well as to give junior analysts an opportunity to lead interviews.

If junior analysts have not previously participated in formal or informal surveys, they typically gain an appreciation of the potential pitfalls in interviewing private participants in the food system, many of whom are illiterate and not strongly numerate. Younger, less-experienced staff begin to appreciate how difficult it is to gather valid and accurate information from farmers and traders and the demands this places on interviewers. This can prove useful when they themselves design a formal survey.

Conclusion

The rapid appraisal of the Nepal vegetable seed marketing subsystem conducted in June-July 1989 was one of several RA exercises carried out as part of an applied research program on the subsystem and related export opportunities. It used in-depth, key informant interviews with subsystem participants, policy-makers, and knowledgeable observers, as well as site visits to farms, markets, and processing facilities, to identify and diagnose constraints on improved performance of the vegetable seed subsystem. Structured informal interview guidelines were devised and helped to guide the inquiry.

A major strength of the vegetable seed RA was that it was an important component of a broader research and development program. The

RA team visited areas that had not been covered in an earlier RA study; focused more on issues of economic organization, marketing channels and costs, and price policy than that study; and incorporated a lot of diffuse but useful secondary data in its report. However, the exercise would have been more effective had economists and vegetable seed specialists been able to participate jointly in the field work; had the team been able to cover a broader geographic area and interview more farmers in remote seed production zones; and had more junior analysts been able to participate in the RA field work in what is typically a valuable on-the-job training experience.

References

Chilton, Michael. 1990. *Proposal for a Pilot Innovation to Improve Vegetable Seed Handling and Marketing Methods in Nepal.* Agricultural Marketing Improvement Strategies Project. Moscow, Idaho: University of Idaho, Post-Harvest Institute for Perishables.

Chilton, Michael, and Rajendra P. Shrestha. 1989. *Report on a Vegetable Seed Production and Marketing Strategy for Nepal.* Agricultural Marketing Improvement Strategies Project (USAID). Bethesda, Maryland: Abt Associates, Inc.

Holtzman, John S. 1986. *Rapid Reconnaissance Guidelines for Agricultural Marketing and Food System Research in Developing Countries,* MSU International Development Working Paper No. 30. East Lansing, Michigan: Department of Agricultural Economics, Michigan State University.

Holtzman, John S., and Ramesh B. Munankami. 1990. *Rapid Appraisal of the Vegetable Seed Marketing System in Nepal.* Agricultural Marketing Improvement Strategies Project (USAID). Bethesda, Maryland, and Kathmandu, Nepal: Abt Associates and No Frills Consultants.

Kumar, Krishna. 1989. *Conducting Key Informant Interviews in Developing Countries.* Washington, D.C.: Bureau for Program and Policy Coordination, USAID.

_____. 1990. *Conducting Mini-Surveys in Developing Countries.* Washington, D.C.: Bureau for Program and Policy Coordination.

Welsh, Tim, and Jamuna Kayastha. 1990. *Market Potential in Thailand for Nepal-Produced Vegetable Seed.* Agricultural Marketing Improvement Strategies Project (USAID). Moscow, Idaho: Post-Harvest Institute for Perishables, University of Idaho.

World Bank. 1990. *World Development Report.* London and New York: Oxford University Press.

Zaman, Samir. 1989. *Observations on Vegetable Seed Production, Marketing, and Importation in Bangladesh.* Agricultural Marketing Improvement Strategies Project (USAID). Bethesda, Maryland: Abt Associates, Inc.

Notes

1. The RA study was conducted shortly after India had closed most of the border crossings and terminated many of the trade and transit privileges accorded Nepal. Fuel was scarce and could only be found on the black market with difficulty and at great cost. The vehicle rental budget was limited, making it prohibitively costly to leave vehicles at roadheads for days while the researchers were trekking to distant villages.
2. Access to information is a property right in many developing countries, particularly where public analysts and officials are paid poorly or paid late.

136 - 56

7

Systematic Observation in the Analysis of Primary Health Care Services

Stewart N. Blumenfeld, Manuel Roxas, and
Maricor de los Santos

In this chapter, Blumenfeld, Roxas, and de los Santos present what is undoubtedly an excellent example of the use of structured direct observation in the development setting. The purpose of this study, an integral part of a larger multinational research project, was to identify deficiencies in the primary health care system in the Philippines. The authors prepared a set of direct observation forms, taking into consideration the activities, tasks, and subtasks that health care workers must carry out in health clinics to accomplish discrete clinical objectives. These forms were closed-ended, and in most cases observations could simply be checked to save time. The authors focused on 18 rural health units and their satellites using a set of performance criteria for direct observation.

As the chapter indicates, the authors were able to identify many operational problems that required immediate attention by the government. For example, health workers were not getting all the information they needed to make correct diagnoses for some conditions such as acute respiratory infections. Many were giving some misinformation about children's nutritional status. Still others often failed to communicate with the mothers to follow through with the requisite treatment at home.

The authors learned three important lessons from the experience that are of wider importance. First, direct observation generates details that cannot be obtained by any other methods, such as field surveys or qualitative interviews. Second, training of workers for direct observation is not as difficult as it seems. Local staff can be trained to observe people without significantly disturbing normal functions. Third, closed-ended observation instruments promote the reliability and consistency of data.

A general observation about this methodology can be made here. Although the authors in this particular case constructed a relatively large sample to improve the "generalizability" of their findings, it does not follow that the methodology cannot be used on a smaller scale. Even when monitoring and evaluation staff do not have time and resources to construct a representative random sample, they will obtain more reliable data by using this approach than if they do not use direct observation forms.

FOR MANY OF THE MAJOR HEALTH PROBLEMS that still kill large numbers of children in the developing countries, efficacious technologies already exist. Immunization can prevent most deaths and serious complications due to such childhood diseases as polio, tetanus, diphtheria, measles, and whooping cough. Oral rehydration therapy can treat or prevent potentially lethal bouts of dehydration due to severe diarrhea. And a conscientious program of growth monitoring can provide early detection of children who are malnourished and therefore at much greater risk of contracting infectious diseases and/or suffering physical and intellectual stunting.

The problem as seen by many who know health systems in developing countries well is that these technologies are not implemented by basic level health workers according to the protocols that make them effective. The central role of the health worker's performance in determining the effectiveness of the service system may be seen when the system is diagrammed as a classic systems model. As an example, Figure 7.1 shows such a model of one important component of a public health care program, the diagnosis of dehydration due to diarrhea and its treatment by means of oral rehydration therapy. The entire process component of the model comprises tasks that must be carried out by the health workers.

Systems Analysis Approach to Problem Identification in Service Programs

A system model makes it clear that the goals and objectives of a service delivery program (which correspond to impacts and outcomes in the system model) cannot be accomplished if the process is poorly implemented or if required inputs are absent. Thus, when *ad hoc* evaluations or routine management information show that targeted objectives are not being attained, identifying the underlying reasons requires identification of missing inputs and analysis of the service delivery process. This chapter concentrates on the process of service delivery; that is, on the activities of the workers who provide health care service.

Figure 7.1 Oral Rehydration Therapy Service Delivery Model

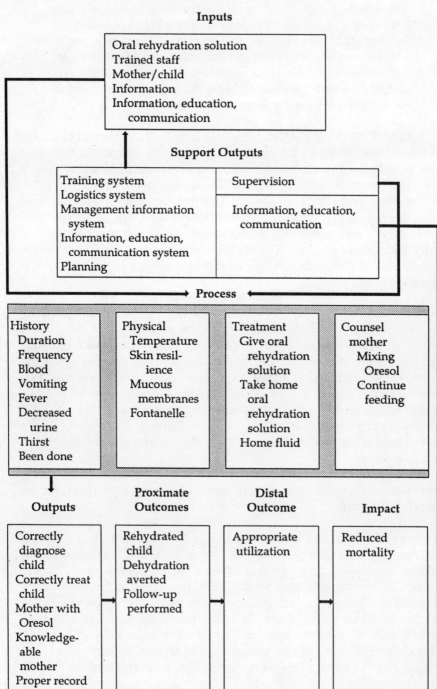

Inputs

Oral rehydration solution
Trained staff
Mother/child
Information
Information, education,
  communication

Support Outputs

Training system
Logistics system
Management information
  system
Information, education,
  communication system
Planning

Supervision

Information, education,
  communication

Process

History
  Duration
  Frequency
  Blood
  Vomiting
  Fever
  Decreased
    urine
  Thirst
  Been done

Physical
  Temperature
  Skin resil-
    ience
  Mucous
    membranes
  Fontanelle

Treatment
  Give oral
    rehydration
    solution
  Take home
    oral
    rehydration
    solution
  Home fluid

Counsel
  mother
    Mixing
    Oresol
    Continue
    feeding

Outputs

Correctly
  diagnose
  child
Correctly treat
  child
Mother with
  Oresol
Knowledge-
  able
  mother
Proper record

Proximate Outcomes

Rehydrated
  child
Dehydration
  averted
Follow-up
  performed

Distal Outcome

Appropriate
utilization

Impact

Reduced
mortality

While collection of statistics on the outputs and outcomes of health service systems is routine in most countries, collection of data on the quality of the services provided by health workers is rare. Instead, service system managers rely heavily on a combination of workers' initial training plus supervision to assure that services continue to be carried out according to specified norms. Our work on the PRICOR Project has shown this reliance to be misplaced.

The PRICOR Project

The Philippines-based study reviewed in this chapter is one of a series of 12 country studies that were carried out under the auspices of the Primary Health Care Operations Research (PRICOR) Project in the period 1986-90.[1] PRICOR's purposes were:
- to develop methods that identify operational problems in the delivery of primary health care (PHC) services;[2]
- to help cooperating developing countries apply these methods to identify operational problems in their basic child survival service programs;
- to assist these countries to carry out operations research in correcting some of these problems; and
- to alert service program managers in the community beyond the specific countries in which PRICOR works to operational problems that seem to exist very widely.

An operational problem is defined as a failure by some component of the health care delivery system—including the service providers themselves—to perform according to prescribed norms. A previous phase of PRICOR had developed operations research methods appropriate for resolving operational problems in these service systems.

The Role of Observational Data

In this phase of the project, an attempt was made to develop a reliable means for quantifying the performance of health workers with regard to how well they carry out the important details of their tasks. However, the PRICOR staff quickly ran into a problem: the specific activities carried out by health workers are not part of standard management information system and are thus not part of a standard record.

Various options presented themselves. One was to interview the health worker and ask him/her to describe in detail what he/she does under specified circumstances, for example, when presented with a child with diarrhea or when he/she is carrying out growth monitoring of a child. However, this was not considered a way to develop reliable information. First, many people do not think in a sufficiently detailed and linear way to assure in exact and detailed account of how they would behave. Thus, they may not articulate the small but often important details. The other side of the coin is that what people say they will do and what they actually do often are very different matters. Another confounding factor is that in dealing with patients, workers often receive behavior-triggering clues from interacting with the patient. Thus, fictitious written or oral case presentation might or might not elicit a true portrayal of the worker's behavior.

An alternative option considered was a variation on the "what if" interview approach, role-playing, in which a live person is presented as having certain symptoms and the health worker is asked to proceed in the presence of observers as if the case were real. This was judged to be a great improvement, because it is more likely to trigger behavior similar to that in a real-life situation. Role-playing has limitations, of course, because certain procedures, such as giving vaccines, cannot be completely carried out. Also, under such contrived circumstances, it is hard to be sure that the worker is not on his/her "best behavior," carrying out every detail of the job in a manner that might not reflect his/her actions under unscrutinized circumstances.

Ultimately, the PRICOR staff decided that direct observation of health workers as they actually perform their duties in a real setting is the best way to actually determine performance. This approach is also rather contrived, but we felt that no worker could keep up a facade when observed in multiple cases, especially in the fairly hurried environment that characterizes many primary health facilities in developing countries. Thus, our main approach to assessing the quality of care was a structured observation and recording of worker activity that looks specifically for key actions that comprise the norms set by generally accepted protocols for providing these services.

Developing Observational Field Instruments

Designers and managers of PHC service systems often believe that delivery of clinical services is a straightforward, relatively simple process that ought to be carried out with little difficulty. In fact, detailed examination of what really is expected of health workers reveals a complex series of actions that afford many opportunities for errors both of omission and commission.

In order to observe service delivery operations systematically, the PRICOR staff first produced a comprehensive list of the broad activities health workers must carry out for each service program component. Each activity subsequently was broken down into its component tasks, and in many cases, these tasks were further disaggregated into subtasks. All of these activities, tasks, and subtasks were compiled in a volume, which we call a thesaurus. A sample page from the thesaurus is presented as Box 7.1. Note the instructions to the user to obtain information through actually observing an immunization session.

Field instruments are developed from the thesaurus. Since health care systems are somewhat different from one country to another, systems analysis designers are encouraged to customize the instruments by extracting from the thesaurus those tasks that fit the particular health care situation to be evaluated. For example, if immunizations are recorded in a special log at the health center rather than on a card retained by a child's mother (as specified in the thesaurus), then determination of what vaccinations the child is due is made by examining those records.

Computerized Forms Design

Carrying out accurate observations in a busy health center with many attention-diverting activities going on requires considerable concentration. It is therefore very important that the data collection forms be easy to follow and mark. We attempted to make our instruments as closed-ended as possible, by minimizing the amount of writing required to fill them in and maximizing the number of observations that could simply be checked. For this purpose, we found computer software specifically designed to create forms very helpful. The program facilitates a neat, uncluttered and unconfusing design and allows easy input of lines between logical sections. The ease with which whole sections of the form can be deleted, expanded, and moved around encourages experimentation with different looks. Most such software allows for easy insertion of checkboxes and provides special characters, such as arrows, to lead the eye from one part of the paper to the next.

Boxes 7.2 and 7.3 are samples of such instruments developed for our systems analysis in the Philippines, created with FormTool software from Bloc Development Corporation. The new generation of forms design software allows forms to be filled in directly on the computer and developed as a database without the additional step of re-entering the data from a paper form.

The Philippines Country Study

Background: The Philippines Health Service System

The Philippine health care system is a mix of private and public providers. In general, wealthier people tend to use the private sector, while

Box 7.1 Sample Pages from the PRICOR Thesaurus

VERSION 1.1   PRICOR   MAY 1, 1988

- *Is the service delivery facility meeting its immunization targets?*

e. Number of immunizations given last year to children under 1 (and/or other age per local policy) per 1000 children under 1 (and/or other age per local policy) in the service delivery facility catchment area by type of vaccine and by vaccine dose (series #) **Service Delivery Facility Document Review**

f. % of immunization of targets achieved last year by type of vaccine and by vaccine dose (series #) **Service Delivery Facility Document Review**

- *Is desired immunization program impact being attained in the service delivery facility catchment area?*

g. Number of new cases of vaccine-preventable diseases in children under 1 (and/or) other age per local policy) last year per 1000 children under 1 (and/or other age per local policy) in the service delivery facility catchment area by type of disease. **Service Delivery Facility Document Review**

2.1 PREPARE VACCINES AND IMMUNIZATION EQUIPMENT AND SUPPLIES

    2.1.1 PREPARE VACCINES (SEE IMMUNIZATION: LOGISTIC SUPPORT)

    2.1.2 STERILIZE NEEDLES AND SYRINGES

- *Do health workers sterilize needles and syringes per standard procedures?*

a. % of immunization sessions* for which needles and syringes are sterilized per standard procedures **Immunization Session Observation**

2.2 IMMUNIZE CHILDREN

    2.2.1 EXAMINE CHILD'S VACCINATION CARD OR QUESTION MOTHER TO DETERMINE IMMUNIZATIONS REQUIRED

- *Do health workers examine children's vaccination cards or question mothers to determine immunizations required?*

a. % of children (immunization session attendees) for whom health workers examine vaccination cards or question mothers to determine immunizations required **Immunization Encounter Observation**

---

*   The term "immunization sessions" refers to single-purpose sessions during which immunizations only are provided, to multi-purpose sessions during which services in addition to immunization are provided and to home visits during which immunizations are provided. An immunization session may include single or multiple immunization encounters.

continued on next page

Box 7.1 *(continued)*

> • *What are reasons for non-immunization of immunization session attendees?*
>
> b. % of children (immunization session attendees) not immunized by reason for non-immunization **Immunization Encounter Observation**

2.2.2   ADMINISTER VACCINES

   2.2.2.1   ADMINISTER RECOMMENDED DOSES FOR ALL VACCINES

   2.2.2.2   USE CORRECT ADMINISTRATION TECHNIQUE FOR ALL VACCINES

   2.2.2.3   ADMINISTER ALL VACCINES WITH STERILE NEEDLES

> • *Do health workers administer all vaccines with sterile needles?*
>
> a. % of vaccine injections given with sterile needles **Immunization Encounter Observation**

   2.2.2.4   ADMINISTER ALL VACCINES WITH STERILE SYRINGES?

> • *Do health workers administer all vaccines with sterile syringes?*
>
> a. % of vaccine injections given with sterile syringes **Immunization Encounter Observation**

   2.2.2.5   PROTECT BCG, POLIO AND MEASLES VACCINES FROM HEAT AND LIGHT DURING USE

> • *Do health workers protect BCG, polio and measles vaccines from heat and light during use per standard procedures?*
>
> a. % of immunization sessions in which BCG, polio and measles vaccines are protected from heat during use per standard procedures **Immunization Session Observation**
>
> b. % of immunization sessions in which BCG, polio and measles vaccines are protected from light during use per standard procedures **Immunization Session Observation**

2.2.3   COUNSEL MOTHER (SEE IMMUNIZATION: SERVICE DELIVERY—3.1 PROVIDE INDIVIDUAL COUNSELING TO MOTHERS OF CHILDREN ATTENDING IMMUNIZATION SESSIONS)

the less wealthy (the bulk of the population) use the public system. The PRICOR Project dealt with the public system.

The public system is hierarchical, with the policy-making officials and staff and overall program managers for the key child survival programs at the top. The job of all these Manila-based officials is to set policies and standards; to develop national goals, objectives and plans; and to monitor overall achievements of the system.

The country is divided geopolitically into 13 regions, each of which has a Regional Medical Office responsible for regional planning within the national framework, but which takes into account allowable local variations, such as special disease problems. A Regional Hospital provides tertiary-level care on a reference basis.

The 13 regions are divided into 79 provinces. A Provincial Medical Office does highly localized planning and monitoring and provides, through the Provincial Hospital, secondary care and ambulatory primary care. Provinces are divided into districts, each with a District Health Office and a small district hospital. Attached to each District Hospital are outreach units called Rural Health Units (RHUs). These number as many as 60 or 70, depending on population and geography. Many RHUs have satellite Barangay (village) Health Stations (BHSs) to help make service even more accessible. Most RHUs are staffed by a physician, one or two Public Health Nurses (four years of training beyond high school), and one or two Rural Health Midwives (two years of training beyond high school). BHSs are always staffed only by a Rural Health Midwife. Some RHMs are assigned to two BHSs, since the BHS may be open only part-time. The Rural Health Midwives (RHMs) are supervised by a Public Health Nurse (PHN) based at the RHU. PHNs are supervised in turn by the physician directly above them.

The Philippine Systems Analysis

PRICOR's mandate from USAID was to focus on the lowest levels in the system, where most primary health care service is provided. In the Philippines, this meant the RHUs and BHSs and their staffs. Discussions with staff of the Undersecretariat for Public Health Services revealed that a number of service programs were not meeting their targets.[3] Four were selected for analysis in four clinical areas: immunization, oral rehydration therapy, growth monitoring, and diagnosis and treatment of acute respiratory infections. In sum, it was agreed that the systems analysis would study performance in these areas of the Public Health Nurses and Rural Health Midwives who staff RHUs and BHSs.

The specific activities observed and the tasks that comprise them may be seen in the data collection instruments shown in Boxes 7.2 and 7.3.

Box 7.2 DOH/PRICOR Systems Analysis

Growth Monitoring: Observation of Growth Monitoring Session

Date (m/d) __/__   Observer (Last name, Initial) _____

District _____ RHU _____ BHS _____

Type of scale used	☐ Child clinical ☐ Adult clinical ☐ Dial spring ☐ Tubular spring ☐ Bathroom ☐ Bar (Espada)
Was the scale turned to 0 at the beginning of the general session	☐ Y ☐ N
HW notation of child's age: How was age determined?	____ mos ☐ By asking ☐ From growth chart ☐ Other _____
Is there a record showing child's date of birth?	☐ N ☐ Y ☐ DOB (m/d/y) __/__/__

When the child was weighed:
  Was it stripped to practical limit?
  Was it relatively still?
	☐ Y ☐ N Weight ___.__ kg
	☐ Y ☐ N

Was the weight read correctly?	☐ Y ☐ N
What kind of record was used?	☐ Growth chart ☐ Log book ☐ Other _____
If this was first-time weighing, did the HW give mother a growth chart?	☐ Y ☐ N-Why _____
Process by which weight and age transferred to record	☐ HW wrote it on chart or in book ☐ HW called it out and someone else wrote it ☐ Other _____

Upon recording:
  Was age recorded accurately?
  Was weight recorded accurately?
	☐ Y ☐ N
	☐ Y ☐ N

Did HW interpret result for mother?	☐ Y ☐ N
Did HW tell mother child needs special feeding or other attention?	☐ Nothing ☐ Feeding ☐ Other _____
Did HW try to verify that mother understood this instruction?	☐ Y ☐ N
Did HW talk about need to maintain breastfeeding or good weaning practice?	☐ Y ☐ N
Did HW ask mother if she had any questions about child's status?	☐ Y ☐ N
Did HW tell mother when to return for next weighing?	☐ Y ☐ N

Box 7.3 DOH/PRICOR Systems Analysis

Oral Rehydration: Observation of Service Delivery

Date (m/d) __/__   Observer (Last name, Initial) _____

District _____ RHU _____ BHS _____

Bgy _____ HW name _____ Position/title _____

Child's age _____ mos.

Did HW ask:

How long child has had diarrhea	☐ Y	☐ N	Comments _____
How frequently child is passing stools	☐ Y	☐ N	_____
If there is blood or mucous in stools	☐ Y	☐ N	_____
If vomiting is also occurring	☐ Y	☐ N	_____
If child has had fever	☐ Y	☐ N	_____
If child has been very thirsty	☐ Y	☐ N	_____
If urine output is greatly reduced	☐ Y	☐ N	_____
What has been done at home so far	☐ Y	☐ N	_____

Did the HW:

Take temperature	☐ Y	☐ N	Comments _____
Examine mucous membranes of mouth	☐ Y	☐ N	_____
Test skin resilience	☐ Y	☐ N	_____
Examine fontanelle	☐ Y	☐ N	_____
Weigh child	☐ Y	☐ N	_____

Child was:

☐ Treated at facility and held for
observation (_____ hours)
☐ Treated at facility and sent home
immediately
☐ Not treated, sent home
☐ Referred to _____

Did the HW test to see that child is able
to take fluid by mouth?   ☐ Y   ☐ N

If treated at facility, was the child given:

Oresol	☐ Y	☐ N	
"Home" solution	☐ Y	☐ N	
Antibiotic	☐ Y	☐ N	If yes, what _____

If child was given Oresol at the facility,
what was used to measure the water?

☐ 1-liter container
☐ Different container, but 1 liter was
estimated reasonably well
☐ Amount of water was obviously
incorrect

If Oresol was given, was the entire packet
used?   ☐ Y   ☐ N

When the child was sent home, was the
mother given:

Oresol	☐ Y	☐ N	
Antibiotic	☐ Y	☐ N	If yes, what _____
Prescription for antibiotic	☐ Y	☐ N	If yes, what _____

For example, in the observation of diagnosis and treatment of diarrhea, the data collection instrument (Box 7.3) directs the observer to note whether the worker asks a series of questions related to prescribing the correct treatment of the case. Other observed items on the form relate to the way the treatment is provided.

By observing the PHNs and RHMs and comparing their work to the norms set for these activities, we expected to identify those weaknesses that were most likely to account for sub-standard target achievement in the system. Knowing those specific areas in which the workers were not performing to standard would enable Department of Health (DOH) management to take corrective actions, such as additional or better training, improving supervision, better planning, or improving the availability of supplies.

Methodology

Sampling Approach. Discussions with the Department of Health's Public Health Services staff led to the conclusion that it was feasible to identify one province that would be reasonably representative of the country, in terms of the type and degree of operational problems to be found. A number of selection criteria were established relating to population health indicators and achievement of service targets in the previous year. A number of provinces fell in the middle range on these criteria. Among these, practical considerations of geographic accessibility, interest and cooperativeness of regional and provincial staffs, and physical security were used as final selection criteria.

Bulacan Province was finally selected. Bulacan is a large province north of Manila that has semi-urban characteristics in the south, near Manila, but is decidedly rural further away. Examination of facility distribution and staffing patterns at the district level revealed no significant deviations from national norms. If anything, in the judgment of the DOH staff, Bulacan might be slightly better off than the national average in terms of the seniority and quality of staff, because it is considered one of the more desirable postings within DOH and thus attracts more applicants. The more objective indices of health, health services, and service outputs, however, placed Bulacan in the middle of the national range. Therefore, DOH and PRICOR made the assumption that the observed level of performance was representative of the middle of the national range.

As noted, the major concern of the PRICOR systems analysis was the quality of the care provided to patients by the Public Health Nurses and the Rural Health Midwives who work at the Rural Health Units and the Barangay Health Stations. Bulacan Province has 54 Rural Health Units.

Resources were not sufficient to study all of them, nor was this considered necessary in order to get a picture of the types of operational problems that were most common throughout the province. Since, according to the service delivery systems model, outcomes are a direct product of process (that is, quality of care), a sampling approach was designed to array the 54 RHUs from "best" to "worst." These qualitative attributes were quantified in terms of key child survival outcome indicators. Using consensus judgment weights supplied by central DOH and provincial health staff, these performance criteria were combined into an index of performance and each of the 54 RHUs was rated on the index.

Based on resources available for the systems analysis, it was judged feasible to examine 18 of the Bulacan RHUs and their attendant BHSs. We decided to "bracket" performance by taking six RHUs from near the top, six from near the bottom, and six from approximately the middle of the performance index. Once again, practical considerations of geographic accessibility and physical security were employed to identify the exact six selected in each category. The 18 RHUs selected had 54 satellite BHSs; these 72 facilities and their staffs comprised our initial sample. However, toward the end of the data collection period, several more RHUs and their BHSs were added in order to obtain more observations of cases of acute respiratory infection and oral rehydration. This brought the total of observed facilities to 90.

Data Collection Instruments. Instruments for data collection were drafted initially on the basis of performance indicators selected from the thesaurus for each of the four interventions. These drafts were presented at workshops to provincial and central managers of these programs, who made the modifications required to fit the Filipino system. For example, there was no point in delving into the adequacy of storage of vaccines at the BHSs, since this is not the Filipino approach. Instead, for vaccination sessions at the BHS, the question became one of protection of the vaccines as they were transported between the RHU and the BHS. The instruments were field-tested in conjunction with the training of the systems analysis staff.

It may be noted (Boxes 7.2, 7.3, and 7.4) that the observation instruments leave little room for subjective judgment by the observer; most items are answered by a simple yes or no. This design is a deliberate attempt to minimize inter-observer variation and to make the methodology practical for those managers who have few highly skilled staff at their disposal. The instruments do not require expert judgments about the quality of a health worker's history-taking technique.

Observation instruments were produced not only to assess direct service provision, but also the performance of the PHNs in their role as supervisors of the RHMs. Box 7.4 shows the instrument used to assess PHNs in this supervisory capacity.

Box 7.4 DOH/PRICOR Systems Analysis

Growth Monitoring: Supervision Observation

Date (m/d) __/ __   Observer (Last name, Initial) _____

Supervisor _____ Title/position _____

Observation of Supervisor/Supervisee Interaction

Supervisee _____ Title/position _____

Site of interaction (☐ Bgy) (☐ BHS) (☐ RHU) _____

Did supervisor examine records to see if most children being weighed on schedule?	☐ Y ☐ N
Did supervisor watch HW zero scale?	☐ Y ☐ N
Did supervisor watch several weighings to determine if weights obtained correctly?	☐ Y ☐ N
Did supervisor spot check to see if ages were correctly determined?	☐ Y ☐ N
Did supervisor spot check to see if weight and age plotted/recorded correctly?	☐ Y ☐ N
Did supervisor listen to HW interpret results to 3 or more mothers?	☐ Yes, and HW did interpret ☐ Yes, but HW did not interpret ☐ No
Did supervisor make any comment to HW about technique or process of weighing?	☐ Yes, praise only ☐ Yes, some corrective comments ☐ No
Did supervisor make any other attempt to verify that HW uses correct technique and/or transmit nutrition messages to mother?	☐ N ☐ Y, What _____ _____

Field Staff and Training. Field staff consisted of seven data collectors and a field supervisor. All were college graduates. Of the seven data collectors, four had backgrounds in nutrition, the others in various social sciences. Five of the seven had had some previous experience doing interviews, but none had had experience collecting observation data. None of the seven were familiar with the health care service system as it functions in the rural parts of the Philippines. The field supervisor, however, was the PRICOR Project Technical/Administrative Advisor in the Philippines, an experienced field person who had worked on other projects dealing with the health care system.

Staff training and instrument-testing were carried out concurrently. Over a three-day period, the staff were briefed on the purpose and

approach of the project, basics of interviewing were reviewed, techniques of unobtrusive observation were discussed, and familiarization
was gained with the instruments. Then the staff were sent to the field to
practice with each instrument while the field supervisor observed them.
Their experiences were discussed and problems, either with the instruments or their own interviewing or observing technique, dealt with.
This training/testing period revealed some interesting problems with
the instruments that had not been foreseen.

For example, it turned out that the PHNs and RHMs had conceptual
difficulties with estimating numeric quantitation in the form of percent-
ages. They were clearly at a loss when asked questions that required
them to select a percentage-type response such as "less than 25 percent,
about 50 percent, more than 75 percent." Eventually, we were able to
work out a verbal continuum with which they seemed comfortable: sel-
dom/occasionally/often/almost always. While this permits only an or-
dinal-level analysis of the data for these variables, it seemed better to
present respondents with a scale they could comprehend rather than
force them to use a scale they could not.

Data Collection. Data collection took place over a 12-week period
(June to September 1988). This is the rainy season in the Philippines and
about one week was lost altogether due to weather problems. A house
was rented in the provincial capital to be used as the activity headquarters and the team residence. One DOH vehicle was assigned full-time to
the systems analysis task. Most of the time the staff were transported
from this headquarters to the particular villages in which they would be
working for the day. Occasionally, team members stayed in local homes
in the area if they were far from the residence. For the most part, each
RHU or BHS was observed for one day. Two or three observers worked
at each session, depending on the size of the facility and the expected
number of cases to be observed.

Each evening, the field supervisor reviewed the instruments completed by the staff, discussed any problems, and made any arrangements necessary for a revisit. There were very few of these required.

One question on everyone's mind was how the RHU staff would
react to being observed as they worked. From the combination staff
training-field trial exercises, two important lessons were learned. At
first, it was obvious that the RHU staff were somewhat uncomfortable
and that it was absolutely vital to reassure them that this was not an
individual evaluation, but rather an effort to help the Department of
Health find out what kind of problems workers in general were encountering in trying to deliver service. In order not to bias health worker
performance, however, they were not allowed to see the data collection

instruments (though staff were instructed not to make a big show of secrecy).

The other lesson learned was that it did not take long for RHU staff to grow used to the presence of the observers and settle into its daily routine. This was probably assisted by the relative youth of the observer teams, their obvious inexperience in service delivery compared to the medical staff being observed, and their overall non-authoritarian, non-threatening demeanor.

Not unexpectedly, it turned out that some information is very difficult for an observer to obtain with certainty. There are some actions of a health worker in dealing with a patient that are very subtle. For example, in dealing with acute respiratory infections, the worker needs to categorize the case as mild, moderate, or severe on the basis of symptoms displayed. This is critical to providing the appropriate treatment. Where clinical records are poorly kept, the worker may or may not do this in his/her head. The only way for an observer to get these data is to ask the worker. Of course, this would remind the worker and bias any further observations. Assessing a child's breathing rate is another critical component for care of respiratory infections, a major determinant of the mild/moderate/severe categorization. Yet a health worker may assess the breathing rate very quickly instead of going through an overt timed count, and if the child is very obviously breathing normally or is very obviously breathing too rapidly, the worker will not be seen to carry out a timed count.

Despite these and other limitations, we feel nevertheless that observation produced most of the information a manager needs to assess the service delivery process. Observers were able to tell unequivocally whether specific points of medical history were asked, whether specific actions were taken during the physical examination, and whether specific counseling messages were addressed to mothers by a health worker.

Data Archiving and Analysis. Although the data collection instruments were designed to be as closed-ended as possible, some open-ended interview questions were inevitable. In order not to lose some of the richness that verbatim responses afford, the data were archived in dBase III Plus to take advantage of the text-storage capability of database management software. Examination of verbatim text did, in fact, prove useful in providing some insights into why certain operational problems were in evidence. For example, it was through these text responses that we discovered how heavily supervisors rely on the original training received by the midwives to ensure that they are doing all the tasks necessary for high-quality care.

For analytical purposes, the data were transferred to the SPSS statistical package. SPSS (or any other statistical software) was not familiar to most staff of the DOH, so data analysis was done mainly—but not entirely—at PRICOR's U.S. offices. To date, data analysis has been restricted to very basic procedures: frequency counts and cross-tabulations. The results of these procedures, however, leave little doubt about, first, the presence of some major defects in the quality of care being provided, and second, the power of observational techniques to identify them.

Results

A sizable literature exists on techniques for measuring inputs, outputs, effects, and even impacts of health service systems. This process, however, usually has been examined more along the lines of worker time-motion and facility patient-flow for the purpose of improving efficiency. Although the World Health Organization's training documents on oral rehydration therapy are comparable, in their attention to the specific process of how this service should be delivered, they are designed for training rather than assessment. Our approach of identifying operational problems by quantifying performance of these subtasks through direct observation of health workers seems to be unique at this time. It is not the purpose of this chapter to carefully delineate the specific operational problems identified for each disease service examined. However, to provide a feeling for the kind of data that systems analysis affords the health care system manager, some examples of the types of problems revealed are discussed in the following paragraphs.

Examples of Problems Observed in Direct Service Delivery

The activities that primary health care workers must carry out to deliver high-quality pediatric services fall into three general categories: diagnosis, treatment, and counseling the caregiver (usually the mother), on what to do for the child at home and what to expect and how to react. For each disease, of course, the specifics of diagnosis and of treatment and the counseling messages are different. It is these specific actions required of the health worker that are listed in the PRICOR thesaurus and that were observed in the systems analysis. The data collection instruments shown in Boxes 7.3 and 7.4 illustrate what specific tasks were observed for growth monitoring and for oral rehydration therapy (used to prevent dehydration due to diarrhea).

Many problems were found in the direct delivery of services. For example, we found that in diagnosing acute respiratory illness patients, both PHNs and RHMs rarely asked if tuberculosis was present in the household—a vital piece of information in determining the treatment regimen. In more than one-third of observed cases, mothers were not cautioned to continue feeding the sick child, even though many mothers tend wrongly to withhold food from sick children. When medicines were prescribed for the child, in 40 percent of the cases the mother was not told the timing and measurement of dosage administration. And in 90 percent of the cases the mother was not counseled to complete the drug regimen, even if the child appeared to be getting better very quickly.

Regular weighing of young children is a key component of a program of early detection and treatment of malnutrition. Moreover, studies have shown that it is important to closely involve mothers in the growth monitoring process, because their participation is one of the best ways to ensure that they continue to bring the children regularly into the clinic and that they take appropriate remedial steps if the child's nutrition level begins to decline. To this end, nearly all countries use a growth card on which the child's weight is plotted against his/her age. The plot is overlaid against colored bands that show normal weight-for-age ranges and make it easy to see when the child is falling below normal. The card is the key tool for demonstrating to a mother the nutritional status of her child and explaining what needs to be done. It is vital, then, for the health worker to get the plotting right and to point out to the mother how her child is doing.

When we observed the weighing and plotting process, many errors were found. For example, in 16 percent of cases the health workers marked either the child's age, or his/her weight, or both incorrectly. In addition, in 90 percent of cases observed, the health worker failed to comment on the results to the mother. Instead of using the weighing and plotting to actively involve the mother in the care of her child, the process was treated very mechanically.

Important details such as these cannot be obtained other than by observation of how workers deliver service. Yet it is exactly these details that are major determinants of whether the care provided is effective. Armed with this kind of information, the service system manager—or for that matter, an immediate supervisor—can pinpoint and correct significant deficiencies in the system as a whole or in a particular individual.

Examples of Problems Observed in a Support System

Health workers alone do not constitute a functional health care service system. They require various kinds of support: a training system (both initial and refresher), logistical support, information, plans, financial support, and supervision. Of all of these, supervision is probably the least understood in truly operational terms. Obviously, no service system is deliberately planned with a weak supervision component. But among service system managers, supervision is almost always acknowledged as one of the weakest links in the chain that ultimately leads to quality care. Rarely, however, is the supervisor's job defined in specific operational terms, and almost never is the performance of supervisors studied in such terms.

The PRICOR thesaurus displays very specific tasks that supervisors are supposed to carry out, broken out in several categories: knowing the details of the job of the person being supervised in operational terms, actively assessing his/her performance against operational norms, identifying gaps and the reasons for them, taking corrective action, receiving and resolving problems, and imparting new information and skills. The PRICOR systems analysis in the Philippines assessed supervisors' performance by observing how they actually carried out the operational tasks that define supervision. Box 7.4 shows what specific tasks were observed to assess supervision of RHM by Public Health Nurses in the growth monitoring program. While the general result—the weakness of supervision of peripheral service providers—was not unexpected, identification of the specific flaws provided important information that could be used in very practical ways by the DOH.

First, the quantification of supervisory performance on specific operational elements added significant impetus to a nascent movement in the Department to take serious stock of the supervision situation and its effect on the quality of care. And second, the data provided useful information for specific corrective actions that might be taken. For example, as has been noted, the assessment demonstrated that supervisors relied too heavily on RHMs' original training for assurance that these workers would continue to provide all the elements of service that they were taught. Non-observational data convinced us that supervisors were not aware of many of the deficiencies in service quality provided by the health care workers they were supervising. But it was the observational data that provided many of the clues as to why. We could document that supervisors do not often *watch* their "charges" to satisfy themselves that the latter are carrying out all the tasks they are supposed to, and they rarely ask them if there are problems for which help is required.

As a result of this systems analysis, several operations research studies are being carried out, both by DOH staff themselves and by outside organizations commissioned by the Department, to develop special training for supervisors, to devise tools to assist with field supervision, and to develop means for supervision of supervisors.

Direct Observation: Summary of Lessons Learned

In this case study, direct observation provided important information about quality-of-care issues that may explain in part why some important objectives of the primary health care system in the Philippines are not being met. For example, nutritionists in developing countries agree that involving mothers in monitoring their children's nutrition status is a key to identifying incipient malnutrition or treating a child for malnourishment. Yet PRICOR staff observed that 90 percent of workers weighing children did not interpret the result to the mother. And, of mothers who brought a child to a facility for treatment of diarrhea, 55 percent were not reminded to continue feeding the child, even though this is an important and standard component of quality service for this problem. This level of detail probably cannot be reliably obtained any other way.

Also, it is possible for observers to do their work without significantly disturbing the system. The key is for the observer to be perceived as non-threatening by those being observed, so this should be a special point of emphasis during training. In some situations, it is even possible for the observers and their activity to be seen as a positive asset. The rapport our young staff established with the health care facilities' staffs was, in many cases, quite warm.

Finally, in order to promote both reliability of the data and inter- and intra-observer consistency, we strongly recommend using instruments designed for maximum objectivity. This has the added advantage of allowing the investigator to employ "non-expert" observers, because little judgment in the substantive area is required. This may also relate to the point above; presumably under some circumstances, an "expert" peering over one's shoulder is likely to generate discomfort and an unnatural situation.

Notes

1. The PRICOR Project is implemented by the Center for Human Services, Inc., Bethesda, Md., and is funded by the United States Agency for International Development, Bureau for Science and Technology, Office of Health, under Cooperative Agreement No. DPE-5920-A-00-5056-00.
2. Services that focus specifically on child survival are a subset of the services that comprise primary health care in developing countries. However, primary health care consists of a broader concept than just direct service provision. It

also includes substantial involvement of communities in management of the service system, an emphasis on disease prevention as much as on treatment, and assured access to service in terms of affordability and geographic proximity. Services generally recognized as central to child survival are: immunization, oral rehydration therapy, correct diagnosis and appropriate treatment of acute respiratory infections, and growth monitoring and treatment of malnutrition. Depending on their own situation, some countries add to the list malaria diagnosis and treatment, as well as maternal health services aimed at preventing low birth weight and neonatal tetanus.

3.   The PRICOR Project in the Philippines is a joint undertaking of the Center for Human Services' PRICOR Project and the Republic of the Philippines Department of Health (Undersecretariat for Public Health Services and Undersecretariat for Management Services).

8

Using Urban Commercial Counts and Marketplace Censuses to Appraise Agricultural Development Projects

Gordon Appleby

In this chapter, Gordon Appleby explains a different type of direct observation method, which he used in the north Shaba region in Zaire. This is one in which proxy indicators were used to assess the impact of an agricultural project covering a large geographical area (15,000 square kilometers). The indicators that Appleby used in this case study were counts of the retail outlets in the region.

The essential premise of this methodology is that successful agricultural development raises farm production and increases farmers' incomes, which in turn create greater purchasing power and thus foster commercial development. In this evaluation, Appleby carried out a systematic count of retail shops, service establishments, and marketplace goods as a measure of levels of commercial activity. The resulting data showed significant commercial growth, in north Shaba. The data also indicated variations in commercial growth which could be a function of project activities. The area that had received greater assistance in terms of roads, seed supplies, and agricultural extension demonstrated greater commercial development.

A word of caution about the application of this methodology is necessary. While agricultural growth generally—though not always—contributes to commercial development, the latter can take place without the former. For example, factors such as the multiplier effect of project expenditures in the region, improvement in transportation facilities, or the growth of manufacturing can contribute to commercial growth. In such conditions, the findings of the study based on this methodology could be misleading. Before using this methodology, investigators should therefore carefully examine the full range of factors that could explain changes in levels of commercial activity.

HOW CAN THE IMPACTS of a long-term agricultural development project covering a large (15,000 square kilometer) area be assessed? And, how can such an assessment be accomplished in a very short period of time?

Urban commercial counts provide a means, albeit indirectly. By way of illustration, this case study presents an example of the use of commercial counts in the post-project assessment of an agricultural development project in Shaba Province, Zaire.

The underlying logic of this approach is simple. Increased agricultural production results in more produce being marketed, which translates into higher farmer incomes and greater commercial activity and development. Not all commercial institutions, however, develop equally quickly. First, marketplaces will offer additional groups of goods (called arrays) and attract more vendors. Then, new and different shops and service establishments will be opened. Finally, new centers will appear in the region. Conversely, a fall in agricultural production means lower rural incomes, less commercial activity—first in the marketplaces, then in the stores and shops, and in time, in fewer centers. In other words, the expansion and contraction of visible retail trade provides a reliable index of rural economic change.

What is required for urban commercial counts is a set of tools for measuring and analyzing commercial development. Fortunately, a set of measures derived from central-place theory can be used for this purpose. Commercial activity, accordingly, is indexed by the number and types of shops and the diversity of marketplace goods and services. By counting the numbers of each type of establishment in each place, the analyst can discern the spatial pattern of regional development. Centers at the same level of development will have similar numbers of each type of retail outlet. Centers at higher levels of development will have more shops of different types and more complex marketplaces, while centers at lower levels of development will have fewer shops and less complex—or diverse—marketplaces. Further, these levels of center development normally pattern regularly in space.

These measures have several advantages for evaluating the impact of agricultural projects. First, they are quantitative. The counts provide a reliable, replicable measure of commercial development. In this regard, commercial counts represent a major advance over much rapid rural reconnaissance, which is highly impressionistic. With commercial counts, the basic data are unassailable; one can query only their interpretation of the data.

Second, because the counts are replicable, they can be repeated—carried out one year and then redone several years later in order to assess the extent of change. The approach can also be used to analyze differences in project impact within a region, as well as changes over time. Third, the method is extremely efficient. Instead of continuous and expensive monitoring of agricultural production—measuring fields, repeatedly inspecting the crops over the growing season, and weighing cuttings to determine yield—one can quickly count enterprises in commercial centers as a proxy measure for the farmer income.

In this case study, a description of the Shaba region and of USAID efforts there provides the context for the present evaluation. The article then presents the general theory supporting this applied approach, that is, the geographical theory of central places. The subsequent section discusses how this theory in fact worked out during data collection and analysis. The penultimate section presents the findings and conclusions of the evaluation and the final section draws several lessons that provide guidelines for potential users of the method.

Country and Program Settings

For a ten-year period (1975-86), the United States Agency for International Development (USAID) supported an agricultural development project in the north Shaba region of southern Zaire. Originally designed as an integrated rural development project, Project Nord Shaba (PNS) was revamped in 1982 as a strict agricultural development project. Various activities such as farmer councils, intermediate technology, and women-in-development efforts were dropped so that project attention could better focus on rebuilding agricultural feeder roads, distributing open-pollinated corn seed, and improving corn cultivation practices. A project management unit and a socioeconomic monitoring cell were also retained throughout the project's life. PNS ended in September 1986, whereupon USAID initiated a kindred activity in the contiguous central Shaba area just to the south.

At the time the project started, north Shaba was one of the most isolated and backward areas of Zaire. There had been a vital commerce in the region based on river and rail transport during the colonial period, but war and rebellion had taken a heavy toll. Bridges had been blown up, isolating large parts of the area. River traffic effectively stopped as river channels silted in, and while the railroad continued to run, its schedule was at best intermittent and undependable. As a consequence, many mercantile firms that had shipped bulk produce out of the area and distributed merchandise to farmers had closed long before.

By the early 1970s, the regional economy of north Shaba had all but collapsed. Many farmers had of necessity reverted to subsistence agriculture. This was particularly true in the more populous western half of the project area, centered on Kongolo. There, most Hemba farmers practiced a mixed cropping system, with corn as a consumption crop. By contrast, in the eastern area centered on Nyunzu, the patrilineally organized Luba practiced a shifting cultivation, with manioc as the dietary staple and corn as a cash crop. The Luba had other advantages as well. They could open up new forest plots every several years because population densities were much lower than in the Kongolo area (3 versus 15 persons per square kilometer). Also, the Luba had access to Pygmy labor, which was not available in the western part of the project area. Thus, there was more production for domestic export in the Nyunzu area than in the Kongolo area, but wholesale trade everywhere was much reduced.

As a result, in 1974 (just before PNS began), there were only two centers in the entire region, Kongolo and Nyunzu. Each was an administrative center with limited public services, such as schools, religious missions, and dispensaries. Both were on the rail line, which in theory made possible shipments to and from the provincial capital of Lubumbashi and into the neighboring Kasai region. Each also had access to a productive hinterland, although the economic reach in each instance was limited to the distance that goods could be headloaded or carried by bicycle. Each had a weekly marketplace as well, the only ones in the region at the time. Elsewhere in the region, villagers practiced subsistence agriculture and had few economic ties outside their villages.

Project Results

Despite these unpromising beginnings, PNS succeeded beyond almost everyone's expectations. By rehabilitating rural roads and distributing improved seed, corn production increased from 30,000 metric tons in 1977-78 to over 100,000 metric tons in 1985-86. Moreover, the quantity of corn marketed increased from 10,000 metric tons just before the project to almost 50,000 metric tons by the time the project ended. Although it is difficult to impute causality for these increases directly to particular project interventions, it is clear that rebuilt roads, improved corn seed, and new agricultural practices—in addition to the strong markets for corn in the Kasais and south Shaba that undergirded a favorable farmgate price—had a decided effect on corn production and marketing in the project area.

These improvements were becoming clear as early as 1982, when the project was evaluated and re-designed. Even then, many end-of-project targets were being exceeded. Thus, at the termination of project activities in September 1986, when the USAID mission in Kinshasa commissioned a post-project impact evaluation, there was interest in the evaluation in assessing what other changes in the PNS area were associated with the sustained ten-year effort.

As part of this impact evaluation, it was quickly decided in the field to focus assessment on commercial development. The notion was that if PNS had succeeded as an agricultural project, it would have set off a process of regional development that would be reflected in the extent of commerce in rural towns. The use of "urban" commerce to measure rural change may seem counter-intuitive, but it is really quite logical. As an evaluation methodology, it is efficient and cost-effective as well. Towns that serve villagers in the surrounding areas depend on and develop in conjunction with their hinterlands. Thus, tracking "urban" commercial development provides an efficient measure of change in surrounding rural areas, because one need go to only one town or marketplace to gauge how the 20 or more dependant villages are faring. By extension, one can cover a region by visiting the towns and marketplaces there, which are much more limited in number than the villages.

Description of Methodology and Rationale

Central-Place Theory

A useful set of field and analytic tools for assessing regional commercial development has been devised in anthropological applications of central-place theory (Skinner 1964, 1965 and Smith 1972, 1976, based on the work of Christaller 1966 and Marshall 1969).

Three observations constitute the basis of central-place theory. First, goods and services that are purchased more frequently can be sold in more market centers. For example, daily necessities, such as bread, eggs, or vegetables will be more widely available than specialized or expensive goods, such as cosmetics, enamelware, plastics, beds, or radios. Second, and for many of the same reasons, goods are added in a predictable manner to any market center's inventory. That is, a town that already offers food staples may add more exotic foodstuffs, as well as clothing, plastic goods, and enamelware. And third, centers at the same level of development will be spaced approximately equally apart, with lower-level centers appearing more densely on the landscape than higher-level centers.

To study this patterning, geographers inventory the types and numbers of shops in each town in a region in order to categorize centers into levels according to the types and numbers of goods and services available in each. The levels of centers are then mapped in order to discern the spatial patterning of centers.[1]

Development studies must include both retail establishments *and* periodic marketplaces, for these are but two parts of a single system. The patterning of shops and markets is usually isomorphic: centers with more stores and services usually also have more diverse marketplaces. Further, the lowest level of marketplace is often found in rural centers that support few or no stores; these markets are effectively an extension of the retail system into the countryside, which cannot support permanent stores. Sometimes, however, the two subsystems are structured differently; analysis of these systems can be more complicated (Smith 1985).

Central-Place Field Methods and Analysis

Three types of commercial count can be completed for all centers in a region: retail shops, service establishments (including truckers), and marketplaces. Tables 8.1 through 8.3 in the following section illustrate categories of enterprises that have proved useful in studies in several parts of the world.

Several methodological comments are in order. First, while these lists are a reasonable starting point, any additional goods or services available in a region must be added to the list. For example, in Shaba there are no wholesale buyers; that is, marketeers who come from towns to buy local produce in bulk—staples, or eggs and cheese, or other products (for example, tamarind, mushrooms, fish)—that is then taken to the towns for sale. Where this wholesale bulking function occurs, it must be included in the market census.

Second, commodities may vary by locale, for example, rice may be the staple in one area, corn in another, and cassava in a third. Where the particular commodities in a class (for example, food staples) vary within a region, it is best to code the specific commodities in each marketplace and later collapse those goods into the generic classification (for example, regional staple) in order to even out the geographic variation.

Third, marketplace goods, shops, and services must be counted only once and always in the same category. This is relatively easy for shops and services, which usually sell a single type of good or service (for example, groceries, dry goods, cloth, watch repair, tailoring). Marketplaces, by contrast, can be very confusing, as many vendors assemble a little bit of many very different goods. Probably the most difficult problem a researcher faces is how to code all the sellers whose arrays comprise a seeming jumble of foodstuffs, goods, or whatever—the *mercachifle* of Spanish America and the *table* of Francophone Africa. These are best coded as "mixed array" under the predominant category of goods handled, for example, foodstuffs or manufactures. This approach will reduce but not eliminate the problem, because some sellers will purvey goods from several (or all) categories of goods. Whatever coding decision is taken, the same rule must always be applied or the results of the counts in different places will be non-comparable.[2]

Finally, not all shops or market arrays are equally important from an analytic point of view. Central-place analysis is relatively insensitive to small errors in the numbers of common establishments and vendors. It matters little whether there are 61, 73, or 92 vendors of local staples in a marketplace if most markets average 20 such sellers, some average 70 or 80, and a very few have 200 or more. By contrast, the presence of "higher-order" goods or services that are usually available only in higher-level centers (for example, cosmetics, radios, beds) is critically important to the analysis, for these commodities (or their absence) differentiate centers by level. Therefore, a special effort must be made to record all of these enterprises. In other words, where precision is required, commercial and market censuses should be carried out. Most times, however, estimates of retail and service establishments by knowledgeable local informants and reasonably accurate market counts will suffice.

To analyze these data, the analyst must: (1) rank goods according to the number of centers in which they appear; and, (2) rank centers according to the number of types of goods they purvey. To do this, goods are ranked within category (that is, retail shops and service establishments, including repairmen) and listed down the left-hand side of the page from most common (appearing in most centers) to least common (appearing in the fewest centers). Similarly, it is usually helpful to list the centers across the top of a sheet of graph paper from high-level (most functions) to low-level (fewest functions). This bookkeeping chore usually requires several attempts before the simultaneous ordering of goods and centers is completed successfully. Tables 8.1 through 8.3 demonstrate common examples of this formatting.[3]

This analysis can be done for an area at one point of time, for several areas at the same time, for one area over time, or for several areas over time.[4] No matter how complex the analysis, the essential measures remain the same—the commercial counts that allow determination of the number of levels and the number of centers in each level, and their distribution over space in relationship to transportation routes. The practical application of these principles and techniques is illustrated in the next section.

Data Collection and Analysis Activities

The post-project impact evaluation for Project North Shaba lasted four weeks—three days in Kinshasa for briefings, ten days in the project zone for field investigations, three days in the regional capital for meetings, and a week in Kinshasa for report writing and meetings. The first several days in the project area were spent attempting to assess the extent of social and organizational change. When it became apparent that whatever social change had occurred in the project area could not be systematically documented in the time available, it was decided to focus on the possibility of "urban" commercial development.

The evaluation team postulated two probable findings. First, it was supposed that increased corn marketing would have given rise over time to greater commercial development throughout the region. Increased corn marketing itself connotes greater commercial activity— during the limited buying season. The important question was, given that there was undeniably a larger, seasonal trade in corn, was there also an increase in urban commercial development, that is, in the numbers and types of shops and markets that operated year-round?

Second, it was supposed that, in view of the project emphasis on corn, those areas that marketed most corn would provide evidence of greater commercial development. As luck would have it, the project area divided into two areas: Kongolo, which was more heavily populated and had more rehabilitated roads, but where corn was initially mostly a subsistence crop; and Nyunzu, which was much less populated, had fewer roads, but produced more corn for sale. Since the quantities of corn marketed had long been much greater in Nyunzu than Kongolo, the initial premise held that commercial development would be greater in the Nyunzu area than in the Kongolo area.

Testing and documenting these expected findings required systematic counts of retail and service establishments and of marketplace vendors' inventories of goods ("arrays") in all centers of the project area. The counts were done with questionnaires and market census forms that were relatively simple to construct.

The questionnaire for urban commercial development was a checklist of all types of retail and service establishments in the region. The interviewer asked informants how many of each type of establishment there were now and how many existed five and ten years before. Of course, the actual conversations were more free-wheeling and open-ended, but the use of a checklist helped ensure that the interviewer did not forget some category or type of shop. It also helped that two evaluators conducted the interview, with one taking the lead in the conversation and the other taking notes and double-checking the information.

Data were collected from several sources. Key informants in each center were asked about the number of shops, retail and service establishments, and truckers in that place over time. The informants, all residents of the place, were merchants or authorities, or even passers-by. The information sought in these interviews was generally known and neither threatening nor overly intrusive, so most any adult could be of help. Even so, it was worthwhile to corroborate the information by interviewing, for example, both an administrative authority and a merchant. Although their numerical answers might not be identical, there was rarely any great difference in the numbers of establishments reported. Moreover, project documents provided important corroborating evidence on these and other matters.

By contrast, marketplaces were actually enumerated by the team, because this information cannot be collected through interviews.[5] Although there are several ways to do a marketplace census, they all amount essentially to counting all the arrays in the market as quickly and accurately as possible. It is usually useful to have a printed form listing all the market arrays that appear in the region. In the Shaba assessment, the enumerator carried this form on a clip board. He or she started in one corner of the market, counted all the vendors of each array in that row or two of sellers, entered the counts on the form, and then moved down to the next tier of rows.

The fact that vendors rent stalls or table space and that vendors selling the same arrays tend to congregate in the same areas of the market helped tremendously in carrying out the census. Nonetheless, there were "problem" areas. For example, women vendors from the same village often sat with their children in a cluster, which makes it impossible to count the actual number of vendors. Fortunately, as has been mentioned, a reasonable estimate of the number of vendors in these clusters sufficed, for these women offered mostly very low-order goods. Once the census has been completed, the enumerator tallied the counts for each array and verified that all types of arrays had been counted.

Marketplace censuses should be done when business is at its peak. In north Shaba, all markets meet daily, although there is variation over the course of the week. On Friday, market vendors are required to perform public service, called *solongo*, which means that the number of vendors might be fewer than usual. Saturday morning is the time when other residents perform *solongo*, so the number of buyers (and hence sellers) might be smaller. Conversely, Sunday is a day of rest when people from outlying villages come to market, so Sunday can be a larger than average market day. Inclement weather introduces another variable.

It would have been ideal to have multiple censuses for each marketplace in order to take all this variation into account. However, with but one week for fieldwork and with the work schedules of the other evaluation team members to consider, only one marketplace census could be scheduled for each place within the mutually agreed-upon team itinerary. Due note was taken of any special conditions that might affect comparability.[6]

Data collection posed other difficulties. Travel in southern Zaire is difficult under the best of circumstances. One village listed in the scope of work proved to be nearly inaccessible at this time of year—the end of the rainy season. The team drove for three hours in the rain to reach it, encountering many difficulties. Happily, however, perseverance paid off, for this village in northern Nyunzu, which once had a thriving commerce and social infrastructure, was now devoid of any commercial activity outside the corn marketing season, despite the immense amounts of corn produced and marketed there. This visit, and others like it to and beyond the limits of the project area, provided critical information to verify the interpretations made on the basis of the commercial counts.

These problems notwithstanding, all the largest and many smaller centers with shops and marketplaces were censured. As has been described, the goods enumerated were ranked according to the number of centers in which they appeared, and centers were ranked according to the number of types of establishments and marketplace arrays that they purveyed. The findings presented in Tables 8.1, 8.2, and 8.3 interpret these data and rankings.

Findings and Conclusions

The Commercial System's Evolution in North Shaba, 1976-87

At the outset of PNS, there were only two "higher-level" centers in the region, and to judge from retrospective interviews with key informants, even these supported only a very feeble commerce. Today, by contrast, there are several levels of market center, each with a limited but active commercial life.

The two original centers, Kongolo and Nyunzu, remain paramount. Both offer the entire range of retail services available in the region, from kiosks through retail shops to wholesale/retail operations with a transport function (Table 8.1). They also provide many other services, such as pharmacies, hotels, restaurants, and the like (Table 8.2). Further, these two centers have the largest and most diverse marketplaces in the area (Table 8.3). The only unexpected finding is that, by 1987, Kongolo surpassed Nyunzu on every index as the major center in the region.

Further, an intermediate level of center has newly appeared in the region. The differences between these places—Sola, Mbulua, and Lengwe—and the two high-level centers are clear. The intermediate centers all have several large retail stores, some local transport services, a few other services, and a marketplace. (In the case of Lengwe, the marketplace was successfully established only four years before, after several decades of fitful attempts.) But none of these functions is as complete as in Kongolo and Nyunzu. In the marketplaces, for example, there are many fewer vendors, and even though the proportion of sellers with manufactures is similar, a much more limited range of goods is available. Sellers in these markets generally have more mixed arrays, combining medicines, hardware and plastics, school supplies, and some clothing. There are no sellers of specialized arrays, such as plastic shoes

Table 8.1 Counts of Commercial Shops and Transport in the PNS Area, by Level of Center, 1987

	Level 1		Level 2			Level 3	
Category	Kongolo	Nyunzu	Mbulula	Sola[a]	Lengwe	Makutano	Butendo
Stores							
Kiosks	50	20	15	0	10	0	0
Retail only	25	15	20	10	5	3	0
Wholesale	6	4	4	1	1	1	0
Transport							
Pickups	4	0	1	0	0	0	0
Trucks	30	12	3	2	0	0	0

a. The center was visited in the early afternoon, when the market was already disbanding. Therefore, there is no market count for Sola.

Table 8.2 Counts of Other Retail and Service Establishments in the PNS Area, by Level of Center, 1987

	Level 1		Level 2			Level 3	
Establishment	Kongolo	Nyunzu	Mbulula	Sola[a]	Lengwe	Makutano	Butendo
Service							
Flour mill	6	7	4	1	1	0	0
Bakery	11	5	1	1	0	0	0
Pharmacy	6	4	4	1	1	1	0
Hotel	3	4	2	0	0	0	0
Restaurant	3	2	1	0	0	0	0
Bar	1	3	0	0	0	0	0

a. The center was visited in the early afternoon, when the market was already disbanding. Therefore, there is no market count for Sola.

Table 8.3 Vendor Counts, by Commodity Array, in Marketplaces of PNS Area, by Level of Market, January 1987

Commodity/service	Level 1		Level 2		Total no. of vendors
	Kongolo	Nyunzu	Mbulula	Lengwe	
Local foodstuffs					
Tubers/grains	63	23	14	3	103
Greens/spices	43	15	6	2	66
Flour	14	5	11	1	31
Forages	13	10	5	1	29
Vegetables/fruit	23	4	1	0	28
Firewood/charcoal	12	10	4	0	26
Palm oil	13	3	2	0	18
Tobacco	4	4	0	0	8
Meat	3	5	1	0	9
Chicken/eggs	1	1	0	0	2
Subtotal	**189**	**80**	**44**	**7**	**320**
Imported foodstuffs					
Dried fish	17	7	8	1	33
Salt	7	5	4	0	16
Bread	5	3	1	2	11
Soap	2	1	5	1	9
Sugar	7	1	0	0	8
Subtotal	**38**	**17**	**18**	**4**	**77**
Manufactures					
Boutique/table	14	14	2	4	34
Used clothing	26	4	4	0	34
Hardware	4	10	3	3	20
New clothing	12	1	4	0	17
Plastic shoes	7	4	0	0	11
Pharmacy	4	2	1	3	10
Cosmetics	1	1	0	0	2
Subtotal	**68**	**36**	**14**	**10**	**128**
Craft goods (basketry, chairs, pottery)					
Subtotal	**5**	**2**	**2**	**1**	**10**
Services					
Finger foods	10	7	5	2	24
Restaurant	3	2	1	0	6
Watch repair	1	1	0	0	2
Tailor	1	1	0	0	2
Bicycle repair	1	0	0	0	1
Subtotal	**16**	**11**	**6**	**2**	**35**
Total	**316**	**146**	**84**	**24**	**570**

or cosmetics. As feeble as this development may be, it is still greater than in any other place in the region, other than Nyunzu and Kongolo.

Significantly, all three of these centers lie on the trunk road. Moreover, these middle-level centers are all located between major centers, which is a predictable pattern in central-place theory.

The third level of center occurs only on the periphery; that is, away from this commercial core. These lower-level centers are few in number and demonstrate very little commercial development. In theory and in fact, there are always more lower-level centers than higher-level centers. In the present instance, there are surely more third-level centers than the evaluation team was able to visit. Nonetheless, each of the villages visited had only one or two small shops on the order of a small general store. Any other third-level centers would likely have similarly limited commerce.

Finally, most villages do not have even a small store. This class of villages, devoid of formal commerce for most of the year, makes up the fourth, and bottom level of the commercial hierarchy. It would probably be the most numerous class had commercial activity been inventoried in all places in the region.

In summary, north Shaba has undergone a commercial renaissance in the last decade. Whereas before there were only two centers along the rail line, several new centers on the trunk road now also perform wholesale and retail functions. Moreover, whereas before there were only two levels of market center—the two bulking centers and all other villages—there are now four levels. Besides the two entrepôt centers on the rail line and the three secondary bulking centers on the trunk road, small commercial centers are now appearing in some villages off the main arteries, so that peripheral villages, especially in the Kongolo area, are now differentiating themselves into two levels—those with and those without year-round commerce and trade.

The change that has occurred is dramatic, given the backward, isolated state of the area at the outset of the project. And the change, small as it may be, could not have been documented without the commercial counts.

Spatial Patterning of Commercial Development

The second finding is that patterns of commercial development vary not simply with corn production (income), but also with population density and transport efficiency. Although this outcome runs counter to the team's initial expectation, it accords perfectly with central-place theory predictions.

At all levels of the commercial hierarchy, market centers in Kongolo—which has long lagged in corn production—are more fully developed than centers in Nyunzu, which has long dominated the corn business. Kongolo town has more wholesalers, more retailers, more transporters, more service personnel, and a larger market than Nyunzu town. Among the middle-level centers, Sola and Mbulula in Kongolo district have larger and more diverse markets, more stores and shops, and more services than Lengwe, which is in the Nyunzu area. Of importance, there are even transporters in the middle-level centers of Kongolo district, but none in Lengwe. Finally, at the lowest levels, some villages in the Kongolo area boast a shop or two, some of which even purchase local produce at wholesale. By contrast, there are no shops in any of the villages visited in Nyunzu, even though some of these places have a large population and show clear signs of once having been small commercial centers.

This consistent difference between the two areas is readily explained. The project rehabilitated far more roads in Kongolo than in Nyunzu, thus opening up more areas for commercial production. This decision is understandable, inasmuch as population densities in Kongolo are almost five times higher than in Nyunzu. Also, even though corn is a consumption crop in Kongolo, farmers in that area practice a much more complex agriculture and typically sell various crops to merchants. Even though the overall value of these other crops—rice, peanuts, and palm oil—does not rival that of corn, in a particular locality, the total income from agricultural production is much greater than that from corn alone.

In other words, the three factors considered fundamental for commercial development in central-place theory—transport efficiency, population density, and income (in this case, from crop diversification), which together determine "demand density"—are all significantly higher in Kongolo than in Nyunzu. As a result, commercial development is greater in the Kongolo area than the Nyunzu area.

Spatial Patterning of Other Regional Changes

Spatial analyses are powerful because they provide an overall framework for interpreting other variations within the region. So little work has been done on this topic that the matter is treated here illustratively, with the example of farmer investment patterns.

Project reports documented that farmers in Nyunzu cultivated larger areas (3 hectares on average) than farmers in Kongolo (1 hectare on average). Although yields were lower in Nyunzu (2.6 metric tons/hectare versus 3 metric tons/hectare), farmers there produced and sold much more corn. In fact, three-quarters of all Nyunzu farmers earned more from corn than the top 25 percent of Kongolo producers. Probably 10 percent of the farmers there cultivate 10 or more hectares in corn, earning as much as US$2000 a year. Nonetheless, patterns of household expenditure have not changed significantly in the region. People basically meet their daily needs, and if they can afford it, they purchase a radio, bicycle, or sewing machine. Only the largest producers can make productive investments as well as consumption expenditures. Such investments are essentially limited to building a house in town, opening a store, and buying a pick-up or used truck. Inasmuch as more farmers in Nyunzu are better able to invest, one would expect greater local investment in that area, compared to Kongolo.

As the commercial counts document, it is the Kongolo area that exhibits greater local investment. Not only is the major center there more developed, but shops are opening in the smaller villages as larger farmers open stores in their natal villages and buy trucks. Evidently, the multiplicity of cash crops allows these local entrepreneurs to bulk produce in quantities too small to attract larger merchants. And the prolonged harvest season for these different crops means that smaller producers have cash available over much of the year, thus supporting local shops. By contrast, in Nyunzu, where corn remains the major—if not the only—commercial crop, marketing is compressed into a few months after the harvest, buying is handled by merchants from the major centers, and consequently, there is much less local commercial development. An entrepreneurial farmer in the Nyunzu area has but one option—to invest in the major town there. Those who have invested locally have failed, for there is simply not enough cash in the countryside for most of the year to support even a small shop. In a very real sense, diversified cropping, as in Kongolo, supports more widespread regional commercial development than mono-crop export agriculture, which, as in Nyunzu, is leading to the rise of a single primary town with a very seasonal commercial pulse.

In summary, urban commercial counts enabled analysis of change within north Shaba over time in response to productive change in the countryside. Fortunately, there were just enough historical descriptions available to piece together a quantitative picture of the pre-project situation that could be compared with the field data collected during the evaluation. Also, north Shaba is sufficiently large that comparison of these counts in the two sub-zones of the project area revealed significant differences in commercial development within the region—differences that will continue unless corrective action is taken. Together, the temporal and spatial comparisons provide a complex, integrative view of the type and extent of change that occurred over the course of the project, in the countryside, as well as in the towns.

This interpretation of the commercial counts gave explicit form to the project personnel's intuitive knowledge of developments in the area. Everyone "knew" that production, income, and commerce had increased, but no one understood the extent of the observable change or its spatial patterning. This central-place interpretation provided a framework for understanding the changes over time that people familiar with the area knew accorded with events.

The interpretation also clinched a major, implicit question in the team's scope of work. That was, apart from the direct consequences of project interventions, had the project sparked a spontaneous process of development? And if it had, what was this process and how could it be documented? It was precisely this question of important, indirect impact that could best be answered through the rapid rural reconnaissance techniques of urban commercial counts.

Guidelines and Suggestions

It is useful to conclude with observations about limitations of this approach and a suggestion for possible uses of central-place methods in other contexts.

First, the use of urban commercial counts and marketplace censuses for rapid appraisal of agricultural development projects presumes that the project being evaluated is the single or at least the major undertaking in the region. In the case of the north Shaba project, no other government or donor program existed, so attribution of the changes in commercial development was straightforward.[7] It obviously would be much more difficult, if not impossible, to allocate impact among several agricultural development projects operating simultaneously in the same region. In other conditions, it might be difficult or impossible to impute causality; that is, to eliminate factors exogenous to the project (for example, illegal or black market trade) as the explanation for improvement in regional conditions.

Second, the use of commercial counts to evaluate an agricultural project presumes that the project is working on crops that are generally important for sale throughout the area. Various types of agricultural projects do not meet these criteria, and could not be evaluated in this manner. Village garden projects for family nutrition, for example, do not aim primarily at increased family income. Similarly, projects that target a specific crop in a delimited area would likely not have a widespread or regional effect. For example, an irrigated rice project of, for example, 50 hectares, could, if successful, have only a local—not a regional—impact on commerce.

These caveats notwithstanding, the field and analytic techniques employed in the north Shaba evaluation are powerful. The approach can, in principle, be used in other contexts, either where the project area is smaller than a region or where the project focus is more on secondary crops. Commercial counts in these situations could contribute to project monitoring and evaluation through the same spatial and temporal analyses as was done for Shaba on the basis of limited but rigorous fieldwork. The need now is for additional applied studies to test the efficiency of the approach under these varied conditions.

References

Appleby, Gordon. 1978. "The Aftermath of Exportation: The Socio-economic Evolution of the Regional Marketing System in Highland Puno, Peru." Ph.D. diss., Stanford University, Department of Anthropology.
_____. 1982. "Price Policy and Peasant Production in Peru: Regional Disintegration During Inflation." *Culture and Agriculture* No. 15 (Spring): 1-6.
_____. 1985. "Marketplace Development in the Gambia River Basin." In Stuart Plattner, ed., *Markets and Marketing: Monographs in Economic Anthropology,* No. 4. Boston, MA: University Press of America.
Christaller, Walter. 1966. *Central Places in Southern Germany.* (Translated by C.W. Baskin.) Englewood Cliffs, N.J.: Prentice-Hall.
Marshall, John U. 1969. *The Location of Service Towns: An Approach to the Analysis of Central Place Systems.* Toronto, Canada: Department of Geography, University of Toronto.
Poulin, Roger, Gordon Appleby, and Cao Quan. 1987. "Impact Evaluation of Project Nord Shaba." Project evaluation report for USAID/Zaire. (photocopy)
Skinner, G. William. 1964. "Marketing and Social Structure in Rural China." Part I. *Journal of Asian Studies* 24:3-43.
_____. 1965. "Marketing and Social Structure in Rural China." Part II. *Journal of Asian Studies* 24:195-228.
Smith, Carol A. 1972. "The Domestic Marketing System in Western Guatemala: An Economic, Locational, and Cultural Analysis." Ph.D. diss., Stanford University, Department of Anthropology.
_____. 1976. *Regional Analysis. Vol. 1.* New York: Academic Press.
_____. 1985. "Methods for Analyzing Periodic Marketplaces as Elements in Regional Trading Systems." *Research in Economic Anthropology* 7:291-337.

Notes

1. While geographers usually analyze urban centers in more developed regions, anthropologists have adapted the theory and its methods to the study of periodic marketplaces; that is, intermittent centers that blip on the landscape once every so many days. Skinner (1964, 1965) pointed the way in a masterful trilogy on the Chinese marketplace system over three great epochs. Smith (1972, 1976) operationalized the approach in a pioneering field study of the very complex marketplace system in highland Guatemala. Subsequently, Appleby used Smith's field methods in studies of the marketplace systems in southern Peru

(1978) and Senegal and The Gambia (1985), besides this study in Zaire (Poulin, Appleby, and Cao 1987). The central-place methods presented here are truly an anthropological innovation.

2. This methodological problem reflects economic reality: where demand is weak, sellers can better maximize their profits by adding different goods to their arrays than by increasing the diversity of a particular good.

3. The classification of goods and services used here contains an implicit categorization of centers into levels that short-circuits the elaborate central-place method (Marshall 1969). The categorization is based simply on the numbers and types of shops and services. In retail trade, for example, a place with only two small retail shops is less developed (that is, less "central" and of a "lower order") than a place with 15 small shops *and* 3 large retailers. This latter center is, in turn, less developed than one with 50 small shops, 15 large retailers, and 5 merchants with not only retail, but also wholesale bulking operations. As has been mentioned, a concordance usually exists between the types and extent of commercial activity. Higher-level centers have more shops with greater capital, more truckers, more service establishments, and more diverse marketplaces than lower-level centers, and the shifts over time are *usually* all in the same direction. Where this concordance does not occur, as sometimes happens, the system is more complexly structure and may require a more detailed analysis.

4. Analysis at one point in time is basically descriptive, for there are no comparative materials. Here one is interested in the number and level of centers and their spatial patterning, quite possibly for use as a baseline in future monitoring of project impact. Temporal or spatial variation allows a more complex analysis based on the same set of measures. If the system has been studied at two points in time, it is possible to discern changes in the regional system by comparing the number of levels of center and their spatial dispersion at each time (Appleby 1982). If parts of the same system are studied at the same time, one can discern intra-regional variation in much the same way. The only difference is that one is comparing different areas within a single system at one point in time rather than the same area at different points in time (Appleby 1985). In the most complex use of this methodology, if one has baseline and post-project data for a region that exhibits sub-regional variation, one can analyze the regional system as it developed over time and discern differential development over space within that system (Poulin, Appleby, and Cao 1987).

5. Naturally enough, people think of marketplaces in terms of the particular goods that one can find there. They do not think of markets in terms of arrays of goods; that is, the inventories carried by individual vendors. To illustrate, one cannot ask whether there is a vendor of plastic pails or hardware (an array of plastics or of hardware), for the answer will almost always be yes if some vendor carries a few pails or some hinges—mixed into an array predominately of other goods such as clothing. In other words, a list of all the goods available in a market is *not* the same, in a central-place perspective, as a census of marketplace arrays. For these reasons, marketplace vendor counts must be carried out by trained teams. Furthermore, retrospective interviews about marketplace composition usually provide little or no usable information. One can ask when the market was successfully established and, maybe, approximately, how large it

was; one cannot usefully ask about the number of types of arrays that were then offered.

6. The team encountered a number of "special considerations" in doing the marketplace censuses. The team arrived in Sola just as the market was disbanding, so the census there was not credible. In Mbulula, it rained suddenly, and the team had to delay its departure until after the market reopened. Later that week, the census of the two markets in Kongolo town could only be taken on a Sunday. Thus, the numbers recorded probably represent the peak business in contrast to the more usual weekday markets studied elsewhere. Such are the exigencies of field work in a time-bound situation.

7. Some critics nonetheless faulted the evaluation for being unable to demonstrate conclusively the role of the project in changing conditions in north Shaba. Common sense argued persuasively for the importance of the project—after all, there had been no other development activity in the region. However, it was then impossible to exclude the possibility of exogenous factors, such as macroeconomic policies. Subsequent design work undertaken in preparation of a follow-on project in neighboring central Shaba project provided the opportunity to prove that PNS—and not other factors—accounts for the changes documented here. Commercial counts done in central Shaba, which would have been subject to the same exogenous factors as north Shaba, documented that this neighboring area scored significantly more poorly on every measure of commercial development. In fact, central Shaba at that time (1987-88) looked very much like north Shaba had *before* the start-up of PNS. Since the same exogenous factors would have been operative in both areas, the difference in commercial development in the two regions can only be explained in terms of project intervention.

9

Participatory Rural Appraisal: A Case Study from Kenya

Charity Kabutha, Barbara P. Thomas-Slayter,
and Richard Ford

In this chapter, Kabutha, Thomas-Slayter, and Ford describe the application of participatory rural appraisal (PRA) methodology to a community development initiative. A multi-disciplinary team consisting of two social scientists, a biologist, an environmental information specialist, and a health and nutrition expert undertook the appraisal in a sublocation in eastern Kenya. To gather relevant data and information, the team conducted key informant and group interviews, direct observation, informal surveys, and literature review. It also developed the village sketch map, village transects, farm sketches, time line, trend lines, seasonal calendar, farm profile, and technical profiles, which were then used by the team to help the community assess its needs, establish development priorities, and formulate action plans.

The value of participatory rural appraisal lies not only in its use of innovative data collection methods, but also in initiating a process that empowers the local community by providing it with vital data and other information that can be used for designing and implementing grassroots development initiatives.

The participatory rural appraisal described in this chapter was conducted in 1988. The chapter was drafted in late 1989. Since that time, much has happened in Mbusyani as a direct result of PRA. Mbusyani Dam has been completely rehabilitated; a new tree nursery has been opened and is operating; several hill slopes have been terraced through the organizing and labor of several women's groups; private farmers have constructed bench terraces on their own land, based on the example of the work of the women's groups; a cluster of several women's groups has raised money and pur-

chased a maize mill that has now been running for two years; and plans are well underway for the rehabilitation of a second dam. Further, several villages adjacent to Mbusyani are now using elements of PRA to help in their own village planning and project design. It has been four years since the original PRA in Mbusyani, and the community groups are carrying on with continued energy.

PARTICIPATORY RURAL APPRAISAL (PRA) uses multi-sector teams to join with village leaders to assess village needs and priorities and subsequently, to create village resource management plans. The plan becomes the basis for action for development projects in the rural community, and enables local institutions, government units, and nongovernmental organizations (NGOs) to cooperate in their implementation. PRA draws upon the knowledge and skills already resident in the village. It also:

- creates a setting in which local residents exchange information with one another and the local technical officers;
- provides a structure for local aspirations and goals to be expressed and implemented;
- provides a ranked list of village project activities that funding agencies can support; and
- sets in place a plan that village leaders and institutions can implement and sustain (Thomas-Slayter 1992).

The PRA approach assumes that popular participation is a fundamental ingredient in development project planning that takes place at the local level. PRA is rooted in the earlier work of Gordon Conway and Robert Chambers' Rapid Rural Appraisal and draws much of its data collection and ranking techniques from their work. PRA assumes that locally-maintained institutions and technologies, as well as sustainable economic, political, and ecological inputs, are fundamental to reversing the general decline in these spheres that Africa has experienced in the past several decades. The PRA approach is built on the premise that individual rural communities reside in discrete ecosystems or microzones—defined by rainfall levels, soil types, elevation and vegetation, and so on—and require particular and unique combinations of farm, health, soil, water, and woodland/grassland management. PRA further assumes that community residents have a good working knowledge of their ecological and development needs, but do not necessarily have the means to make all this information systematic, or—based on this information—to mobilize their communities to take action to solve problems.

A combined team of officers from Kenya's National Environment Secretariat (NES) and Clark University (Worcester, Massachusetts), with assistance from technical officers from Kangundo Division, Machakos District, field-tested Participatory Rural Appraisal (PRA) in Mbusyani Sublocation in July/August 1988. While collaboration on resources management between NES and Clark has been underway for several years, development of the PRA approach is new.

The purpose of the Mbusyani study, then, was to learn whether a rapid appraisal team consisting of NES staff, Clark University representatives, technical officers, and community leaders could gather data, define problems, rank solutions, and devise an integrated village plan for natural resources management in a relatively short time period, with substantial community participation. The basic questions to be tested included:

- Data: To what extent did Mbusyani residents possess sufficient data on which to build a practical resource management plan?
- Participation: Would use of participation as a means for gathering data and setting priorities be manageable, both in terms of organizing infrastructure and eventually developing an agreed-upon plan?
- Village leaders and institutions: To what extent would a PRA approach capture the attention of village leaders who are in a position to manage such an approach?
- Donor and NGO assistance: Would the preparation of an agreed-upon village resource management plan provide documentation that would attract NGO or donor assistance?
- Sustainability: Would village groups, once mobilized and familiar with the PRA process, use it to sustain resource management activity and design new plans?

The NES team that carried out the pilot PRA consisted of a social scientist with extensive agricultural experience (the team leader), a biologist, a social scientist, an environmental information specialist, and a village health worker and nutritionist. The team worked closely with extension officers for technical assistance, particularly in regard to water resources and conservation. The team also drew heavily on the energy and assistance of local leaders in Mbusyani, including formal leaders such as the assistant chief, as well as informal leaders, such as heads of women's groups.

PRA normally has eight clearly-defined steps (Kabutha, Thomas-Slayter, and Ford 1990), though the procedures can vary greatly, depending on local need and preferences of the team. These steps include:

- site selection and clearance from local administrative officials;
- preliminary visit;
- data collection: spatial, time-related, social, and technical; focusing especially on problems of the community;
- synthesis and analysis;

- setting problems in priority order and exploration of opportunities to resolve them;
- ranking opportunities by priority and feasibility and preparing a Village Resource Management Plan (VRMP);
- adoption of the VRMP; and
- implementation.

These eight steps as carried out in Mbusyani included:

Site Selection

In the case of the Mbusyani study, the head of the farmers' cooperative union for Mbusyani, the assistant chief, and ten leaders from women's groups in the sublocation came to Katheka Sublocation (where NES and Clark University representatives had carried out a research exercise, training sessions, and demonstration days in 1987 and 1988) to see how village groups here had organized programs and projects to ease pressure from human activity on local natural resources. The Mbusyani group was so impressed with Katheka's achievements that they invited NES to visit their sublocation to determine if similar work could begin in Mbusyani. Thus, NES went to Mbusyani because the local leaders had requested it.

The PRA site, Mbusyani, is a sublocation consisting of eight villages in Kenya's semi-arid zone. It lies 90 km east of Nairobi in Kakuyuni Location, Kangundo Division, Machakos District. The terrain is hilly, the climate dry (average rainfall is 400 to 600 millimeters per year), and the elevation is about 1500 meters. The population in 1990 was estimated to be 8,000.

The residents of Mbusyani are Akamba, a group of agro-pastoralists who have lived in Machakos since the seventeenth century. Some Mbusyani households have family ties in the sublocation that date back three or four generations. Due to increasing pressures on the land in neighboring regions, many have moved into Mbusyani in recent years, occupying land that previously was used for rotational grazing. Today, people in the area derive their livelihoods mostly from subsistence agriculture and cash remittances, though about 20 prosperous farmers sell coffee as their primary source of income.

The extension of farming and the subsequent constriction of grazing lands are two forces that have led to accelerated resource degradation, including loss of ground cover, soil erosion, and reduced water availability in the region in general, and in Mbusyani in particular. These forces, coupled with erosive soils, steep hill slopes, and torrential seasonal rainfall have created a situation in which the community's natural resources are vulnerable. There are many dimensions to this predicament, including health problems such as bilharzia, food storage needs, access to reliable water sources, high rates of soil loss, and declining water supplies.

NES made a preliminary visit on May 31, 1988, and spent a half day meeting with leaders. After extended discussions among NES and Mbusyani leaders, all agreed to go ahead with a PRA. The village leadership understood what would be expected of them, especially in terms of organizing groups of leaders and residents for discussions with the PRA team. The NES pledged that it would assist with gathering data, organizing the data into a format from which village groups could rank priorities, and helping to prepare a village resources management plan. It was stressed that responsibility for implementation of the plan would be placed primarily with community leaders, with assistance coming from technical extension officers, the NES, and donor or NGO groups that might be identified.

Data Collection

The team gathered four basic data sets, in addition to routine secondary information (see the appendix). These included spatial data, time-related information, data on institutions and social structure, and technical information. All turned out to be important in carrying out the PRA and eventually formulating the resources management plan. The total time for the PRA team and community group for the data gathering exercise was six days.

Data Synthesis and Analysis

Once the data were collected, the PRA team spent a day meeting by themselves to organize the information. They made large charts and tables of trend lines, institutional arrangements, the transect, and so on, and then compiled a list of all the problems mentioned in any of the data-collection exercises. The team then split up into pairs. Each took a particular problem (water, for example) and in each instance summarized the problem, in some cases by subdividing by ecological zone; matched opportunities or potential solutions to each problem; and listed opportunities for each problem on large pieces of paper, big enough to be seen in a large meeting.

Ranking Problems

The next day, villagers met together to rank their problems. The meeting was held in a primary school classroom near the sublocation's market. Data gathered in the preceding exercises were displayed in the form of charts and graphs on the walls, including the trend lines, transect, sketch map, and others. The charts containing the lists of problems and opportunities were placed at the front of the room. The NES team leader chaired the meeting. Participants included the six team members from NES; nine technical officers representing soil, water, forestry, agriculture, village health care, community development, and livestock; a number of village elders and community leaders; the assistant chief for the sublocation; and leaders from eight women's groups.

There are many ways to rank problems in this context. The literature on PRA and *The Participatory Rural Appraisal Handbook* offer many suggestions (Kabutha, Thomas-Slayter, and Ford 1990). In most cases, community groups have simply voted to derive a list of most-severe to least-severe problems. Sometimes, the voting places clusters of problems in categories of severity; other times, it is a numerical ranking of severity. In one case in Pwani (Kenya), the community agreed on one set of rankings the first day and then, after intense discussions, established a totally different rank order for problems the following day.

In the case of Mbusyani, villagers voted. Given that all problems of a community cannot be solved in one effort, there is a need to organize these problems into sets of issues that can be dealt with step by step over an extended period of time. The ranking process in PRA seemed to help and has therefore become an important exercise in Mbusyani's efforts to help itself. The outcome in Mbusyani was an ordering of problems that villagers and technical officers agreed were the most severe and in greatest need of attention. The task was essentially completed by lunch time. While there were several high-priority problems that were mentioned a few times, the overwhelming and most frequently-cited issue was water.

Ranking Opportunities

In the afternoon, the same group reassembled and discussed possible solutions; in this case, to the water problem. The PRA team had previously listed recommended solutions, ranging from boreholes to rehabilitating rock springs. The NES/PRA team leader chaired the meeting. The means for bringing order and a systematic approach to the ranking was the use of an "Options Assessment Chart" developed by Gordon Conway and Robert Chambers. The team leader used the criteria of stability, equity, productivity, sustainability, *and* feasibility to help the group place weighted values on each possible solution and eventually to arrive at a unanimously agreed-upon set of actions, including development of a new well, rehabilitating two small reservoirs and water catchments, terracing a badly-eroded hill slope, and continuing with efforts of reforestation. Technical officers played an important role in this discussion so that solutions would be feasible in technical, economic, ecological, and social terms. There was some initial difficulty using the Options Assessment Chart, mostly because the terms (for example, sustainability) did not translate well into Kikamba, the local language. However, the team worked closely with the village leaders and eventually a ranking emerged.

Adopting a Village Resource Management Plan (VRMP)

According to the original schedule, the group was to reassemble the following morning and create a village resource management plan. However, several leaders and especially the water engineer felt there was insufficient technical information to develop a comprehensive plan. The water engineer returned the following week and, joined by the entire PRA team and the Mbusyani Resource Management Committee, visited all potential water points in the sublocation and expanded considerably upon the technical feasibility document. Figure A9.9 in the appendix includes excerpts from the technical survey.

Two weeks later, the entire sublocation committee again assembled and, using data that the water engineer's survey had developed, organized a comprehensive water and natural resources management plan for Mbusyani. The plan indicates what tasks are to be carried out, what materials will be needed to do the work, who will do it, and what—if any—external assistance will be needed.

A brief extract from the plan is shown in Figure 9.1.

Implementation

Implementation in Mbusyani has moved forward, not always on schedule, but with considerable commitment from all parties involved. The assistant chief has been the prime mover, with major cooperation and support from many different constituencies in the sublocation. The first task, a well at Kithini Springs, went quickly, with labor and local materials from the community, and cement rings and skilled labor from the Ministry of Water Development. No external funds were required.

The second project, rehabilitation of a reservoir at Mbusyani Dam, was more ambitious. Women's groups supplied labor and dug dozens of fence post holes to erect a sturdy fence to protect the watershed area. The groups also dug several meters of bench terraces and planted many trees as a means of curbing erosion and siltation in the reservoir. A local NGO heard of the project and agreed to provide fence posts, wire fenc-

---

Figure 9.1 Village Resources Management Plan (extract)

WATER: Zone I

Source: By Priority	Estimated Requirements	Committee Responsibility	Projected Time
Kwa Nzau Well	1. Hand pump 2. Cement rings 3. Cement and cover 4. Sand 5. Ballast 6. Labor	1. External 2. MOWD 3. External 4. Community 5. Community 6. Community	Immediately

WATER: Zone II

Kwa Kiluli Dam rehabilitation	1. Posts and wire 2. Terracing 3. Afforestation 4. Spillway protection	1. External 2. Community 3. Community 4. Community	Work will start on June 20, 1989, on the spillway.
Kwa Kiluli Well	1. Hand pump 2. Cement rings 3. Cement 4. Sand 5. Ballast 6. Labor 7. Cover	1. External 2. MOWD 3. External 4. Community 5. Community 6. Community 7. External	Immediately
Yenyeni Springs Well rehabilitation	1. Dig well deeper 2. Protect site 3. Technical design 4. Hand pump 5. Sand 6. Ballast 7. Cement 8. Wire and poles 9. Rings and cover	1. Community 2. Community 3. MOWD 4. External 5. Community 6. Community 7. External 8. External 9. External	Work to assemble materials will start on June 19, 1989. Actual building will start when water level drops, and digging can begin.

ing, and tree seedlings for Mbusyani Dam. The NGO also wrote a successful proposal to a UN agency, using data developed during the PRA exercise, and noting how the work on the dam was part of the larger village plan to bring sustained production to its natural resources. The funds provided additional fencing and a means for scooping silt from the bottom of Mbusyani and Kakuyuni reservoirs. While the paperwork has taken 18 to 20 months, the project is now getting underway.

A third element of implementation was developing soil control on a badly-eroded hill slope. The Ministry of Agriculture donated tools to carry out this work, and an additional allotment of tools has been obtained through a private donor. Women's groups have provided many hours of volunteer labor for the effort and planted hundreds of trees along the new terraces.

Twenty-four months after adopting the plan, Mbusyani has made considerable progress, though the work is not yet finished. It is unclear whether the enthusiasm and work energy that has been maintained over this 24-month period will continue. It is equally unclear whether the small external inputs, such as hand tools from the Ministry of Agriculture, fencing and posts from an NGO, cement rings from the Ministry of Water Development, and funds from the UN have been critical to the success, or whether the community would have been able to organize alternative means to acquire these inputs on their own.

Findings and Conclusions

The introduction of this case study set out five clusters of questions to be tested by the field methodology. Findings from the Mbusyani exercise (and reinforced by subsequent PRA field exercises) are covered in the following sections.

Data

Mbusyani residents know a great deal about their community. The time line and trend analyses revealed an intimate awareness of what past circumstances had been. The seasonal calendar indicated an integrated understanding of past problems and present needs. Yet in spite of these good data, there were gaps in the information base on topics normally assumed to be important in development planning. Villagers were generally unaware of quantified information, for example, statistics on rates of soil loss or percentage changes in infant mortality. They were also weak in anticipating the economic and technical feasibility of proposed solutions. Finally, they were mostly uninformed about ways to find technical and financial support to implement their hopes and aspirations.

Even so, these data gaps seemed to pose no serious problem in formulating the village resource management plan. Given long-term involvement with the community, villagers had sufficient data to rank problems and consider solutions. Extension officers provided technical and economic information as needed. As a result of the experience, the community was able to rank solutions in ways that reflected their own knowledge base, integrated with technical and economic considerations provided by members of the PRA team.

In the judgment of the PRA team, the villagers, in association with extension officers, had access to sufficient data to formulate sound resource management plans.

Participation

PRA provides an organizational structure that focuses and systematizes grassroots participation. In the present case, Mbusyani residents responded actively at every level. For example, there was no shortage of elders to describe past events and present trends; people were interested in the seasonal calendar exercise; and discussion was prolonged when the relative importance and relationships among institutions in the sublocation were considered. During the formal meeting to finalize Mbusyani's VRMP, discussion was vigorous and often intense. While women were sometimes reluctant to speak in the presence of male extension officers and local officials, they did speak up with conscious encouragement by members of the PRA team and specific support methodologies. By the end of the sessions, the women participants made their feelings well known.

Two elements seem to have structured the participation. First, data-gathering from village groups sent a message that the PRA team had interest in knowing what the community knew. As the participatory data-gathering continued, a momentum began to build. At no point were there ever more than 300 or 400 people involved in the process, out of a total population of 8,000 (or roughly 4,000 adults). Thus, it would be inaccurate to say that the entire community participated. Yet significant numbers did participate on a sustained basis, suggesting that the process was important in attracting the attention of the community.

Second, the task-oriented and visual nature of the PRA was important. Village residents could see what the researchers were collecting and felt they could comment, for example, on whether the trend line was being accurately drawn. The interactive and tangible nature of the data demystified the research process and made the community feel a sense of ownership of the PRA from an early stage.

While there are certainly other elements in explaining why Mbusyani has implemented its resource management activities, the PRA team agreed that the structured and systematized participation has been one of the most important.

Village Leaders and Institutions

Locally-initiated plans require committed and skilled local leaders to follow up on the recommended initiatives. In the case of Mbusyani, the assistant chief demonstrated these qualities admirably. He called meetings, organized work groups, attended local committee discussions, and kept good records. He also served as liaison for dealing with external groups such as NES or the NGO. His leadership, while not necessarily flashy or charismatic, was steady, reliable, and thorough. This consistency in the assistant chief's leadership in follow-up is a fundamental element in explaining why the PRA research has produced results.

It must be stressed, however, that the assistant chief was not the only leader in the formula. To date, he has managed none of the money that has been raised. All funds have been administered by one of the external agencies (for example, the indigenous NGO) or by the Mbusyani Women's Group. Thus, a second crucial quality of local leadership is the skill and commitment that leaders of a half-dozen women's groups have brought to Mbusyani. They have carried out bench terracing, fence-post installation, sand and gravel collection, and tree planting. They are now collecting money for a maize grinding mill and are gathering funds for a cost-sharing acquisition of tools. As is the case with the chief, the women's leaders are not necessarily charismatic. Instead, the explanation for their success in leadership lies in simply following through with assigned tasks and delivering services on time.

The assistant chief, the women's group leaders, and the community institutions are essential elements in the Mbusyani project's effective management. Given the recent shift in the development field in Kenya toward decentralization of development planning, through the District Focus, there is clear evidence that PRA provides a methodology that enables rural institutions to function more effectively. The PRA team agreed that cultivating such leaders and institutions in new communities will be a fundamental element in expanding the work of local sustainability.

Donor and NGO Assistance

A problem prevailing in much of rural Africa is one of dependency on outside help. Rural communities wait, beg assistance from donors, or implore help from politicians to get water systems, agricultural supplies, and the like. This "client" relationship is demeaning and perpetuates a second-class status for rural communities. PRA suggests there is a great deal that rural communities can do for themselves.

The process of ranking needs and designing solutions in Mbusyani placed initiative in the hands of the rural groups in ways that identified:

(1) what steps community groups themselves could take; (2) what services and materials they could organize from local extension staff; (3) the role of NGOs; and (4) how requested donor assistance could complement items (1) through (3).

Mbusyani's experience suggests that when a community raises external funds, these funds actually reach the intended beneficiaries. At present, donors are not set up to respond to rural requests. While the structures for such support are potentially available, the present process of project identification and design tends to rely on centralized and external agencies. Thus, while PRA shows that a "bottom-up" approach in village assessment produces tangible results, there is equal need for donors and governments to restructure a portion of their efforts to respond to such locally identified project designs.

Sustainability

The crux of the issue in rural development is how long Mbusyani will carry on without continued encouragement or help from NES, an NGO, or other external sources. It is too early for a final judgment. However, a number of interesting and perhaps significant results have been observed.

First, much of the PRA follow-up has been carried out by the community itself. Bench terracing, fence-post installation, watershed rehabilitation, and well-digging have been completed independently of outside help.

Second, a local Kenyan NGO discovered Mbusyani's VRMP and turned it into a fundable proposal. While delays within the UN bureaucracy dampened the initial enthusiasm, the funds were eventually allocated, and both the NGO and Mbusyani are benefiting. There will probably be additional such "joint" ventures as well.

Third, both the Ministry of Agriculture and the Ministry of Water Development have been moved to provide assistance that would not necessarily have been forthcoming otherwise. In both cases, they did so because the community was organized and the ministries knew that any supplies made available would be put to good use.

Costs

The experiment in Mbusyani took place quickly (in less than 10 days), was inexpensive (less than $1,000 in new money), participatory, and provided the community abundant and systematized data that has led to the VRMP. If the total cost of this PRA were to be calculated, including staff time, estimates would include:
• The time of 3 NES officers, at 15 to 20 days each,

- The time of 3 extension officers, at 10 days each,
- A corps of perhaps 10 village leaders, at 10 days each,
- An extended cluster of secondary village opinion-makers and "movers" of about 25 people, at 3 to 4 days each,
- A much larger community group of perhaps 400, who attend one or more of the data-gathering or ranking meetings, at about 2 days each.

Thus, the PRA methodology has been effective, at least in one community, in turning data into action, using minimal funds.

PRA in Perspective

PRA is a new way to look at village data, rural priorities and aspirations, and potential interventions. It offers possibilities for restructuring the way rural planning and resources management take place. Yet nothing in this case study should be interpreted to mean that the PRA process can replace national and district planning, data collection, and analysis by various government agencies, technical and economic feasibility studies, environmental impact statements, or extension services provided by technical officers. Rather, PRA should be considered as a supplementary methodology that gathers site-specific data, integrates sectors, actively involves beneficiaries in the planning process, links extension services directly with rural communities, and sets in place an "implementable" plan of action that local institutions can take seriously. As the development community searches for means to introduce sustainable development, the PRA methodology appears to bring a mix of elements not present in most donor- and government-initiated methodologies. To this extent, PRA warrants further testing and refinement in various ecological, cultural, economic, and political settings.

References

Chambers, Robert. 1983. *Rural Development: Putting the Last First*. Essex, U.K.: Longman Scientific and Technical.

Chambers, Robert, Arnold Pacey, and Lori Ann Thrupp, eds. 1989. *Farmer First: Farmer Innovation and Agricultural Research*. London: Intermediate Technology Publications.

Conway, Gordon R., and Edward B. Barbier. 1990. *After the Green Revolution: Sustainable Agriculture for Development*. London: Earthscan.

Davis-Case, D'Arcy. 1989. *Participatory Assessment, Monitoring and Evaluation: A Field Manual*. Rome: Community Forestry Unit of the Food and Agriculture Organization.

_____. 1990. *The Community's Toolbox: The Idea, Methods and Tools for Participatory Assessment, Monitoring and Evaluation in Community Forestry*. Rome: Community Forestry Unit of the Food and Agriculture Organization.

Eastman, Ron, Richard Ford, Anne Gibson, and James Toledano. 1990. *An Intro-duction to Geographic Information Systems for Resources Management.* Worcester, MA: SARSA.

International Institute for Environment and Development. January 1990. *Manual on RRA and Related Approaches.* London: RRA Notes (Number 8), pp. 30-35.

Kabutha, Charity, Barbara P. Thomas-Slayter, and Richard Ford. 1990. *Participatory Rural Appraisal Handbook.* World Resources Institute, in collaboration with Kenya's National Environment Secretariat, Egerton University, and Clark University. (Also contains the full Mbusyani Village Resource Management Plan, pp. 72-80.)

Kabutha, Charity, and Richard Ford. October 1988. "Using Rapid Rural Appraisal to Formulate a Village Resources Management Plan." *RRA Notes* (Number 2). (Contains a detailed description of the ranking procedure, and an example of the Conway/Chambers Options Assessment Chart.)

Korten, David C. 1990. *Getting to the 21st Century: Voluntary Action and the Global Agenda.* West Hartford, CT: Kumarian Press.

Mascarenhas, James, et al., eds. August 1991. *Participatory Rural Appraisal: Proceedings of the February 1991 Banglore PRA Trainers Workshop.* London: RRA Notes (Number 13), IIED.

Molnar, Augusta. 1991. "Community Forestry: Rapid Appraisal." Rome: Community Forestry Unit of the Food and Agriculture Organization.

Rocheleau, Dianne. *Land-Use Planning with Rural Farm Households and Communities: Participatory AgroForestry Research.* Working Paper No. 36. Nairobi, Kenya: International Centre for Research on Agroforestry.

Thomas-Slayter, Barbara P., and Isabella Asamba. 1991. *From Cattle to Coffee: Transformation in Rural Machakos.* Worcester, MA: ECOGEN Case Study Series, Clark University.

Thomas-Slayter, Barbara P. 1985. *Politics, Participation, and Poverty: Development Through Self-Help in Kenya.* Boulder, CO: Westview Press.

_____. November 1989. "Implementing Effective Local Management of Natural Resources: New Roles for NGOs in Africa." *Human Organization* 51(2): 136-143.

Appendix: Information Gathered

Box A9.1 Information about the Village Sketch Map

Definition: The sketch map is a spatial representation of the commu-
                nity.

Purpose: It provides reference points within which data collection,
                analysis, and planning take place.

Process: Whereas the assistant chief already had a 1:50,000 topo-
                graphical map, he did not have a detailed map of the
                sublocation nor did he have any definition of micro-
                ecological zones within the sublocation. The team traced a
                base map, using the 1:50,000 topo map as a guide. Then the
                PRA team, two village elders, and the assistant chief drove
                all roads and lanes in the entire sublocation—a trip of about
                2 hours—recording information and talking with people, as
                appropriate.

Result: The map exercise identified three micro-zones, defined
                largely by elevation, soils, and rainfall. The Upper Zone
                Has somewhat higher rainfall, generally fertile soils, and
                potential for growing coffee. The Lower Zone is generally
                drier, has few water sources, and generally lower agricul-
                tural potential.

Usefulness: Knowing about micro-zones, disparities in wealth, differ-
                ences in land use, and variations in resource access pro-
                vided an opportunity for the assistant chief, women's
                group leaders, and the PRA team to locate areas where lo-
                cal leaders thought there were particular problems. Having
                this initial visual reference provided common ground for
                the team and local leaders to exchange information. The
                sketch map also suggested how the team should go about
                preparing the transect (next exercise).

Assessment: Preparing sketch maps as a first step has proven to be a
                dramatic and visually important way to announce to the
                community that something is going on. Several PRAs have
                had excellent responses in having the communities prepare
                their own sketch maps. The exercise is one of the most
                important PRA data-gathering tools.

Time: The mapping exercise took half a day.

Figure A9.1 Village Sketch Map

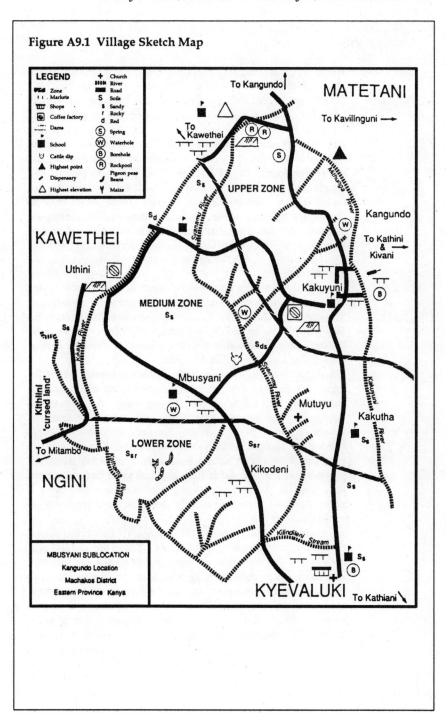

Box A9.2 Village Transect

Definition: A transect is a cross-section of the community, showing ecological, cultural, economic, and land use conditions.

Purpose: The transect identifies types of land use, local perceptions of
problems, and village views of opportunities to solve them.
It helps the team to verify the validity of the sub-zones,
which the sketch map has defined. There are several goals in
using the transect. First, the transect confirms sub-zones set
out in the sketch map. Normally, the PRA team pencils in a
rough track on the sketch map that will cut through the differing micro-zones in the community. These zones may be
distinctive in many ways, including their ecology, cropping
patterns, economic activity, wealth, ethnicity of residents, or
type of land tenure system. Using a transect enables the
team to double-check the approximate zonal estimates in the
sketch map.

Second, the transect enables the team to begin looking for
both problems and opportunities on a zone-by-zone basis.
The core of PRA is developing collaboration among community institutions to define and act upon their needs, as these
institutions perceive them. The transect is the first formal
data collection step in this process.

Third, the transect exercise is an important entry point for
team members to interact with a broad cross section of the
community in totally non-threatening ways. As team members walk the transect line, they will encounter farmers,
school children, water carriers, animal cart drivers, people
headed for market, cattle herders, and more. The occasion of
building the transect allows team members to ask these villagers what kind of yields they had last year, how prices are
changing for maize or fertilizer, whether the water table is
rising or falling, and how they describe their most severe
problems.

Experience in doing several PRAs suggests that these casual
conversations yield huge dividends. There are several reasons why. For example, a casual conversation on the road
and in an anonymous setting may yield an honest response
about prices or problems, whereas a formal sit-down interview may encourage cautious answers. Further, a chance
meeting on a village path may bring together two or three
totally disassociated residents candidly discussing, for example, the current fuel wood or forestry situation, without

continued on next page

Box A9.2 *(continued)*

fear of reprisals from higher authorities. Finally, informal transect conversations call forth comments from people who might not normally speak up in a community meeting or any kind of an interview. Women, impoverished residents, ethnic minorities, or youths may speak out amid the anonymity of the transect path, but remain silent in an interview.

Process: While some PRA teams will walk a straight line from one side of a community to the other, intersecting all micro-zones, the Mbusyani team chose a different tactic. The distances were great and the goal of the transect was to understand transactions within each micro-zone, so the team broke into three smaller units and explored routes, as noted on the sketch map. The sub-groups joined with elders and asked questions as they walked. In each case, the sub-groups started at the highest point in the micro-zone and fanned out from that area.

Results: The transect provided a detailed look at land use practices, present problems, and potential solutions. It also enabled the team to confirm that considerable variety in ecology and land use practices was present in the sublocation.

Usefulness: Preparing the transect enabled the PRA team to become acquainted with details of the micro-zones. As the sub-groups walked through the community, they observed, recorded data, and stopped and talked with whomever they met. A list of problems and opportunities for the sublocation began to emerge.

Assessment: The transect is on a par with the sketch map in order of value to the PRA team. It allows cross-zone comparisons, highlights diversity in problems and opportunities, and draws out humble elements of the community. It has, like the sketch map, earned a solid place in the array of PRA's information-gathering tools.

Time: Given that the team split into three sub-groups, it took only half a day to gather the data. Then, one member from each sub-group sat together in the evening and prepared the composite transect that appears in this study (Figure A9.2).

Figure A9.2 Composite Transect

Soil	Loose, deep red soil	Sandy soils and small patches of red soils	Shallow sandy soils; rocky in most parts
Water	About 3/4 of households have shallow wells, area also has 3 dams and 1 spring	A river infested with bilharzia, 2 poorly maintained dams	Water in Kilindiloni River, salty; River Kathana, bilharzia; roof catchment
Vegetation	All natural vegetation cleared to give way to settlement	High proportion of natural vegetation, acacia, lantana, canola grasses	Natural vegetation consisting of acacia, shrubs, and grasses
Social-economic indicators	1/2 of household heads in wage employment, majority mabati roofs, brick or stone walls	1/2 of households tin roofs, 1/2 thatched, brick walls	Mainly grass, thatched houses
Food crops	Maize, beans, bananas, pigeon peas	Maize, beans, pigeon peas, fruits, bananas	Maize, beans, bananas, fruits, pigeon peas
Cash crops	Coffee	Coffee	Coffee
Achievements (last 5 years)	Soil conservation tree planting, water development: wells, roof catchment	Soil conservation, water development: dams	Some soil and water conser-vation
Forestry/ Agro-forestry	Widespread agro-forestry greuillea, eucalyptus mangoes, papayas	Minimal tree planting: mangoes, papayas	Very little tree planting
Resources management	Terracing, embankment reinforced with multi-purpose grasses	A lot of bench terracing	Limited soil conservation
Problems	Inadequate water, education, health facilities, famines, lack of dip facilities	Water, famine, inadequate education and health facilities	Water, transport, and food
Opportunities	Rehabilitation: 3 dams 1 spring, external assistance, tools, market	Water development: dam, well, roof catchment, government assistance	Water development: dams, roof catch-ment, external assistance

Box A9.3   Information about the Farm Sketch

Definition: Farm sketches are hand drawings of farm layout and use and include cropping patterns, buildings, tree locations, and water sources on individual farms.

Purpose: They illustrate relationships between resource management practices and a variety of variables, including income, education, and ecology for a representative sample of households in the community.

Process: The PRA team broke into smaller units and visited farms along the route of the three transect paths, paying attention to examples of the variety of ecology, incomes, land uses, and family sizes present in the community. Team members prepared sketches by walking around the farms with household heads. In subsequent PRAs, the teams have combined the exercises of farm sketches, farm interviews, and the transect, just to save time.

Results: The farm sketches showed individual farm management practices and enabled the team to compare facilities and strategies among the three micro-zones.

Usefulness: It became clear that the Upper Zone was, on a relative basis, more affluent than the Lower Zone, had better-managed farms, produced more, and provided higher incomes than in the other two zones. The farm sketches (coupled with the farm interviews noted below) confirmed these differences.

Assessment: The utility of the farm sketch depends on the particular PRA. In most PRA exercises, data have been gathered as a means of stimulating and planning community-based enterprises such as water resources, marketing, forestry, soil control, transport, etc. There has been relatively little "on-farm" work resulting from existing PRAs. Thus, the sampling technique for picking 6-10 individual farms for sketches and interviews has been generally qualitative (class, ecological zone, size of holding, type of land use, family size) rather than precisely quantitative (precise income, yields per acre, percentage of income derived from farm). To date, the generalized sampling has served PRAs well, as the site selection can be determined during the transect and sketch map activities. If *individual farm strategies* are to become a vital element of the PRA village action plans, it will be necessary to consider more systematic sampling techniques in choosing farm sites.

Time: Farm sketches took an entire day, even with the team breaking into three sub-groups. Combining different data-gathering exercises, as noted above, has enabled later PRA teams to gather all interviews and all sketches in one day.

Figure A9.3 Farm Sketch

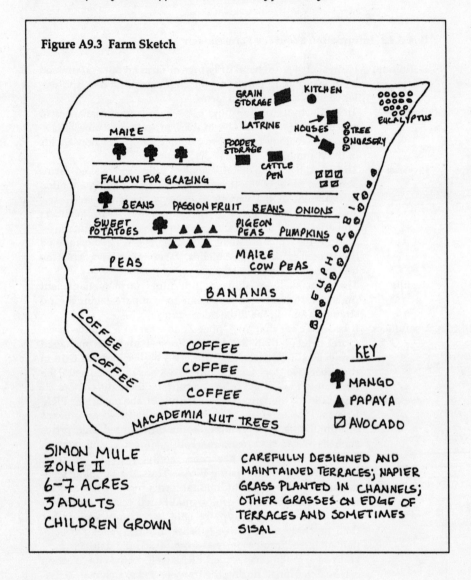

KEY

🌳 MANGO

▲ PAPAYA

▨ AVOCADO

SIMON MULE
ZONE II
6-7 ACRES
3 ADULTS
CHILDREN GROWN

CAREFULLY DESIGNED AND
MAINTAINED TERRACES; NAPIER
GRASS PLANTED IN CHANNELS;
OTHER GRASSES ON EDGE OF
TERRACES AND SOMETIMES
SISAL

Box A9.4 Information about the Time Line

Definition: The time line is an aggregate of past events, as influenced by present conditions.

Purpose: The goal is to learn from the community to understand what it considers to be important in its history. The time line provides an insight into the community's historical perspective on current issues.

Process: A PRA team meets with residents to discuss what they consider to be the most important events in the community's past and to prepare a time line. It is important to note that groups assembled for data-gathering should reflect the age, ethnic, gender, class, and educational diversity of the community. Data are gathered in group meetings with explicit attention paid to including community residents from different backgrounds and perspectives. Problems and opportunities are discussed in these meetings.

Depending on the size of the community, three or four groups are organized, representing different sub-zones. For example, in Mbusyani, with a population of about 8,000, the PRA team split into four groups and asked the assistant chief to arrange for groups (about half elders for the time line) to come to four local market centers to meet the visitors. The role of elders, both male and female, is important in Africa, where age is so highly respected. Further, the elders carry some of the community's history with them and personify some (but not all) of the values, priorities, and aspirations of the community. They lend a sense of continuity to community action that has been sorely lacking in many development interventions.

The goal for the time line is to understand what the community considers to be important in its history. A PRA team learns from discussions among small groups, with emphasis on community elders. These discussions stimulate exchanges about problems and achievements as far back as the most senior local residents can remember. In Mbusyani, the elders presented a vast store of information (see below) that normally might not be offered to a visiting researcher or project design team.

Results: The community emphasized earlier problems that either they had experienced or that they remembered previous generations describing. Drought is an important element of Mbusyani's past, as is famine. The exercise pointed out to

continued on next page

Box A9.4 (continued)

	the PRA team that problems of aridity and periodic drought were not new to the community.
Usefulness:	The time line exercise worked effectively in Mbusyani. Residents became deeply involved in describing their experiences, especially their hardships. The exercise drew heavily on the elderly, who are not always consulted by planners and project designers. The exercise also helped to confirm some of the emerging hypotheses about the nature of Mbusyani's problems, as well as aspirations.
Assessment:	While not as central to PRA as transects and sketch maps, the time line serves an important purpose, that of informing elders that their views are important. One of the features of rural African development is the age of the younger, Western-trained NGO and extension officers versus the accumulated wisdom of village elders. The time line has been an important element in several communities to open dialogue between these two age groups.
Time:	The time involved in Mbusyani was a full day, though normally half a day is enough.

Figure A9.4 Time Line

1836	Yangoyo famine
1850	Ya Kiasa famine
1861	Mutulungo famine
1870	Ngelete famine
1880	Ndata famine
1885	Kyumbe (Dance)
1897	Rinderpest outbreak
1898	Yua Ya Munyili, Mbalia and Kilumi Dance
1898–1900	Mission at Muisuini—Kangundo
1899	Railway line at Konza
1906–1910	Immigration from Mbooni, Chief Ntheketha
1910	Ndata Ila Yaumie
1910–1911	Yua Ya Ndata (Maharagwe) famine
1912–1914	Money introduced
1914–1918	Destocking by white man—Malua
1914–1918	Men carried to war
1915–1918	Compulsory school
1918	Diarrhea
1918–1919	Epidemic lung disease of domestic animals—Munyili
1928–1929	Nzalukangye famine
1930–1931	Locusts
1931	Kuthulia Kikuyu, fencing with sisal
1939–1940	Muindi Mbingu campaigned against forced destocking
1939–1945	World War II
1942	Munyoloko famine, enforced conservation measures
1943–1945	Mwolyo
1949–1951	Dams started
1950	Mbua Ya Kanzi, Mabolelo floods
1950–1951	Drought after floods, forced destocking
1951–1952	Mbua Ya Kavisi
1952–1954	Emergency
1960–1961	Food for work
1962	Yua Ya Ndeke, bumper harvest, projects on service dams started
1965	Yua Ya Atta
1973	Drought, eclipse of the sun
1978	Earthquake
1980	Nikw'a Ngwete
1984	Drought, army worms
1984–1985	Cholera outbreak, epidemic on lemon trees
1987	Noukengwatie

Box A9.5 Information about Trend Lines

Definition: Trend lines plot village perceptions of change over time in key sectors.

Purpose: PRA assumes that local communities have a good grasp of changes over time within their own villages and that these data are fundamental in helping communities plan management strategies for their resources. Trend line discussions bring together all ages and groups in the community, including men and women, to elicit their perspectives on "the way things are going." The trend lines demonstrate village perspectives over 20 years on changes in resource issues such as rainfall, crop production, soil loss, deforestation, health, population, and other topics of community concern. They complement the time lines. A PRA team organizes groups of residents and leaders for this exercise.

Process: In recruiting trend line groups, less emphasis is placed on elders than for the time line groups. More attention is paid to those currently using the land. The reason for this is that time lines go back as much as a century, whereas trend lines look only at the recent past and how it is changing.

Normally, villagers talk about trends in some basic sectors such as soil loss, rainfall, income, education, population, and food production. But the open-ended style of PRA enables villagers to add new categories for trend analysis. For example, in Mbusyani, local leaders charted their problems and discussed whether they had more problems in recent years or earlier. This discussion unlocked a range of perspectives that might never have surfaced in a more formal interview or questionnaire setting. Further, the discussion among villagers concerning whether the trend line is going up or down revealed an inner core of villagers' feelings about basic issues in youth unemployment, the need for vocational training, constraints of land, and the grinding poverty that many villagers faced. A team leader from NES led the discussion, using chalk and a blackboard (the meeting was held in a school classroom). The groups developed trend lines for population, rainfall/water availability, land productivity, formal education, tree planting, soil conservation, and erosion control.

Result: Trend analysis helped the team to: (1) learn from the community how they perceive change over time in various sectors; (2) integrate key changes into a village profile; and (3) organize the range of opportunities for the community to consider.

continued on next page

Box A9.5 (continued)

Usefulness: Several of the earlier data collection exercises had focused on opportunities to solve problems. This exercise expanded the list, clarifying local perceptions of important changes within the community.

Assessment: The trend exercise turns out to be one of the most important opportunities to open discussions on village problems. Rather than ask direct questions, as with questionnaires and surveys, the trend lines allow a PRA team to draw out information about problems indirectly. Further, the trend lines enable community members to talk about interventions that did and did not work in previous attempts at—for example—and productivity, soil erosion, water development, and more. It must be born in mind that these exercises are measuring perceptions, not actual performance. However, given the goals of PRA to use data-gathering and analysis to stimulate communities to plan and to act, local perceptions are exceedingly important.

Time: The trend analysis took half a day.

Figure A9.5 Trend Lines

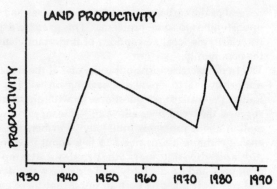

LAND PRODUCTIVITY

1945   A bumper harvest due to good rains
1977   Increase in yields due to training carried out at Machakos Farmers Training Centre. Free seeds were provided (beans and maize) and free fertilizer as well
1988   Increase in productivity due to: application of chemicals; manure; fertilizers applied to shambas in 1987 were not used by crops due to shortage of rains plus destruction of crops by cutworms, crickets, and stalk borer

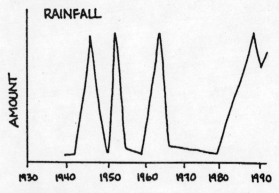

RAINFALL

1940–1942   Mbulunga famine
1943–1945   Mwolyo famine
1960   Maa Ya Ndege (famine due to floods, food brought by airplane)
1978   Nikwa Ngwete famine

Box A9.6 Information about the Seasonal Calendar

Definition: A seasonal calendar is a snapshot of village activities, problems, opportunities, and possible interventions, represented over the course of a year.

Purpose: It enables a PRA team, using group discussions, to learn about land use, hunger seasons, farming activity, times when disease is more prevalent, food surplus, and cash availability. The seasonal calendar also adds to information about village views of problems and opportunities.

Process: The assistant chief assembled a group representing different age, gender, and leadership perspectives. The PRA team leader asked questions about what activities were most important during the year and when they happened. The responses helped the team to prepare a profile of activity in the village on a monthly basis.

One of the valuable contributions of the seasonal calendar is the chance to link problems and opportunities to an annual cycle. For example, in some communities, dilemmas such as human and animal diseases or seasonal hunger occur virtually every year. In times of drought or blight, these problems may start earlier and last longer. But they recur year after year. Other problems, such as access to fuelwood or the need for building materials for water storage, persist at a sustained level throughout the year.

Results: The seasonal calendar presented large quantities of diverse information in a time frame. It compared village activities, month by month, across sectoral boundaries. These annual cycles helped to determine, for example, labor availability, timing for project activity, potential absorptive capacity for new activities, times of disease and food shortage, and variations in cash flow.

Usefulness: The calendar was one of the chief determinants to show that water scarcity seemed to be at the core of many of the community's problems. Regardless of season, water appeared to be a persistent problem.

The seasonal calendar ranks with the village sketch maps, trend analysis, and transect as one of the four basic exercises to grasp the "big picture" of the community. It may be the most helpful tool for integrating problems, opportunities, and potential actions into a single visual framework that communities can discuss. Experience indicates that the seasonal calendar is critical to the success of the PRA.

Time: Group discussions on the calendar took half a day.

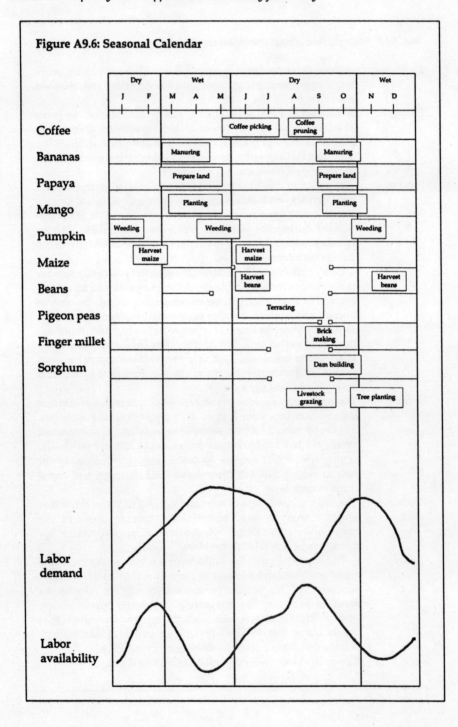

Figure A9.6: Seasonal Calendar

Box A9.7 Information about Farm Interviews

Definition: Farm interviews collect detailed information for a small number of households. They supplement the farm sketches (see Box A9.3).

Purpose: The interviews yield socioeconomic information. Topics include the nature of resource management practices, the characteristics of the particular farm household, and the respondents' observations on household and community problems. These interviews offer the team an opportunity to hold discussions with residents who might not normally be included among the leaders or other group meetings.

Process: Household heads were the same as those selected for farm sketches. They represented a cross-section of the community by gender, class, and ecological micro-zone.

Results: While the farm interviews yielded good data on family size, income, education levels, numbers of livestock, etc., the prime use was to confirm the growing list of problems and opportunities. The interviews, representing the diversity of the community, reinforced the hypotheses that water was a problem for the entire sublocation, but was especially severe for households in the lower and poorer zone.

Usefulness: The most helpful dimension was to assure that problem definition and eventual program activity would be sensitive to issues of equity in the sublocation.

Assessment: The commentary on farm sketches (Box A9.3) is equally applicable here.

Time: Farm interviews take one day if they are integrated with the farm sketches.

A full questionnaire is found in the *PRA Handbook,* pp. 43-47.

Figure A9.7 Farm Interview (excerpt)

This Household Data Form is to be completed for each interview and submitted to the PRA team leader at the end of the day. It records basic household data. The remaining information is to be collected as Field Notes, using the categories described in the Questionnaire Guidelines.

Name _____ Position in household _____ Zone _____

Male _____ Female _____ Age _____ Marital status _____

Highest level of education attained for husband and wife:

husband _____ wife _____

Place of origins of parents and grandparents?

How many children have been born to you?

How many children are living?

How many children are living with you on the farm?

How many people in total are living on the farm?

Does anyone in this family have a job outside Kyevaluki?

Do they help sometimes with such things as school fees or money for fertilizer?

Box A9.8 Information about Village Institutions

Definition: Groups of residents rank community institutions in order of importance and construct diagrams that indicate the relationships between and among village units.

Purpose: An understanding of institutional roles and relationships is fundamental to sustainable development. The analyses helped the PRA team to: (1) learn about the activities of groups and organizations within the community; (2) understand how the community views these institutions and how they rank them according to their contribution to community development; and (3) assess the relationships among these institutions by creating a diagram of institutional interactions.

Process: The team first compiled a list of all institutions (church groups, women's organizations, cooperatives, etc.) in the sublocation. Meeting with clusters of men and women in four different sites of the sublocation, the team asked residents to rank the importance and cooperation of village institutions. To facilitate this process, the PRA team leader brought 30 to 40 circles, cut from paper. Roughly a third of these were small circles, a third were medium-sized, and a third were large. The team leader asked group members to place names of the community's institutions on the labels, using large circles for the influential groups and smaller circles for the less important ones. This exercise alone can frequently consume one or two hours, as there is often intense discussion among villagers about which groups are the most important.

Next, the group leader asked villagers to arrange the circles to show how different institutions in the community cooperate to get things done. If two groups worked closely together, the circles would be placed to overlap one another. If the groups had no record of collaboration, circles would be placed separately from each other.

Results: The Mbusyani discussions created four diagrams, one each from the four discussion groups, showing institutional relationships. While details varied, they all identified the important role of women's groups, as well as of government institutions in Mbusyani.

Usefulness: Responses on the social and institutional analysis are revealing, in part as they provide direct information (institutional structure) and indirect data (which groups will work to-

continued on next page

Box A9.8 (continued)

gether). For Mbusyani, they confirmed that the women's groups were the best bet to supervise follow-up work, raise and manage funds to do the work, and to cooperate with the assistant chief to plan new activities. In another community (not Mbusyani), the institutional analysis revealed that no village group trusted the assistant chief and would work with him. Many other examples of such insights could be cited. The point of the village social analysis is the depth of understanding and the action imperatives that can be derived from a half-day discussion of the village's social and political profile, as perceived by representatives from the community.

Assessment: While the sketch map and seasonal calendar reveal important physical information, the institutional diagram has become a central device for gathering social and institutional data. The results have offered valuable insights into the interworkings and often closely guarded details of community life. The structuring of an implementation plan often reflects the institutional information revealed in this exercise.

Time: The exercise took half a day.

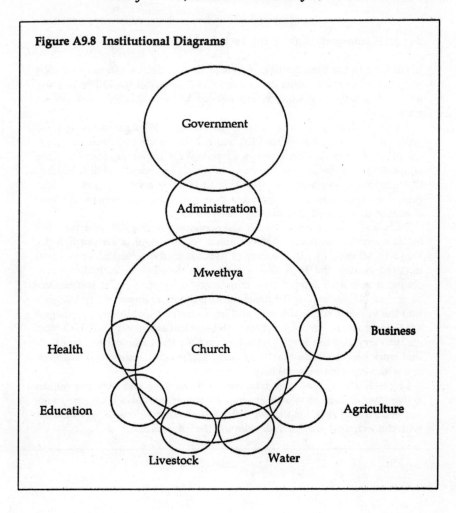

Figure A9.8 Institutional Diagrams

Box A9.9 Information about the Technical Survey

In addition to the time, spatial, and social data, technical officers on a PRA team assemble information on economic and technical feasibility, i.e., water, soils, forestry, agriculture, etc. needed to help villagers rank project activity.

Technical data are fundamental to the successful design and implementation of an action plan. Most PRA teams will include two or three technical officers who can do surveys of potentials in water, forestry, crop adaptations, marketing, etc. In cases in which a particular skill is lacking, the team PRA specialist has been able to identify a local expert, in most cases for no additional money other than providing transport and sometimes the cost of food and lodging for a few days.

Technical assessments consider the economic, ecological, and technical implications of alternative interventions (Figure A9.9 is an example for water in Mbusyani). In the case of Mbusyani, the technical survey was initiated during the PRA and a few more detailed investigations concluded a few days later. After conducting several PRAs, it has become clear that: (1) the technical data are among the most important to integrate into the villages' socioeconomic and institutional capabilities; (2) villagers are the key agents, in cooperation with technical extension and NGO officers, to carry out the implementation; and (3) the technical interventions that work best are those that community leaders can understand and manage with very little external help.

The technical survey may take two or three days and may not require active involvement of village groups. However, previous PRA experience has shown that it is helpful for village leaders or elders to work closely with the technical groups in developing the information.

Figure A9.9 Technical Survey

Water Sources in Mbusyani (excerpt)

Kithini Springs:	Located in the upper area of the sublocation; flows all year; serves 1,000 people. The spring is located off the road in a high, hilly area.
Kakuyuni Dam:	Built by self-help efforts in 1969-70. It is located along a tributary of the Syanamu River (seasonal). The dam was constructed with large rocks and cement. It no longer holds much water because of leakage. There is still some water being retained in the dam, as witnessed by the cattails growing in the catchment area and by vegetables growing along the water access way. If rehabilitated, this dam could supply water for the secondary school, Kakuyuni market, and households in the area.
Kivuenani Well:	This water source is called a well because there is no outlet. Water availability is seasonal, as the source is replenished only by rainfall. The communal usage is not high because this source has a low flow and is in the Upper Zone where other water sources are more plentiful.
Syanamu Sub-Surface Dam:	Near the coffee factory south of Kakuyuni market. It is a sub-surface dam in good condition. The cement and rock wall has recently been completed. However, there are problems with the quality of the water. It is saline and unsuitable for human consumption, but is used for cattle watering and for the coffee factory. There is also bilharzia in the water.
Kwa Muikuyu Spring:	A stream and rock dam located in the middle part of the sublocation along a tributary of the Syanamu River. The spring area has been surveyed and is demarcated as a communal water resource. The spring is highly productive and serves many people in the sublocation, despite high prevalence of bilharzia.
Kwa Kituma Well:	Built by the coffee society. The water is pumped into the well through a channel originated in the Syanamu River. This is poor quality water and is only used by the coffee factory.

212-end
N/A

Selected Bibliography

Burgess, R.G., ed. 1982. *Field Research: A Source Book and Manual*. London: Allen and Unwin.

Casley, Dennis J., and Krishna Kumar. 1988. *Project Monitoring and Evaluation in Agriculture*. Baltimore, Maryland, and London: Johns Hopkins University Press.

_____. 1989. *The Collection, Analysis, and Use of Monitoring and Evaluation Data*. Baltimore, Maryland, and London: Johns Hopkins University Press.

Chambers, Robert. 1981. "Rapid Rural Appraisal: Rationale and Repertoire." *Public Administration and Development* 1 (2):95-106.

_____. 1992. *Rural Appraisal: Rapid, Relaxed and Participatory*. Sussex, England: Institute for Development Studies.

Conway, Gordon. 1985. "Agroecosystem Analysis." *Agricultural Administration* 20: 31–55.

Finsterbusch, Kurt. 1976a. "Demonstrating the Value of Mini-Surveys in Social Research." *Sociological Methods and Research* 5(1).

_____. 1976b. "Mini-Surveys: An Underemployed Research Tool." *Social Science Research* 5(1).

Krueger, Richard A. 1988. *Focus Groups: A Practical Guide for Applied Research*. Beverly Hills, California: Sage Publications.

Kumar, Krishna. 1987. *Conducting Group Interviews in Developing Countries*. Washington, D.C.: Agency for International Development.

_____. 1987. *Rapid, Low-Cost Data Collection Methods for A.I.D*. Washington, D.C.: Agency for International Development.

_____. 1988. *Conducting Key Informant Interviews in Developing Countries*. Washington, D.C.: Agency for International Development.

_____. 1990. *Conducting Mini-Surveys in Developing Countries*. Washington, D.C.: Agency for International Development.

International Conference on Rapid Rural Appraisal. Papers presented at the conference in Khon Kaen, Thailand, September 2-5, 1985.

Lincoln, Yvonna S., and Egon G. Guba. 1985. *Naturalistic Inquiry*. Newburry Park, California: Sage Publications.

Miles, Matthew B., and A. Michael Huberman. 1984. *Qualitative Data Analysis: A Sourcebook of New Methods*. Beverly Hills, California: Sage Publications.

Patton, Michael Q. 1980. *Qualitative Evaluation Methods.* Beverly Hills, California: Sage Publications.

_____. 1982. *Practical Evaluation.* Beverly Hills, California: Sage Publications.

Spradley, James P. 1979. *The Ethnographic Interview.* New York: Holt, Rinehart, and Winston.

Sudman, Seymour, and Norman M. Bradburn. 1988. *Asking Questions.* San Francisco and London: Jossey-Bass Publishers.

Van Maahen, John, ed. 1983. *Qualitative Methodology.* Beverly Hills, California: Sage Publications.

Whyte, William Foote, ed. 1991. *Participatory Action Research.* London and New Delhi: Sage Publications.

Yin, Robert. 1984. *Case Study Research: Design and Methods.* Beverly Hills, California: Sage Publications.

Contributors

GORDON APPLEBY received his Ph.D. in anthropology from Stanford University and has over 20 years of experience in international development. He has worked for the USAID/S&D's Office on Agriculture on small-farm research and extension, headed the planning unit of a river basin development organization in West Africa, and consulted on a number of projects in agriculture, rural development, and the natural resources. More recently, Dr. Appleby was the director for the Environment and Natural Resources unit at the Academy for Educational Development (Washington D.C.), where he managed a project using social marketing techniques for agricultural extension. Presently, he is working as a short-term consultant for the World Bank, USAID and other international agencies.

JILL E. ARMSTRONG is an associate professor and a community nutrition specialist in the Department of Food Science and Human Nutrition at Washington State University. Her research interests include community nutrition, social marketing, and international development. Dr. Armstrong has conducted community nutrition assessments in Antigua, the West Indies; among the Hmong people in the Pacific Northwest; and in cross-cultural studies with multi-ethnic groups.

STEWART BLUMENFELD received his doctorate from the University of California at Los Angeles, where he subsequently served on the faculty for ten years. From 1979 to 1983, he was seconded from UCLA to USAID's Office of Nutrition to develop and manage a project aimed at developing an improved methodology for evaluating nutrition intervention programs. In 1983, Dr. Blumenfeld joined the University Research Corporation's Center for Human Services (Bethesda, Maryland), and is currently the Deputy Director of the Center's Quality Assurance Project.

CECILIA CABAÑERO-VERZOSA, a health communications expert on the staff of the Academy for Educational Development, has managed multinational health interventions on diarrheal disease control, immunization, nutrition, family planning, water, and sanitation. In 1992, she became Deputy Director for Technical Services of a global communications program, Health Communication for Child Survival (HEALTHCOM). The countries in which she has conducted field work or managed projects include Bangladesh, China, Honduras, India, Indonesia, Kenya, Malaysia, Nepal, Nigeria, Peru, the Philippines, Sri Lanka, Swaziland, and Thailand. Ms. Cabañero-Verzosa received her M.A. in public administration from the University of the Philippines.

DENNIS J. CASLEY retired from the World Bank as chief of the Operations Monitoring Unit in the Central Operations Department. Earlier, he headed the Monitoring and Evaluation Unit in the Bank's Agriculture and Rural Development Department. Mr. Casley has been involved in development programs for about three decades, particularly in Africa. His most recent publications (co-authored with Krishna Kumar) are *Project Monitoring and Evaluation in Agriculture* and *The Collection, Analysis, and Use of Monitoring and Evaluation Data*, published by the Johns Hopkins University Press for the World Bank.

RICHARD FORD is a professor of history and international development and a director of the International Development Research Program at Clark University (Worcester, MA). He has carried out extensive field work and published numerous articles and assessments of community-based development in several parts of Africa, as well as in India, the South Pacific, and among Arab settlements in Israel. He was a member of the first Participatory Rural Appraisal Team in Kenya and co-author of the *PRA Handbook and Implementing PRA*, as well as of other evaluations, case studies, and handbooks on PRA.

ROBERT J. HAGGERTY, trained in food science and human nutrition, has been involved since 1985 in the development of a systematic method of post-harvest loss assessment. This work has been done with the Postharvest Institute for Perishables at the University of Idaho and Washington State University. Mr. Haggerty presently coordinates international activities in food science and human nutrition in the College of Agriculture at the University of Idaho.

JOHN S. HOLTZMAN, an agricultural economist, is the technical director of the agricultural group at Abt Associates, Inc. (Bethesda, Maryland) and also served as the research director of the Agricultural Marketing Improvement Strategies (AMIS) Project. AMIS used rapid appraisal methods in many of its diagnostic studies of agricultural marketing in developing countries. Before joining Abt Associates, Dr. Holtzman was on the faculty of the Department of Agricultural Economics at Michigan State University, where he worked on the food security research program funded by USAID.

CECILE M. JOHNSTON received her Ph.D. from the University of Michigan in experimental psychology. She coordinated the formative research effort on the USAID-funded HEALTHCOM II Project. She has extensive research expertise in marketing analysis, strategic planning, advertising effectiveness, communications, and consumer research.

CHARITY KABUTHA is the former deputy head of the planning unit for Kenya's National Environment Secretariat, Ministry of Environment and Natural Resources. In that capacity, she served as the leader of the original PRA team for several Kenya-based studies, including Mbusyani. She is also the co-author of several articles and reports on PRA, including *Participatory Rural Appraisal Handbook; Conducting PRAs in Kenya*. Ms. Kabutha now works for UNICEF, where she is program officer for projects on mother and child health in western Kenya.

OLABODE O. KAYODE is a lecturer in health education at the University of Ilorin, Nigeria. He received his M.P.H. degree in health education from the University of North Carolina and has consulted with many USAID-funded international development projects, including HEALTHCOM. Mr. Kayode has authored reports on health education, particularly nutrition, and on weaning foods and water-related parasitic diseases.

KRISHNA KUMAR is a senior social scientist in USAID's Center for Development Information and Evaluation. He has taught at Michigan State University and the East-West Center, and has consulted extensively with international donor agencies. Dr. Kumar has published eight books, dozens of monographs, and numerous articles in professional journals on development problems and evaluation methodology. His two recent books (co-authored with Dennis J. Casley) are: *Project Monitoring and Evaluation in Agriculture* and *The Collection, Analysis, and Use of Monitoring and Evaluation Data*, both published by the Johns Hopkins University Press for the World Bank.

MANUEL ROXAS received his M.D. degree from Manila Central University and his M.PH. from the University of the Philippines Institute of Public Health. He has worked at various levels of the Philippine Department of Health, from direct service provider, early in his medical career, to the highest policy-making level as Undersecretary of Health for Public Health Services. Dr. Roxas was co-principal investigator for the PRICOR Project in the Philippines.

MARICOR DE LOS SANTOS, a sociologist, has designed, managed, and supervised field data collection activities and data analysis for a number of projects. In 1987, she joined the PRICOR/Philippine Project as a technical advisor and helped design and manage the field phase of research as described in the case study in this book. Ms. de los Santos provided technical assistance to local investigators carrying out operations research studies for the Philippines Department of Health under the PRICOR Project.

THAYER SCUDDER is a professor of anthropology at the California Institute of Technology, and has directed the Institute for Development Anthropology (Binghamton, NY) for several years. He has consulted extensively with major international donor agencies, particularly USAID, the World Bank, and FAO, and has published numerous articles and several authoritative books based on his extensive field work in Africa and Asia. His most recent book, *African River Basin Development*, was published by the Westview Press in 1991.

BARBARA P. THOMAS-SLAYTER is an associate professor of international development at Clark University and director of the International Development Program there. She has published on participation, resource management, and gender, with particular emphasis on Africa and Asia. Her book, *Politics, Participation, and Poverty: Development Through Self-Help in Kenya*, assessed community institutions and their capacities to carry out self-help activities. Dr. Thomas-Slayter was a member of the first PRA team and co-authored the *PRA Handbook*.